Water, Sovereignty and Borders in Asia and Oceania

In the twenty-first century, water is an increasingly contested and scarce resource in an era of climate change and rising water demands related to global urbanisation and industrial agriculture. There are conflicts over rivers in the Middle East and in South Asia, fishermen are imprisoned for crossing the invisible borders of national oceanic economic zones, and in China and Australia, regional populations, city dwellers and colonised indigenous peoples are engaged in battles over internal rivers.

This book restores water, both fresh and salt, to its central position in human endeavour, in ecology and in the environment. It explores the roles that water, in both rivers and oceans, has played in shaping and challenging national and international demands for precise borders and clear-cut sovereignties. This book draws on water's many formations and representations, exploring human relationships with an essential component of life and a major factor in contemporary politics. The topics range from oceans and rivers to lagoons, billabongs and estuaries in Asia, Oceania and the West Pacific. In interdisciplinary and cross-disciplinary analyses of the many facets of water and its crucial role in everyday life and in geopolitics, the contributors address the physical descriptors of water and interrogate its politicised administrations.

Water, Sovereignty and Borders in Asia and Oceania identifies new discursive possibilities for thinking about water in theory and in practice. It presents discourses that address the multiple crises of water access and availability in an economically booming region and thus should be of interest to scholars of Asian Studies, Geography, Environmental and Cultural Studies.

Devleena Ghosh is an Associate Professor in the School of Social Inquiry at the University of Technology Sydney, Australia. Her research interests are in Indian Ocean studies, postcolonial studies and the cultural history of migration. She is currently involved in a joint project researching Intercolonial Networks in the Indian Ocean. **Heather Goodall** is a Professor of History in the School of Social Inquiry at the University of Technology Sydney, Australia. Her research interests include place and contested histories, indigenous histories, environmental history, cross-cultural research, international activism and new media. She is currently engaged in a research project focussing on Australia's relations with the Indian Ocean Region. **Stephanie Hemelryk Donald** was formerly Director of the Institute for International Studies at the University of Technology, Sydney, Australia and is now a Professor of Chinese media studies at the University of Sydney.

Routledge studies in physical geography and environment

This series provides a platform for books which break new ground in the understanding of the physical environment. Individual titles will focus on developments within the main sub-disciplines of physical geography and explore the physical characteristics of regions and countries. Titles will also explore the human/environment interface.

1 **Environment Issues in the Mediterranean**
J. Wainwright and J. B. Thornes

2 **The Environmental History of the World**
Humankind's changing role in the community of life
J. Donald Hughes

3 **History and Climate Change**
A Eurocentric perspective
Neville Brown

4 **Cities and Climate Change**
Harriet Bulkeley and Michele Betsill

5 **Little Ice Ages**
Ancient and modern
Jean M. Grove

6 **Himalayan Perceptions**
Environmental change and well-being of mountain peoples
Jack D. Ives

7 **The Natural History of the Earth**
Debating long-term change in the geosphere and biosphere
Richard John Huggett

8 **Aviation and Climate Change**
Lessons for European policy
Alice Bows, Kevin Anderson and Paul Upham

9 **Water, Sovereignty and Borders in Asia and Oceania**
Edited by Devleena Ghosh, Heather Goodall and Stephanie Hemelryk Donald

OCEANS AND RIVERS IN ASIA AND OCEANIA
PACIFIC OCEAN
CHINA
Beijing
KOREA
JAPAN
Yellow R
Yangtze R
Brahmaputra R
PAKISTAN
Indus River
Jamuna R
Ganges R
Teesta R
Meghna R
Mekong R
TAIWAN
Mumbai
INDIA
Arabian Sea
Bay of Bengal
GOA
SRI LANKA
VIETNAM
MALAYSIA
MARSHALL ISLANDS
KIRIBATI
INDIAN OCEAN
Timor Sea
KIMBERLEYS
Broome
Fitzroy River
FIJI
COOK ISLANDS
AUSTRALIA
Perth
Darling River
Sydney
Georges River
Murray River
NEW ZEALAND
KEY
① BANGLADESH
② BHUTAN
③ BURMA
④ CAMBODIA
⑤ LAOS
⑥ NEPAL
⑦ THAILAND

Water, Sovereignty and Borders in Asia and Oceania

Edited by Devleena Ghosh,
Heather Goodall and
Stephanie Hemelryk Donald

Routledge
Taylor & Francis Group
LONDON AND NEW YORK

First published 2009
by Routledge
2 Park Square, Milton Park, Abingdon, Oxon OX14 4RN

Simultaneously published in the USA and Canada
by Routledge
270 Madison Ave, New York, NY 10016

Routledge is an imprint of the Taylor & Francis Group, an informa business

Typeset in Times by Wearset Ltd, Boldon, Tyne and Wear
Printed and bound in Great Britain by TJI Digital, Padstow, Cornwall

British Library Cataloguing in Publication Data
A catalogue record for this book is available from the British Library

Library of Congress Cataloging in Publication Data
Water, sovereignty, and borders in Asia and Oceania/edited by Devleena Ghosh, Heather Goodall, and Stephanie Hemelryk Donald.
p. cm. – (Routledge studies in physical geography and environment; 9)
Includes bibliographical references and index.

1. Water rights–Asia 2. Water rights–Oceania. 3. Water-supply–Asia–Management. 4. Water-supply–Oceania–Management. I. Ghosh, Devleena. II. Goodall, Heather.
HD1698.A1W38 2008
333.910095–dc22 2008027315

ISBN10: 0-415-43726-1 (hbk)
ISBN10: 0-203-88467-1 (ebk)

ISBN13: 978-0-415-43726-4 (hbk)
ISBN13: 978-0-203-88467-6 (ebk)

Contents

Figures

Contributors

Shapan Adnan is an Associate Professor in the South Asian Studies Programme of the National University of Singapore. His research interests include peasant economy and capitalist development, domination and resistance among the peasantry, ethnic conflict and land rights of indigenous peoples, critiques of flood control structures, determinants of fertility and forced migration, and critiques of the development business. Among his books are: *Annotation of Village Studies in Bangladesh and West Bengal: A Review of Socio-economic Trends over 1942–88*, *Floods, People and the Environment: Institutional Aspects of Flood Protection Programmes in Bangladesh*, and *Migration, Land Alienation and Ethnic Conflict: Causes of Poverty in the Chittagong Hill Tracts of Bangladesh*.

Kate Barclay is a Senior Lecturer in the International Studies Program at the University of Technology Sydney. She researches the social, political and economic aspects of fisheries in the Asia Pacific region. She has published *A Japanese Joint Venture in the Pacific: Foreign Bodies in Tinned Tuna* and *Capturing Wealth from Tuna: Case Studies from the Pacific*, and a video documentary *Rich Fish* about southern bluefin tuna industries. Her current research interests include fisheries interactions in northeast Asia, and their effect on sustainable fisheries development in the Pacific.

Jon Barnett is a human geographer and an Australian Research Council Fellow in the School of Social and Environmental Enquiry at the University of Melbourne. His current ARC project aims to identify the risks climate change pose to the social systems in the Pacific Islands and ways of managing these risks. He is also engaged in a collaborative research project on the water problems of Northern China. His recent fieldwork has concentrated on the South Pacific, China and East Timor. He is on the editorial boards of *Global Environmental Change*, *Journal of Human Security*, *Geography Compass* and *Pacific Ecologist*.

Allison Cadzow is a Senior Research Officer for the Parklands, Culture and Communities Program at the University of Technology Sydney. Together with Heather Goodall, she produced the website *Gold and Silver: Vietnamese*

Migration and Relationships with Environments in Vietnam and Sydney for the Migration Heritage Centre (NSW). She co-researched an exhibition on the environmentalist Marie Byles and is currently assisting with a biography of the Aboriginal performer, Jimmy Little.

Paul D'Arcy is a fellow in the Australian National University's Division of Pacific and Asian History. He researches and teaches Pacific and environmental history, as well as conflict resolution and development in the Asia Pacific region. He has published *The People of the Sea: Environment, Identity and History in Oceania* and *Peoples of the Pacific: The History of Oceania to 1870.*

Stephanie Hemelryk Donald was formerly Director of the Institute for International Studies at the University of Technology, Sydney and is now a Professor of Chinese media studies at the University of Sydney. Her books include *Picturing Power in the People's Republic of China*, *Media in China*, *Little Friends: Children's Media Culture in China*, and *Tourism and the Branded City: Film and Identity on the Pacific Rim*.

Brian Finlayson is an Associate Professor in the Melbourne School of Land and Environment at the University of Melbourne. Brian is a geomorphologist and hydrologist and has written books on hillslopes, global hydrology and stream hydrology. He is co-Director of the Centre for Environmental Applied Hydrology.

Devleena Ghosh is an Associate Professor in the School of Social Inquiry at the University of Technology, Sydney. Her research interests are in Indian Ocean studies, postcolonial studies and the cultural history of migration. She is the co-author of *Colonialism and Modernity*, co-editor of *Cultures of Trade: Indian Ocean Exchanges* and editor of *Women in Asia: Shadowlines* (forthcoming). She is currently involved in a joint project researching Intercolonial Networks in the Indian Ocean with Heather Goodall, Stephen Muecke and Michael Pearson.

Heather Goodall is a Professor of History in the School of Social Inquiry at the University of Technology, Sydney. Her research interests include place and contested histories, indigenous histories, environmental history, cross-cultural research, international activism and new media. Her books include the award-winning *Isabel Flick: The Many Lives of an Extraordinary Aboriginal Woman* and *Invasion to Embassy: Land in Aboriginal Politics in NSW from 1770 to 1972*. She is currently engaged in a research project focussing on Australia's relations with the Indian Ocean Region.

Janice Gray is a Senior Lecturer in the School of Law at the University of New South Wales, Sydney. She designed, introduced and taught one of the first postgraduate courses in Water Law. She has presented and published nationally and internationally on Water Law, Property Law, Equity and Native Title. J. Gray *et al. Property Law in New South Wales* was first published by

Butterworths in 2003 with a revised second edition in 2007. Her recent research has been on legal regimes for sewer mining.

Douglas Hill is a Lecturer in the Department of Geography at the University of Otago, New Zealand. His research focuses on rural development in West Bengal, the geopolitics of water resources in the Ganges–Brahmaputra and Indus basins, maritime labour in Calcutta and the transformation of urban space in India.

Philip Hirsch is a Professor of Human Geography in the School of Geosciences at the University of Sydney and Director of the Australian Mekong Resource Centre. He has worked on and in the Mekong region for more than 25 years and has published widely on environmental issues, development and natural resource management in the region. His current work on water governance and agrarian change includes field-based projects in a number of Mekong countries.

Tony McAvoy is a Wiri man and his grandfather's country is the area around Clermont, Queensland, northwest of Rockhampton. His grandmother was a Kullilli woman from Thargomindah, southwest Queensland. He worked as a solicitor in Queensland, in private practice and for the Aboriginal Legal Service, before moving to the NSW Department of Aboriginal Affairs to gain experience in government policy analysis and development. He was admitted to the NSW Bar in 2000 and specialises in assisting indigenous people in the pursuit and recognition of native title rights and interests.

Jeff Malpas is a Professor of Philosophy and ARC Professorial Research Fellow at the University of Tasmania and also Distinguished Visiting Professor at LaTrobe University. He has an international reputation for his work across a number of areas in philosophy, particularly those relating to issues of place, space and environment. His most recent book is *Heidegger's Topology* (MIT, 2006).

Stephen Muecke is a Professor of Cultural Studies, Australian Professorial Fellow and Fellow of the Australian Academy of the Humanities. His long-term research interests are indigenous studies, transnational cultures, fictocritical writing, travel writing and new ethnography. His books include *Ancient and Modern: Time, Culture and Indigenous Philosophy* and a biography of David Unaipon. With Devleena Ghosh, Heather Goodall and Michael Pearson he is currently researching the interconnectedness of the Indian Ocean region from a cultural studies perspective.

Dirk H. R. Spennemann is an Associate Professor of Cultural Heritage Management in the School of Environmental Sciences at Charles Sturt University. His main research interests are in the area of future studies, focussing on heritage futures by examining the conceptual understanding of heritage issues and the future recognition of heritage sites.

Sandy Toussaint is an Adjunct Professor at the Universities of Western Australia and Melbourne. She has undertaken ethnographic research among indigenous and non-indigenous groups in the Kimberley since 1981 and published widely on applied and theoretical matters related to the anthropology of cultural environments (waters and lands), native title and customary law, health and medicine, and the implications of interdisciplinary research.

Mark Wang is an Associate Professor in the Melbourne School of Land and Environment at the University of Melbourne. Mark is a human geographer whose research interests include urbanisation and development in Asia. He is currently engaged on an ARC research project exploring the operation of Chinese labour markets and the relationship between migrant workers' spatial/social mobility and skill accumulation. He is an Honorary Professor of China Three Gorge University and is on the editorial boards of the *International Development Planning Review* and *Chinese Geographical Science*.

Michael Webber is a Professorial Fellow in the Department of Resource Management and Geography at the University of Melbourne. He is an economic geographer, the author of ten books and over 100 academic papers, whose long-term interests centre on the organisation of work and labour markets, and their relationship to equity and exploitation. Since the early 1990s, he has worked on these issues in China. For the past five years he has also been working with colleagues in Melbourne and China on water supply in China, in particular on managing the delivery of irrigation water to farmers in northern China in a way that is socially sustainable.

Acknowledgements

This book had its genesis in a symposium initiated and convened by researchers (Kate Barclay, Stephanie Hemelryk Donald, Devleena Ghosh, Heather Goodall, James Goodman and Stephen Muecke) from Trans/forming Cultures, the Centre for Culture and Communications at the University of Technology, Sydney in 2005. Other participants were drawn from a number of active Australian research networks associated with the Centre, including the China Node of the Asia-Pacific Futures Research Network, the South Asia Network and the Research Initiative on International Activism. This symposium was made possible by the generous funding of the Australian Research Council through the Asia-Pacific Futures Research Network and the International Centre of Excellence in Asia-Pacific Studies, Australian National University.

This book brings together some of the articles presented at that symposium along with other invited pieces relevant to the theme of water, borders and sovereignty. The editors gratefully acknowledge the cartographer, Ian Faulkner, for creating a marvelous map to tight deadlines and Lola Sharon Davidson whose assistance, editing and indexing skills were invaluable.

Introduction

Fresh and salt

Devleena Ghosh, Heather Goodall and Stephen Muecke

> Nothing in the world is more flexible and yielding than water. Yet when it attacks the firm and the strong, none can withstand it, because they have no way to change it. So the flexible overcome the adamant, the yielding overcome the forceful. Everyone knows this, but no one can do it.
>
> Lao Tzu

Amphibious stories

Water, whether fresh or salt, has been an essential part of human culture and history. Each story of livelihood extracted from water tells of the ebbs and flows of the creation of the national and global economy, made by people with cultures, not just capital. For example, the Indian Ocean is not just the Indian Ocean rim, a regionalization based on capital flows, with an empty centre. An historical and cultural perspective such as Gilroy's pinpoints how traditional economic ideas are inadequate to explain historical developments (Gilroy 1993). The neoclassical and Marxist 'labour theory of value' doesn't apply well to forests, rivers or the sea, and current notions of economic development conflict with ecological stability. This book attempts to restore water, both fresh and salt, to its central position in human endeavour, ecology and environment.

Water, like all other elements essential to and intertwined with human lives, is made meaningful by people in various ways. For example, many people saw (and still see) water as a 'force of nature', governed only by deities like Neptune or Varuna, moving according to its own chaotic, complex and rhythmic logic. When we read water, we focus on aspects we can observe and understand; the currents and tides, things which will move us if we sail it in our specially designed ships. Over generations we build up knowledge of the relations of wind and water; and we store this knowledge in texts. We can calibrate the tides and the monsoonal seasons. Free of the manipulative agency of humans, bodies of water, rivers and oceans, still remain, of necessity, readable. Yet we can take another step in this fluid philosophizing and assert that we *have* made modifications to oceanic and riverine architecture: yes, *maybe* we have made them physically different and hence more humanly meaningful than we thought. For example, the coastline of Singapore is no longer fractal. That means every inch of it has been made geometric (a natural and fractal coastline is defined as one whose length increases, towards infinity, as one's capacity to map it increases). The Singapore coastline is all straight lines. In this example, human beings have added another dimension to an always-changing environment. Whether simple or complex, these attempts to add an element of control, artificial elements, point to the moral of this story, that no material can be totally controlled and hence made to deliver up exact meanings every time. This manipulation of material is only ever a question of scale. Human agency is one part of the mix of agentive factors, as Actor Network Theory suggests. Both rivers and oceans are actors, not singular ones, but ones in a complex set of actions without intention.

There has been an intellectual tradition in European thought which would make the division between a physical world (in action, in movement) describable by natural laws; and on the other a world of representations, meanings and stories, which is the world of human creation and reflection. So it is in language that the great narratives about the ocean have found form – the *Lusiads*, the stories of Sindbad, and so on. This artificial binary, the one between the physical and the representational, between science and art, asks the question: which is the more powerful way of telling the story of water: the humanistic or the scientific? This is a question that has to be asked if we are to work towards an 'ecology of practices' and the ethical management of natural resources (Stengers 2005). Shiv Visvanathan, in discussing his teacher Seshadri's conception of the laboratory says, 'Science becomes an inventive morality play around the dreams of energy in India and neither tradition nor modernity is privileged in this agonal struggle'. When Seshadri wanted to start his scientific problems autobiographically, with 'here and now' problems, everyone thought he was crazy. But he wanted to 'create a science that was muscular, not machismo, a science that thought with its hands, a science that was more sexual and sensual, a science that was sensitive to suffering' (Visvanathan 2008).

There is, thus, no innocence in the words we use to turn the great wheels of science. Visvanathan goes on,

> [T]here is more violence tucked in words like health, poverty and energy than in the worst annals of crime. Once you introduce words such as history, development and progress into poverty and suffering, you economize and scienticize it on Judeo-Christian time.
>
> (Visvanathan 2008: 12)

We have to remember such things as they rush to build a dam on the Mandovi River in the hinterland of Goa (or as we rush to stop it), and we have to bear in mind another contingency, the 'morality play' of global exploitation run out of the North 'on Judeo-Christian time', with a narrative about apocalypse, redemption and the chosen people. The critique of such narratives, which use religious characters to drive developmental modernization for corporate profit, has to be incisive and political. Visvanathan again: 'Jawaharlal Nehru's oft-quoted statement "Dams and laboratories are the temples of the new India" was an idiotic combination of Comte and Fabian socialism' (Visvanathan 2008: 13).

Oceans: division not separation

> We are in a certain sense amphibious, not exclusively connected with the land, but with the sea as well.... The sea and the land in which we dwell furnish theatres for action, limited for limited actions and vast for grander deeds.
>
> (Strabo, cited in Semple 1931: 59)

In 'Different Spaces', Michel Foucault, in 1964, developed his idea of heterotopia: 'An ensemble of relations that define emplacements that are irreducible to each other and absolutely non superposable.' A train, apparently, is such a bundle of relations 'since it is something through which one passes; it is also something by which one can pass from one point to another, and then it is something that passes by' (Foucault 1998: 178). But having announced at the beginning of the essay that at the end of the nineteenth century we were leaving behind the great period of History and temporal accumulation and were embarking on an adventure of Space, 'juxtaposition, of the near and the far, of the side-by-side, of the scattered', he finishes with a nostalgic glance back at the great colonial era of sea travel and the ship as an extreme type of heterotopia,

> A piece of floating space, a placeless place, that lives by its own devices, that is self-enclosed and, at the same time, delivered over to the boundless expanse of the ocean, and that goes from port to port, from brothel to brothel, all the way to the colonies in search of the most precious treasures that lie waiting in their gardens, you see why, for our civilisation, from the sixteenth century up to our time, the ship has been at the same time not only the greatest instrument of economic development ... but the greatest reservoir of the imagination.
>
> (Foucault 1998: 184–5)

He speaks here not without irony – and Eurocentrism. But what he offers, with the tool of heterotopia, is the notion of multiplicities in cultural traffic, where there is movement of objects, movement through objects, and lines of cultural force that make things move in certain directions because they are predisposed to do so. A story is just one way of predisposing the flow of objects along certain cultural directions, representing the intersection of codes, structuring as it does the potentialities of human imagination into the real relations of objects, giving them special values.

Steinberg, in his book *The Social Construction of the Ocean*, analyses such values, values that humans, singularly or collectively, ascribe to oceans. He offers three perspectives for the basis of most human–marine interactions: the ocean as resource provider, the ocean as transport surface and the ocean as battleground or 'force field'. The sustainable management of oceanic resources and its distribution is a major issue in current geopolitics. In the early part of the twentieth century, the oceans provided mainly fish as resource and avenues for commerce or war. However, in the twenty-first century, the need to accommodate traditional tenure systems and production practices with emerging resource needs, political power differentials and technological advances, as well as to adjudicate between those who need to use the same ocean space for different purposes, has made for particularly complex negotiations, especially where the actors are territorially bounded states (Steinberg 2001: 11).

In modern geopolitics, the ocean is no longer an unmanaged space, but subject to regimes of private and public ocean law. The coastal areas, like land, may be claimed and controlled by individual states, while the 'freedom of the high seas' supposedly reigns on the deep ocean, to enable the unhampered movement of shipping. However, there has been, for a long time, an extensive set of maritime law relating to the conduct of shipping in international waters (Steinberg 2001: 15). The political and jurisdictional aspects of the law of the sea affect its commercial and economic use and vice versa (Gold 1981, quoted in Steinberg 2001: 15).

If space is a product of social, political, cultural and economic relationships, even the farthest oceanic space is not just an arena for trade and connection but a deliberately crafted social construction of society. Our imagining of the sea affects us in ways of which we may not be conscious. Society's idealizations of the sea are central to 'the institutions and structures that govern their lives' (Steinberg 2001: 191). Hau'ofa calls the Pacific a 'sea of islands', noting that the myths, legends and oral traditions, and the cosmologies of the peoples of Oceania show that 'their universe comprised not only land surfaces, but the surrounding ocean as far as they could traverse and exploit it' (Hau'ofa 1994). This also fits very well with what we know of early Indian Ocean practice where oceanic wayfinding still comprised of

> navigation by 'reading' the stars, sun, ocean swells, wave patterns, cloud formations, wind directions, colour of the sea, flight of sea birds, and integrating all this information with the aid of a mental compass to determine or maintain a sailing course toward an unseen or unknown land target.
>
> (ASAA 2001)

The nation-state model leads us to be trapped in a land-based, territorial mindset. The dichotomy of both borders and sovereignties arises from the fact that most of the globe's oceans lie outside of national territorial zones and elude national histories. CIA planning documents, for example, map the whole of the world's surface, including seas, placing every bit of it under the control of individual nations (Steinberg 2001: 174). The view of the ocean as a frictionless medium, ripe for capitalist transportation, co-opts the representations of the sea as uncontrolled, mysterious, a wild and untameable force of nature. This notion of the sea as a *mare librum*, a free, unregulated space for the smooth flow of commercial shipping, clashes with other claims of capital such as deep sea mining (*United Nations Convention on the Law of the Sea*, 1983, Part XI). There are warnings that nation-states may extrapolate the act of historical enclosure from land to sea (Denman 1984; Eckert 1979; Booth 1985) as the most efficient way to govern this unregulated medium. In 1998, *The Economist* (1998: 4) argued that the sea 'must become ever more like land, with owners, laws and limits'.

Such enclosures are already happening to some extent. Ruth Balint (2005) in her prize-winning work, *Troubled Waters*, recounts how the changing of maritime boundaries in the Timor Sea between Australia and Indonesia transformed Indonesian fishermen into illegal invaders in spite of the fact that they were continuing to do exactly what they and their families had been doing for generations. Many of them, says Balint, cannot read maritime charts and are often unaware that they have strayed outside the legal boundaries (Balint 1999: 30). They navigate their boats in a very different universe than the one constructed by international laws of boundaries and sovereignties. Their maps and radar systems are the stars, the wind, currents and landmarks, experience, stories and myths: a radically different kind of knowledge and imagination.

Rivers without borders

> A long time ago, when man did not obstruct rivers to suit his petty needs, the river channels served as goodwill ambassadors to extensive geographical areas – a river originating in one country flowing through another, joining another river, forming a filigree of merging and diverging rivers – with the social and cultural heritage of one region blending into another, each drawing on the rich yet varied perspectives in the whole process of cultural evolution.
>
> (Jasimuddin 1977)

The Cadigal and Wangal Wangal people, the traditional owners of the Sydney country, were water people. The rivers and the ocean, the beaches and wetlands all around, were their country as much as the earth on which the city was built. We know this from the survivors of those communities who have continued to live in Sydney and from the ways those traditional owners inscribed the places which related them to the waters. They engraved designs and figures onto the rocks of the headlands, they amassed huge middens with the bounty of generations of harvests and they relaxed together in water-fronted sandstone caves where they stencilled the marks of many hands on the walls to record their shared pleasure. In Australia, we start public events by acknowledging our debt to them but, in the present, we extend this crucial practice to recognize also the many Aboriginal people who, displaced from their own homelands, came to Sydney where they took up the responsibilities of the local traditional owners who were decimated by colonial impact. Some came along the coast, and experienced the confluence of fresh water flowing to the salt sea, but others came from inland, and knew fresh wide, meandering rivers with very different fish, birds and stories. For all of them, water was and remains central to their economy, social life and stories.

The stories embody the rich, complex but unstable meanings with which water is invested. The everyday language used to talk about water is embedded with historically specific dimensions of this complexity. When the invading British arrived in Australia, water baffled them: at once obvious and familiar, it always acted in a contrary way. Fresh water was of course a biological and agricultural need, and salt water was a long heritage for seafaring peoples, like the British colonists who were in desperate need of regular ocean communication. But because the water in this southern colony did not behave at all in ways the settlers knew, they left us a vocabulary for inland rivers and fresh waters which bears the marks of their confusion and surprise.

Like colonial race relations, Western thinking about nature has tended to be posed around dichotomies, assumptions of separation and clear boundaries. The notion of fresh and salt is an example of the expectation of clear boundaries between the two, although, of course, the European experience of estuaries already prepared the settlers for a liminal zone of intermixture and indeterminacy. In Australia, the confusion between fresh and salt goes much further in space and time than estuaries. Here there are salt springs, many of which line riverbanks. Some rivers are in fact largely fed from underground water sources rather than from rain (Boulton and Hancock 2006).

In Australia, naturally occurring salt water flows into the largest of the inland rivers, the mighty Darling and the Murray, in a salting process that has been adjusted and regulated by the occasional high floods and constant 'freshes' that flow down the waterways for centuries. But with the rising impacts of Western agriculture, and most recently of industrialized irrigated farming, the salt springs have been compounded by the salt from a rising water table under the planted paddocks, leaving ugly white salt scalds and unusable sour ground where dead trees mark the way the salt flows into the main river, poisoning it as it goes. Salinity on land and increasingly saline 'fresh' inland rivers have become the marker of an ominous future in Australia's once fertile wheat bowl.

In addition to this, water flowed in Australia in such bizarre and unexpected ways, and lay in shapes and channels so unfamiliar, that the English had to borrow local words even to speak about the waters they saw. Of all the topics for which the settlers felt they needed to learn indigenous vocabulary, that of water led to more permanent incorporation into English than most others. So we now talk about billabongs, gilgais and warambools without a notion that they reflect the settlers' incomprehension of the way water worked in Australia.

But in some places water doesn't seem to be there at all. Can a place be a river if it has no water? Yet the ancient riverbeds are key elements of life in central Australia, where water continues to flow beneath the ground but only occasionally above it. These are wide expanses of sand that mark the water's power when it is flowing. For the rest of the time these smooth, sandy beds allow a fruitful camping place, mercifully free from thorns and snakes, a welcome space of comfort for people to meet, share food, stories and ceremonies around the hearth and sleep safely till dawn in the cool sand.

Where the rivers do flow they are wildly variable and unpredictable and have been so for millennia. This has generated a complex dependent ecology of plant and animal life forms that are adapted to variability. The shifts to regular flows which have come from dams and irrigation pumps have choked off the freshes and floods which stimulate breeding cycles, starving the native species of the signals they need to regenerate and survive. And in flood, the rivers are not confined by any stable or reliable banks, but instead flow widely across the country, filling up channels which lie waiting, sometimes for decades, for this regeneration. Other times the waters flow in unpredictable ways, linking up distant watercourses, flowing in unexpected directions and with a whole rainbow of different colours as silt is carried down from separate floodplains to be mingled and again become 'black soil' once the flood has passed. Nor is the flood gone when the water appears to have flowed on. The black soil holds water deeply trapped within its clay structure, so it is fertile and sought after, despite its boggy qualities. And the waters that create it stay on in the imagination of the farmers when they talk about it, however dry it seems to be, as 'sweet ground', 'that flooded country'.

Yet despite drawing on local language to name water and its flows, the colonizers also left traces of their engagements in other colonies. The word 'tank' for example, so common now in rural Australia as a man-made dug-out depression to store water, sounds like English, but in fact derives from the Gujarati *tankh* (perhaps the Sanskrit *tagada* for 'pond') and is used to describe the extensively developed systems of water storages in India (Powell 1991; Ransom 1988: 663). Such borrowings reveal a shared English experience across the colonies of the Empire, which most Australian researchers conclude signals the engineering and modernizing role the British took on in the colonies. This was particularly pertinent in the case of water; the damming and channelling of rivers was a key aspect of 'the white man's burden'. But such words as *tank* arrived long before the British engineering profession developed (Powell 1976: 18). In fact the English were only the agents of transfer, bringing to Australia the long established local Indian technologies for rainwater harvesting and distribution. 'Sinking a tank', an important profession in rural Australia, is seldom recognized as imported Indian knowledge. So the vocabulary of water reflects the deepest complexities of colonialism, not only the exercise of colonial power over people and nature, but the multi-directional learning and appropriation which has shaped the futures of both colonized and colonizers.

The histories exposed in the language of water and rivers leads us directly to question the meanings inscribed in it. While these meanings diverge between waters considered to be 'fresh' and those that are 'salt', their complexity is common to them both. The shared human need for water as an essential biological demand has generated a rich and multilayered engagement with water in individual psychological and social terms. This is inflected by cultural processes, so that the ways in which different national or religious cultures understand water may not only be varied but can be in intense conflict, changing over time and in the course of such conflicts. So migrancy, the flow of new people into a relationship with water, will bring new ideas, new interactions and potentially, new conflicts over borders, boundaries and ownership.

The articles in this book have been specifically written across disciplinary boundaries. The authors have scaled the borders of philosophy, geography, history, cultural studies, political economy, anthropology and law. This endeavour reflects the holistic nature of water, fresh or salt, a fluid and protean element that cannot be confined to singular territorial sovereignty, ownership or discipline. Any story of water, to be significant, has to work in the borderlands, articulating various factors and narratives, to create representations and harness forces that give some sense of the crucial enmeshing of water in our everyday lives.

Some articles in this book focus on specific interplays between sea and hinterland; between farmers (fresh water) and fisherfolk (salt). Others explore relationships such as trade, seasonal transhumance and management of riverine and tidal estuaries. Still others explore the contested sovereignties that occur when those who have traditional title or traditional livelihoods depending on water come into conflict with the seductions of modernization.

Many papers in this volume engage directly with the question of meanings, but do so in very different ways. Jeff Malpas addresses the philosophical and experiential dimensions of water, exploring how the fluidity of water, both materially and conceptually, has played a key role in allowing people to nurture their understandings of places. Malpas argues for the ambiguity of water in its many forms, as offering both borders and highways, and in doing so constituting the places around it.

Where Malpas explores freshwater questions, Paul D'Arcy and Dirk Spennemann interpret the meanings of water for Pacific peoples, whom the Western imaginary associates with tiny islands. D'Arcy, however, like Hau'ofa, sees them as occupying a 'sea of islands', a broad expanse of dwelling across oceans that act as highways not barriers. He argues that until recently the oceans were seen by Islanders to be corridors and connectors and that island societies in the Pacific were defined by the skills of seafaring across the hospitable oceans rather than the exposed earth of the islands. These broad concepts have been limited as international legal borders are focussed onto land masses to define 'nations' at the same time as the knowledge and confidence which seafaring Islanders once had is being eroded by the shifting demands of Pacific modernities. For Spennemann, however, the core of each Pacific island is the lens of freshwater which saturates the central heart of the island, allowing plants, animals and humans to survive in what would otherwise be a fatally saline environment. Spennemann's paper demonstrates that, yet again, issues of political sovereignty and international law are in conflict with local knowledge and in this case with the science of water and geology, in a tense engagement which means literally life and death for people and Pacific nations.

Kate Barclay focuses on a bigger player in the modern era of the Pacific, showing how Japanese ideas of maritime sovereign rights evolved through various factors; imperial expansion, defeat in war, Japan's postwar re-emergence as a world fishing power, the development of the United Nations Law of the Sea and finally Japan's declining status as a fishing power. She demonstrates how Japanese fishing interests came to configure the Asia-Pacific region as their territory in terms of resource exploitation, using the protection afforded by Japan's military. The Japanese empire was in many ways a naval and fishing empire and the Japanese considered that entitlement to fisheries resources should belong to those with a history of using those resources, as opposed to those controlling the sovereign right within the waters. Barclay contends that, once this understanding is deployed, Japan's position in contemporary international fisheries negotiations becomes much more comprehensible.

Ghosh and Muecke's article explores the 'modern' exploitations of hydro-environments that operate on land *and* sea, land *and* river, focusing on the rich ambiguities and interplays between salt and fresh environments. Fisherfolk all over the world, whether they fish in fresh or salt water and across physical or geopolitical boundaries, work within an increasingly fragile ecology. Ghosh and Muecke trace some aspects of the changing labour practices and environmental contexts in the present day lives of fisherfolk in the Mumbai and Goa area, demonstrating the imbrication of the activity of fishing with the changing ecologies of the coast and the modernization of India's economy specifically through industrialization and tourism. Their article concludes that the complex material transformations generated by the modernizing of ocean use are paralleled in the debates about what constitutes the 'modern', the 'urban' and the 'traditional'.

For each of the authors contributing to this volume, the questions about the meaning of water are not only philosophical and imaginative, but also intensely political. They have consequences in the everyday world, in which real people bear the costs of the power struggles occurring over the politics of mobilizing the meanings of rivers and oceans. Janice Grey and Tony McAvoy address questions around whether water is regarded as a commons and by whom. Grey traces the way legal structures in Australia, and particularly in New South Wales, were generated from a piecemeal inheritance from the United Kingdom, interacting with the intractable physical environment in Australia with its limited and variable surface waters and with the intensifying penetration of a globalizing market. The outcome has been a shift from public ownership of the rights to access water to an intensifying commodification of water and a privatization of the rights to its access. McAvoy, an indigenous lawyer and environmental advocate, takes up the implications of these changing land and water laws for the complex societies of Aboriginal people, like the Cadigal and the Wangal Wangal peoples of Sydney and many others across the continent, for whom water holds a very different set of meanings. McAvoy considers the problems arising from the sudden creation of a property market in water after the recognition of rights in land arising from the 1983 NSW Land Rights Act and then the Native Title judgement of the Australian High Court in 1992. He asks whether there can be legal or political strategies that allow recognition of and respect for the cultural meanings of water that continue to be of central importance to

Aboriginal people in contemporary Australia. Phil Hirsch considers management of water as an international commons in a transboundary river in the long Mekong River complex in South East Asia. Local people along the length of the river have long-established approaches to managing water as a commons but these have been significantly affected by bureaucratization, infrastructure issues and commodification. Hirsch argues that transboundary basin organizations can both enhance and undermine governance for the common good, depending on how they deal with commonality of interests in freshwater at various scales, but that the appearance of overall success in basin-level management can hide some troubling ways in which water as a commons is eroded in the process of development.

Goodall and Cadzow undertake a close study of internal colonialism and borders in Australia by examining a river community in Sydney. They investigate how an urban area that was densely colonized could nevertheless shelter a nucleus of undefeated indigenous people who eventually reasserted their right to be heard in their own country. Salt Pan Creek was central to the story of Aboriginal re-assertion in Sydney over 200 years. It was no accident of geography that the site for such a rich tradition of resistance to the colonial enterprise should have been a watercourse. Rivers, creeks and waterholes have been key sites of conflict because their resources were necessary to both settlers and Aboriginal people. They were also seen by settlers as the means to mark out the dividing lines between them and the conquered peoples. Goodall and Cadzow demonstrate the ways in which the experience of independent and vigorous community life in this urban borderland generated a visionary and committed leadership that continued to shape Indigenous politics in Australia to the present day. Similarly, Sandy Toussaint reflects on the shaping of borders, like waters, by different vantage points and experiences. Borders, she says, may demarcate a landscape, provide protection or symbolize state authority and disciplinary expertise. Similarly, saltwater oceans, freshwater rivers and cognate waterways have the capacity to define environments, embody both safety and danger or provide a threshold for complex expressions of conflict, power and control. Her article explores some of these issues through an ethnographic focus on the Kimberley region's Fitzroy River in northern Western Australia, based on an incremental sovereignty framework. She discusses ideas connected to the conceptualization of the river and the way in which various groups who have immediate or vicarious relationships with it inscribe it with meaning.

Finally, the question of the relation between water and borders, whether international or regional, is tackled directly by Webber *et al.* within China in relation to the Yellow River and the Yangtze and by Hill and Adnan in relation to the massive, trans-border river systems in South Asia. Webber *et al.* undertake a careful analysis of the political impact of the proposed governance and engineering decisions involved in the management of water in the Yellow River valley, where the implications of transfers of water from one region to another will have major effects on the people of both river valleys. Doug Hill examines the recent changes in the complex management of the Indus River in the west, shared since Partition in 1947 between India and Pakistan, and the Ganges–Brahmaputra–Meghna basin in the east, where the governments of India, Nepal and Bangladesh are all involved in decision making. These rivers continue to flow through largely agricultural economies, and the contesting interests at work in pressuring governments over river control are different from those operating in economies like China and Australia where industrial uses and energy production make ever higher demands on river systems. Nevertheless, the rising pressures of highly capitalized development strategies, like intensifying agriculture, as well as the political impact of displacements of populations, have generated recent shifts in cross border decision-making on rivers which, particularly in the east with the Farakka Barrage, have generated new tensions. Just as significantly, Hill points out that the management of surface waters is open to negotiation through the multilayered processes of formal agreements. However, with the increasingly evident limitations of those waters under the pressures of developmental strategies, there has been a major increase in the exploitation of ground water, which is far less accessible either to the quantification of its depletion or to negotiated agreements over sustainable and equitable rates of extraction. So the use of water has escaped the legal and political boundaries established over fresh river water or salt seawater, detaching it from political borders and shaping it once again as 'a commons' but a limited one, vulnerable to uncontrolled exploitation. Shapan Adnan's article identifies the constraints faced by a state that undertakes water management programs on river systems shared with other sovereign states. Such constraints can arise from cross-border contentions as well as internal contestations by concerned social groups. Adnan explores these internal and external constraints in the specific context of water management and flood control programs in the Ganges–Brahmaputra–Meghna delta within the boundaries of Bangladesh. His analysis focuses on the roles of intellectual critiques of flood control from academics and professional groups, resistance to harmful project structures by adversely affected people at the grassroots and wider society, and interventions in shared rivers by upper riparian states. He demonstrates that the floodplain peasantry and the planners and policy makers held very different cultural views about the use and management of water. People's cultural understanding about floods and water use were pitted against a technocratic culture of flood control and river management, which had total confidence in the powers of modern technology, but little understanding of the traditional knowledge system and resilience of the floodplain peasantry. He concludes that government and donor agencies were eventually compelled to make drastic policy changes regarding flood control largely owing to the grassroots contestations by people adversely affected by flood control structures.

While directing their primary focus to the themes of freshwater or salt, commons or borders, all these chapters have engaged deeply with the problems of the complex and shifting meanings of water and the intensely politicized context in which the conflicts over these meanings are played out. They each demonstrate that water debates, whether conducted in the spheres of politics or economics and in the language of science, social science or the humanities, have real consequences for real people. The hand stencils of the Cadigal and the Wangal Wangal people on the sandstone cliffs around Sydney Harbour and its rivers do more than foreground the complex cultures of Aboriginal Australia, they demand we consider the very human qualities of our interaction with water at the same time as we seek to grasp its ecological as well as its political dimensions.

All the articles work at the changing intersections of personal meanings and economic forces and demand reflective consideration, along the lines Malpas suggests, to appreciate the ways in which water and place are mutually constitutive. Such consideration would realize that the processs of creating 'facts' about water, fresh or salt, comprises value judgements. Facts, like values, have a history, and emerge only within the habitus of an ecology of practices and wider power relations. Through their analyses of certain 'critical sites' in the history of modernization and colonialism, the writers in this volume illuminate our understanding of the way in which humans and water are always working together, without a subject–object distinction, unable to dissociate themselves from that relationship, one of both material and symbolic dimensions. An interdisciplinary and cross-disciplinary approach to the study of water implies a study of the ethics and practices within ecologies. It does not say that 'we' have to intensify our care or scrutiny of 'nature'; it says we have to move *certainty* about the production of risk-free objects (with the mantra of the infinitude of all resources and the clear separation between things and people) to *uncertainty* about such relations whose unintended consequences threaten to disrupt all orderings, all plans, all impacts (Latour 2004: 25).

Bibliography

Asian Studies Association of Australia (ASAA) (2001) electronic Newsletter, June.

Balint, R. (1999) 'The Last Frontier: Australia's Maritime Territories and the Policing of Indonesian Fishermen', *Journal of Australian Studies*, December.

—— (2005) *Troubled Waters: Borders, Boundaries and Possession in the Timor Sea*, Sydney: Allen & Unwin.

Barlow, M. and Clarke, T. (2002) *Blue Gold: the Battle against Corporate Theft of the World's Water*, London: Earthscan Publications.

Booth, K. (1985) *Law, Force and Diplomacy at Sea*, London: Allen & Unwin.

Boulton, A. J. and Hancock, P. J. (2006) 'Rivers as groundwater-dependent ecosystems: a review of degrees of dependency, riverine processes and management implications', *Australian Journal of Botany*, 54.

Denman, D. (1984) *Markets under the Sea? A Study of the Potential of Private Property Rights in the Seabed*, London: Institute of Economic Affairs.

Eckert, R. (1979) *The Enclosure of Ocean Resources: Economics and the Law of the Sea*, Stanford, Calif.: Hoover Institute Press.

Economist, The (1998) 'Survey: "The deep green sea"', 23 May.

Foucault, M. (1998) 'Different Spaces' in J. D. Faubion (ed.) *Michel Foucault: Aesthetics, Method and Epistemology, Essential Works of Foucault, 1954–1984*, New York: New Press.

Gilroy, P. (1993) *The Black Atlantic: Modernity and Double Consciousness*, Cambridge, Mass.: Harvard University Press.

Hau'ofa, E. (1994) 'Our Sea of Islands', *The Contemporary Pacific*, 6 (1): 148–61.

Jasimuddin (1977) 'Murshida Gaan', Dhaka, www.hinduonnet.com/folio/fo0107/01070260.htm accessed 30 May 2008.

Latour, B. (2004) *Politics of Nature: How to Bring the Sciences into Democracy*, Harvard, Mass.: Harvard University Press.

Powell, J. M. (1976) *Environmental Management in Australia, 1788–1914*, Melbourne: Oxford University Press.

—— (1991) *Plains of Promise, Rivers of Destiny: Water Management and the Development of Queensland, 1824–1990*, Bowen Hills: Boolarong Publications.

Ransom, W. S. (ed.) (1988) *The Australian National Dictionary*, Melbourne: Oxford University Press.

Semple, E. C. (1931) *The Geography of the Mediterranean Region: Its Relation to Ancient History*, New York: Henry Holt.

Steinberg, P. (2001) *The Social Construction of the Ocean*, Cambridge and New York: Cambridge University Press.

Stengers, I. (2005) 'Introductory Notes on an Ecology of Practices', *Cultural Studies Review*, 11 (1).

United Nations (1983) *The Law of the Sea: Official Text of the United Nations Convention on the Law of the Sea with Annexes and Index, A/CONF.62/122*, United Nations, New York, www.un.org/depts/los/index.htm (accessed 30 April 2008).

Visvanathan, S. (2008) 'Between Cosmology and System: The Heuristics of a Dissenting Imagination', www.ces.fe.uc.pt/emancipa/research/en/ft/sonhos.html accessed 30 May 2008.

1 The forms of water

In the land and in the soul

Jeff Malpas

Water, its presence or absence, and the forms in which it appears, is fundamental to each and every place on earth. Indeed, along with soil, air and light, water is elemental to place, and so also to all life and dwelling in place. Moreover, human life is itself essentially determined through its entanglement in place and places, and so is constituted, if indirectly, perhaps, through water and its forms. The centrality of place that I am alluding to here arises out of a conception of the relation between human being and place, according to which who and what we are is fundamentally determined by the places in which we live – and this is so even while places are also shaped by the lives that are formed within them.

The idea that human life and being may be bound to place in this way is a common theme in much contemporary thought and practice, from anthropology and geography to art and architecture.[1] The idea of a close connection between human life and land is especially prominent, of course, in the thinking of many indigenous cultures – in, for instance, that of the North American Indian as well as of the Australian Aborigine (Myers 1991; Rose 1991) – but it is not a feature of indigenous culture alone. Not only is the idea of such a connection quite widespread in a way that is independent of culture and history, but there is good reason to suppose that our being bound to place is an essential feature of our being human. The evidence to support such a view is various, but depends essentially on recognising the way in which our identities are dependent on the possibilities of action that are available to us and the way those possibilities for action are themselves dependent on the spatio-temporalised forms of our immediate environment (Malpas 1999). Put simply: what we are depends on what we can do, and what we can do depends on where we are situated. It is not merely, then, that we look to the places in which we live as that by means of which we explicitly articulate a sense of ourselves, but more than this, the very shape of our lives is determined, implicitly and explicitly, by the possibilities that are given in and through the places in which we live and our interaction with those possibilities and places.

I have used the term 'topography' to describe the particular mode of inquiry, as well as method, that takes such constitution of the human in relation to place as a central theme (Malpas 1999: 39–41, 2005). Of course, the idea of topography itself calls upon the notion of place, of *topos*, and so my claim is not only that we are ourselves constituted in and through place, but that the relations involved here are themselves essentially the relations exemplified in the structure of place. Place thus provides a twofold key to understanding the constitution of human life and, more broadly, of the world within which that life appears.

But how does place appear, in what forms, and how do places structure themselves? These sorts of question can be addressed at a number of different levels. For instance, at a more abstract level, I would argue that places are structured and articulated in and through narrative – though I would need to say a fair bit about what narrative means here (Malpas 1999: 179–87).[2] At another level, places are essentially understood through ideas of pathway and track, of border and crossing, of site and situation. And at yet another level again, our thinking about place takes shape in our thinking about various 'features' or 'elements' of place – building and street, bridge and road, earth and sky, hill and mountain, valley and plain, river and lake, swamp and floodplain, estuary, coast and sea.

It is when we look to these latter elements that the fundamental role of water in place comes to light. It is through the forms of water, as also through the forms of earth, light and air, that places come to have the particular character that belongs to them. Indeed, reflecting on Veronica Strang's pioneering investigation of the 'meaning' of water (Strang 2004), we may say that the meaning of place is itself significantly constituted through the meaning – and meanings – of water. Moreover, while the various forms of water contribute to the constitution of different places, perhaps the role of water as a basic and determining element of place should also be seen to determine places as themselves, essentially fluid and dynamic.

The various forms of water at issue here have to be understood in terms of the way those forms shape kinds of actions and modes of agency. This is evident, for instance, in the contrast, especially important in Australian Aboriginal cultures in northern Australia, between saltwater and fresh (Sharp 2002). We may think of these as constituting two entirely different 'worlds', but if we do, then we must think of these different worlds as coalescing around different modes of living, acting, moving as these are associated with coast and sea, river, creek and waterhole. Similarly, the contrast between water that is temporary and permanent, also important in Australian Aboriginal culture and thought, brings with it different modes of living through the different forms of movement and action that arise in relation to each of these.

Particular forms of water, and not only these contrasting 'worlds', are similarly tied to different formations of place. The river, for instance, functions as a boundary, as well as a point of crossing over (indeed, the way water functions to mark transition is an important feature of the way water presents itself in almost all its forms); it is also a means of transportation, and so a means of connection as well as separation. As boundary and connection, as highway and divide, the river constitutes places in and around it in particular ways that are directly determined by the shaping of agency and movement. The sea also functions as both boundary and highway and, like the river, it constitutes its own place. But inasmuch as sea stands in contrast to the land, as salt stands in contrast to fresh, so the sea stands in opposition to the land as another realm with its own ordering, its own resources, its own threats and bounties, its own cycles, movements and patterns of activity. These various forms of water, salt and fresh, transient and permanent, sea and river, are articulated through the actions and movements correlated with them, but those actions and movements, and so the character of those forms of water and their places, are also articulated through narrative, story, myth, metaphor and image. Moreover, this is not merely a feature of indigenous understanding, but of understanding as such – our connectedness to place, and the character of place, is worked out through narrative, and in those narratives of place, narratives of water play as central a role as the forms of water play in the constitution of place.

As the forms of water determine the identity of places, so they also determine identity as such. We can see this at work in a host of different instances and examples. In Europe, rivers have played a central role in the constitution, not only of the European landscape, or even of European regions and nations, but of European identity as such. Thus, in the work of Friedrich Hölderlin, we find poetic meditations on the Danube, also called the Ister and the Donau (the variation in names tells us something about the different faces of the river), as well as the Rhine, as they stand in relation to the idea of Germany and of German culture (Hölderlin 1984). The Danube, in particular, appears in Hölderlin as the conduit that brings Germany into its own through bringing Germany into conjunction with its other, namely, the Greek – the Danube connects occidental and oriental, the domestic and the foreign (Young 1999).

The role played by the Danube and the Rhine in Europe is not obviously replicated in Australia. George Seddon writes that

> The Nile, the Rhine, Ganges, Mississippi all have a historical, social, economic and political significance. The only river in Australia of which that can be said is the Murray. Australia is organised around ports, roads and rail, not along rivers.
>
> (Seddon 1998: 51)

Seddon is right that rivers do not have the same role in the constitution of Australian places and so also Australian culture and identity – the Murray is the obvious and perhaps solitary exception here (Sinclair 2001) – as do the Rhine, the Nile or indeed the Danube. And while ports, roads and rail have an obvious significance in Australian life, I would argue that the different forms of water to be found in Australia as opposed to, for example, Europe, are just as important in making Australian places and Australian life.

Water does not figure in the constitution of places only as a feature of the land – river, lake, swamp and so forth – nor only in its contrasting form as sea, but also in its appearance as a feature of the sky – as mist, rain (in all its varieties), sleet, snow and, one must also say, as drought. Indeed, the appearance of water in its cyclical, seasonal variability is a key aspect of the way place is determined in Australia. To some extent this is embodied in indigenous thinking in the form of the water-spirit, that is the Rainbow Serpent who not only forms springs and waterholes by his movements across the land, but also alternates between activity and rest, abundance and scarcity.

It is easy to overlook the forms of water that are associated with the seasons and so also with the sky. Yet these forms can be just as important as those forms that appear on the land or as the sea. Think of the difference between the misty, rain-soaked Irish landscape and the tropical world of torrential rains and humidity that is to be found in parts of Northern Australia. Indeed, the ways in which water appears in the air and through the forms of weather, and not only as a feature of the earth and land, reinforces the key role of water as an element in place. Yet it also indicates the extent to which human engagement with water occurs at a very basic experiential level. We feel water through all of our senses: when we feel the wetness of mist on our skin, when we breathe in the humidity of a tropical evening, when we see the refraction of light through water droplets in a rainbow, when we hear the fall of rain on a tin roof (Strang 2004: 49–79).

The different forms of water are constitutive of the character of different places. Yet as places are constitutive of our own identity – we are who and what we are in and through the places we inhabit – so the forms of water enter into and are constitutive of the soul no less than of the land and the place. In drinking, bathing, and in all the various uses to which water is put, then, not only do we satisfy certain basic physiological and practical needs, not only do we draw upon an element of the natural environment, but we also enact and reinforce the fundamental relatedness that obtains between us and the place and places in which we dwell. To think through the significance of water in human life thus involves more than just considerations of health or of economics – it touches on our very constitution as human, since it touches on our constitution in and through place.

Here, I suggest, is the real core of the idea of water as a 'commons' – the 'commons' is not just that which is common to all as some sort of shared possession, but rather that which is common in such a way that all partake of it, all are determined by it, all are already given over to caring for it, insofar as they are already given over to caring for themselves. This is why the Cochabamba Declaration made by the indigenous people of Bolivia in December 2000 rightly has as its first statement not merely a statement concerning water as a physical necessity for life, but concerning water as sacred to life: 'Water belongs to the earth and all species and is sacred to life'.[3] It is the sacredness of water which is taken as the basis for the imperative to conserve, reclaim and protect it.

The second sense of 'commons' that is at issue here is, it seems to me, often overlooked or ignored in favour of the more pragmatic, instrumentalist conception of the 'commons' as some form of common 'property' or 'resource'. We might distinguish between these two senses of 'commons' in terms that also mirror two different senses in which we may also understand our relation to land or to place: as that which belongs *to us* or as that *to which* we belong. It is this second sense that, I would suggest, is the more fundamental.

The experience of water, or of the forms of water, and of the relation between water and the other elements of place, is a central element in the experience of place as such, and so also of the experience of ourselves and the world. Water is an increasingly important focus for political and environmental concerns, but water is not merely a commodity or a resource to be used and managed – not even when the management is ecologically sensitive. Water is more than just a commodity or resource. To attune ourselves to our essential inter-relatedness to place, and our own entanglement in it, to attune ourselves to the 'spirit' *of place*, is also to attune ourselves to the 'spirit' *of water* and to its forms.

Notes

1 See the bibliography for some recent works on this subject.
2 I take narrative to include not only explicitly presented narratives that appear in the form of stories that are told to be heard or read, but also the implicit narratives encoded in patterns of action or the layout of a particular space.
3 The Cochabamba Declaration, made on 8 December 2000, in Cochabamba, Bolivia:

> We, citizens of Bolivia, Canada, United States, India and Brazil: Farmers, workers, indigenous people, students, professionals, environmentalists, educators, nongovernmental organizations, retired people, gather together today in solidarity to combine forces in the defence of the vital right to water. Here, in this city which has been an inspiration to the world for its retaking of that right through civil action, courage and sacrifice, standing as heroes and heroines against corporate, institutional and governmental abuse and trade agreements which destroy that right, in use of our freedom and dignity, we declare the following:
>
> For the right to life, for the respect of nature and the uses and traditions of our ancestors and our peoples, for all time the following shall be declared as inviolable rights with regard to the uses of water given us by the earth:
>
> 1 Water belongs to the earth and all species and is sacred to life, therefore, the world's water must be conserved, reclaimed and protected for all future generations and its natural patterns respected.
> 2 Water is a fundamental human right and a public trust to be guarded by all levels of government, therefore, it should not be commodified, privatized or traded for commercial purposes. These rights must be enshrined at all levels of government. In particular, an international treaty must ensure these principles are noncontrovertable.
> 3 Water is best protected by local communities and citizens who must be respected as equal partners with governments in the protection and regulation of water. Peoples of the earth are the only vehicle to promote earth democracy and save water.

Bibliography

Adams, P.C. (ed.) (2001) *The Textures of Place: Exploring Humanist Geographies*, Minneapolis, Minn.: University of Minnesota Press.
Casey, E.S. (1999) *The Fate of Place*, Berkeley, Calif.: University of California Press.
Dean, T. and Millar, J. (2005) *Place*, Artworks Series, London: Thames and Hudson.
Entrikin, N. (1991) *The Betweenness of Place*, Baltimore, Md.: Johns Hopkins University Press.

Feld, S. and Basso, K. (eds) (1998) *Senses of Place*, Santa Fe, N. Mex.: School of American Research Press.

Harries, K. (1998) *The Ethical Function of Architecture*, Cambridge, Mass.: MIT Press.

Hayden, D. (1995) *The Power of Place: Urban Landscapes as Public History*, Cambridge, Mass.: MIT Press.

Hölderlin, F. *Hymns and Fragments by Friedrich Hölderlin*, trans. R. Sieburth, Princeton, N.J.: Princeton University Press, 1984.

Jackson, J.B. (1996) *A Sense of Place, A Sense of Time*, New Haven, Conn.: Yale University Press.

Malpas, J. (1999) *Place and Experience*, Cambridge: Cambridge University Press.

—— (2005) *Heidegger's Topology: Being, Place, World*, Cambridge, Mass.: MIT Press.

Myers, F.R. (1991) *Pintupi Country, Pintupi Self: Sentiment, Place and Politics among Western Desert Aborigines*, Berkeley, Calif.: University of California Press.

Read, P. (2000) *Belonging: Australians, Place and Aboriginal Ownership*, Cambridge: Cambridge University Press.

Relph, E. (1976) *Place and Placelessness*, London: Routledge & Kegan Paul.

Rose, D.B. (1991) *Dingo Makes Us Human: Life and Land in an Australian Aboriginal Culture*, Cambridge: Cambridge University Press.

Seamon, D. and Mugerauer, R. (eds) (1989) *Dwelling, Place and Environment: Towards a Phenomenology of Person and World*, New York: Columbia University Press.

Seddon, G. (1998) 'A Snowy River Reader', *Landprints*, Cambridge: Cambridge University Press.

Sharp, N. (2002) *Saltwater People: The Waves of Memory*, Crows Nest, NSW: Allen & Unwin.

Sinclair, P. (2001) *The Murray: A River and Its People*, Melbourne: Melbourne University Press.

Strang, V. (2004) *The Meaning of Water*, Oxford: Berg.

Tuan, Yi-Fu (1990) *Topophilia*, New York: Columbia University Press.

Young, J. (1999) 'Poets and Rivers: Heidegger on Hölderlin's "*Der Ister*"', *Dialogue* 28: 391–416.

2 Variable rights and diminishing control

The evolution of indigenous maritime sovereignty in Oceania

Paul D'Arcy

Pacific Islanders' control of their maritime spaces has varied considerably across time and space over the last 200 years since the increase of a permanent Western presence in Oceania.[1] Colonial rule introduced new systems of maritime sovereignty and new priorities, although these did not totally supplant indigenous systems of tenure. Political independence for most in the 1970s, and the establishment of internationally recognised legal principles of maritime sovereignty in the 1980s, enhanced most Pacific Islanders' maritime territory and the rights they held over them. However, changes to maritime technology and the maritime economy have created a large gap between Pacific Islanders' enhanced sovereign rights and their ability to monitor and harvest their territorial waters. In addition, many Pacific Islanders are either minorities in settler colonies or still controlled by foreign minorities in much of Oceania. Here, restrictions to their maritime sovereignty derive more directly from political marginalisation.

The neglected past: Pacific Islanders' dominion of the sea

Modern studies of sea tenure in Oceania significantly understate the importance and extent of sea tenure prior to colonial rule, especially the fluidity and contested nature of maritime spaces. They generally portray maritime tenure as a relatively static set of rules, rather than an evolving process. Most of these studies were undertaken in the post-war colonial era or since independence by anthropologists. This depiction is now under challenge by recent studies emphasising sea tenure as a fluid process.[2] In this sea of islands, to use Tongan author Epeli Hau'ofa's apt description of Oceania, the sea was crucial to the lives of coastal peoples (Hau'ofa 1994). In the absence of well-developed roads and beasts of burden, the sea was the main form of transport, especially for bulk cargoes. Rugged island interiors and few large, continental islands meant that any journey of any significant distance required a sea passage. Off-island trade goods enhanced the range of status and functional items available for exchange to ensure intra- and inter-group harmony or to pursue political ambitions. The wealth of most near-shore fisheries, especially the highly productive reef and lagoon complexes surrounding many islands of the Western Pacific, meant that fishing activities and tenure units were generally much more concentrated than elsewhere in the world. They were also keenly contested on occasion (D'Arcy 2006a: chs 2 and 3).

Groups controlling coastal areas usually extended their claims of tenure to areas immediately offshore. User rights for coastal land and near-shore resources were mapped out with equal precision down to the level of individual family holdings. Specific maritime features also served as markers for sea boundaries. After describing how the boundaries of the Palauan district of Ngeremlengui ran from mountain peaks to two river mouths, for example, American anthropologist Richard Parmentier details how they ran out towards two points on the reef (Parmentier 1987: 198n1). Most inshore waters were partitioned into areas controlled and fished almost exclusively by the same local community. Fishermen rarely strayed beyond their own area within the near-shore zone. When fish were caught outside of one's own kin group area, it was usual to present part of the catch to local residents. These presentations were usually made to the head of the kin group, although each coral bank, fish weir and other fishing spots within their marine territory were associated with specific families. These subgroups also made presentations to paramount leaders. Refusal to provide tribute entitled the paramount to dispossess the offending group of its maritime territory, although there is no record of any such confrontation. Chiefs on most atolls had rights to material that drifted ashore. This right was based on chiefs' sacred association with gods and ancestral figures who dwelt in the sea or sky.[3] They also had the right to declare particular zones of the lagoon or reef as theirs to regulate and control. This might be done for a short time to conserve marine resources, or permanently to control a rich fishery. Chiefs on high islands held similar rights. They had exclusive use of certain fisheries, and the right to expropriate part of any catch. These expropriations were often conducted for religious reasons, and came with an expectation that chiefs would be generous in redistributing their share, particularly in times of want.[4]

Sea tenure extended beyond these intensively used and intimately partitioned inshore waters, although the record is less detailed for areas further offshore. Few claims of tenure are recorded in areas out of sight of land but, in those that are, access rights appear to have been less exclusive than those nearer to shore. The open ocean is usually described as a fishery open to all by modern commentators,[5] but there were exceptions. Ethnologist Abraham Fornander records fishing grounds three miles offshore in Hawai'i that were still deemed to belong to the chief and people of the nearest coastal residential unit, the *ahupua'a* (Thrum 1919: 186–7). The difficulty of monitoring and protecting offshore areas meant that information on Hawai'ian *ko'a* (offshore fishing grounds) was kept secret by individuals to prevent others from exploiting them. Fishermen would only approach these grounds under cover of early morning darkness, and wait until they were well away from the site before hauling in their catch (Barrere 1976: 78–9). The most thorough study of high island offshore tenure is archaeologist Robert Hommon's study of Hawai'i. He noted that Hawai'ian chiefs occasionally extended their control beyond one island, but found no explicit statement about control of the seas between islands. Hommon asserts that political control was expressed through the limitations and prohibitions that Hawai'ian chiefs were able to impose on activities at sea. He notes that chiefs were able to ban canoe travel at certain times of the year. There were also seasonal bans on fishing for certain species. Fishing for periodically banned species occurred up to 15 miles from the coast, and canoe travel included passages across sea channels up to 117 kilometres wide (Hommon 1975: 96–8, 100–1, 183–97).[6]

Pacific Islanders living on smaller, coral islands such as atolls had an even closer and more extensive relationship with the sea. Many coral islanders maintained tenure claims further offshore. The most detailed studies deal with the Western Carolines, where the sea was crowded with fishing banks, reefs and smaller, uninhabited atolls that were regularly exploited. Evidence collected around the turn of the twentieth century reveals that Puluwatese fished on Oraurau-feis (Manila Bank) southwest of Puluwat, Suat Reef (Enderby Bank) to the northwest, Asebar Reef in the east and Maianjor to the southeast. All these fisheries were less than a day from Puluwat. Canoes would leave about midnight to arrive at the fishing grounds early the next day. After fishing for the remainder of the day they departed in the evening and arrived back at Puluwat the following day. Most of these fishing grounds lie between 20 miles and the 100 miles average overnight sailing range from Puluwat (Damm *et al.* 1935: 50, 56; Marck 1986).

Maritime rights needed to be constantly protected and asserted. Confrontations occurred along borders and within maritime territories, and ranged from low level raiding of individual fish traps to attempts to permanently seize control of enemy fishing grounds. Polish ethnographer Jan Kubary noted that in Palau it was 'considered perfectly natural to rob the traps of the weaker neighboring villages, although the same offence practiced against kin or fellow villagers would not be accepted' (Kubary 1896: 148). When the trader Andrew Cheyne visited Yap in 1864 he found that the people of Tomil and Weeloey were at war after the Tomil people killed two Weeloey men over a fishing ground dispute (Cheyne 1864: entry for 21 February). On other occasions groups attempted to forcibly seize fisheries. The districts of Ko'olau and Kona on the Hawai'ian island of Moloka'i went to war over a disputed fishing ground. Kona emerged victorious in battle and held onto the fishery (Fornander 1969: 282).

A significant amount of fighting took place at sea. Its nature varied between localities from harassing individual canoes passing through inshore waters to open battles between fleets of specialised war canoes (D'Arcy 2006a: 104–9). Despite limited populations and resources, many island communities deployed impressive naval forces. In the 1770s Captain Cook witnessed a Tahitian fleet of 160 large war canoes and 170 sailing canoes. He estimated that the fleet carried over 7,000 men. This was a significant achievement given that the total population of the coalition contributing to it probably numbered in the tens of thousands (Cook in Beaglehole 1961: 385–6; Oliver 1974: vol. 1, 30–3, 405). Beachcomber William Lockerby sailed with a Fijian expedition in 1809 that transported almost 3,000 men in 136 canoes (Lockerby in Imthurn and Wharton

1925: 41–2, cited in Clunie 1977: 22). Fleets elsewhere in Oceania were much less substantial, but could still be important tools.

Naval power was an asset for ambitious political leaders. Throughout Oceania efforts to concentrate power were constrained by political and geographical fragmentation. The main stable social and political units were highly localised kin groups. In an island with poor overland communications and no beasts of burden, sea power conferred mobility. With a fleet, rulers became less remote in perception and reality to those contemplating rebellion. Those with naval forces could harass enemy coasts at will if not met by naval forces of comparable strength. While an army could contest landings, canoe-borne opponents could soon outdistance them, and move on to attack unguarded coasts.

Competing tenure regimes under colonial rule

Indigenous naval power was unable to fend off the foreign military and naval forces that eventually imposed colonial rule over all of Oceania. The Chamorro of the Mariana Islands were the first Pacific Islanders to lose their sovereignty to Europeans when Spanish forces conquered their islands in the seventeenth century. New Zealand Māori and Tahitian Maohi were next to experience a gradual erosion of sovereignty after military confrontation with Westerners in the 1840s. Most Pacific Islanders only nominally came under Western or Japanese colonial rule in the last three decades of the nineteenth century. In most cases, relatively brief and incomplete military victories by the colonisers were followed by prolonged and only partial consolidation of rule characterised by limited foreign settlement and limited resources for administration. The incomplete nature of conquest and consolidation meant that indigenous tenure and use of the sea continued to varying degrees alongside the rules and practices of the new colonisers. Pacific Islanders' maritime interactions and tenure eroded and transformed as new rules governing access, new technologies and changing economic circumstances altered Pacific seascapes. Four major changes occurred during the era of colonial rule. Colonial rules of access were imposed upon traditional tenure. The imposition of a post-conquest colonial peace served to fix formerly fluid and contested maritime tenure. Inter-island and inter-archipelago travel was restricted by colonial prohibitions or colonial boundaries. Lastly, maritime pursuits were also influenced by the decline of seafaring and canoe-making skills in much of Oceania under the influence of changes to maritime technology and the maritime economy.

The lack of administrative resources and land-focused priorities meant that colonial ordinances relating to maritime activities did not necessarily supplant existing indigenous tenure regimes. Colonial governments often declared all waters and lands seaward of the high water mark to be government property. However, such actions were often followed by recognition of customary rights to varying degrees, or at least by tolerance of continued harvesting of traditional resources by local kin groups (Crocombe 2001: 308). Geographer Moshe Rappaport's study of Tuamotu Islanders' loss of lagoon tenure rights during French colonial rule represents the more disruptive extreme of the spectrum. French authorities undermined local communities' collective control of lagoon resources by bringing in compulsory private registration of land in 1847. Many missed the registration deadline and lost their rights according to this new alien system. The remainder had their rights removed in 1890 when the French governor decreed all waters to be public domain under the control of the French administration. Tuamotuan protests were ignored, and henceforth those wishing to exploit lagoon and sea resources required official permission (Rappaport 1996: 35, 37). In contrast, British authorities in the Gilbert Islands (modern day Kiribati) allowed customary marine tenure to prevail until the 1940s. A Native Land Commission subsequently acknowledged only certain aspects of marine tenure however. It recognised descent group ownership of constructed assets such as fish traps and fish ponds, for example, but neglected to emphasise customary obligations of lineage heads to use these assets for the good of the whole lineage (Teiwaki 1988: 40; Thomas 2003: 21).

By the Second World War the colonial peace had had a profound effect on Pacific Island maritime tenure. Modern studies of marine tenure from the post-war colonial era largely reveal what had become, by then, a system of fixed social and political principles. Groups are portrayed as holding different rights to resources on the basis of relative status, with little sense that the system was flexible or open to challenge. There was some continuity from the pre-colonial past however. The distinction between frequently used near-shore waters and other seas remained. Most fishing was concentrated close to shore because of the productivity and shelter of lagoons and other inshore waters. These studies generally conclude that fishermen recognised distinct and specific tenure zones near to shore, while the open sea was much less tightly controlled. Groups held access rights by virtue of their membership of social groups, although ownership was vested in groups ranging from families up to the community as a whole. The smaller the basic tenure group, the more subdivided the inshore fisheries (Sudo 1984: 205, 226–7). Ulithi in the Western Carolines has one of the most thoroughly studied systems of sea tenure from this post-war period. Studies found land holdings divided into small sections of valuable taro land and larger straight-edged blocks of other land held by individual lineages. Its large lagoon was divided into larger, district blocks, with the most powerful lineage in the district controlling access to all resources within it. The lagoon was divided into 14 lagoon sections and 18 reef sections. Maps of marine tenure on Ulithi and most other atolls show marine divisions as straight-edged blocks of territory incorporating the whole lagoon (Lessa 1966: 12–13; Sudo 1984: 218–19; Ushijima 1982: 35–75).

Colonial prohibitions on inter-island canoe travel were widespread – from the British Gilbert Islands to French Polynesia (Lewis 1978: 93). Arbitrary colonial boundaries divided the Pacific into spheres of European interest, while policies eroded Islanders' means of independent travel. Pockets of Islander seafaring survived the colonial era reasonably intact – especially on small, isolated islands. *Proa* (traditional sailing canoes) were still being built and navigators trained in the traditional manner on Micronesian coral islands in the 1970s when independence was being mooted (Lewis 1978: 108–10). Beyond these enclaves, regular Western shipping services and the peace imposed by colonial authorities also provided new opportunities to travel, albeit ones over whose timing and directions Islanders had no control. They travelled according to the demands of an increasingly global market economy and steam-driven timetables that defied the seasonal and tidal rhythms that had previously governed Islanders' travel, alongside cultural priorities and values (Howard 1995: 131; Couper 1973: 235–46; Purcell 1976: 191, 194; Yanaihara 1938: 62, 150).

Social, economic and technological changes also reduced Pacific Islanders connections with the sea during the colonial era. Population losses due to Western diseases during and preceding early colonial rule reduced pressure on resources. New opportunities for employment in the modern cash economy coupled with the imposition of colonial taxes created the opportunity and necessity of moving beyond local subsistence economies, as well as the opportunity to travel and gain the income needed to acquire Western goods. Western boat technology and fishing equipment such as goggles and synthetic nets sped up the decline of traditional maritime manufacturing industries such as canoe making. The cost of such goods relative to locally made equivalents meant that not everyone could afford them. Divisions occurred within some communities as traditional collective approaches to maritime tenure and activities weakened in the wake of combined economic, technological and legal pressures (Crocombe 2001: 308; Couper 1973: 234–6, 239–43; Nason 1975).

Pacific Islanders and the UN Convention on the Law of the Sea (UNCLOS)

While many first generation leaders of independent Pacific nations were negotiating the terms of their independence and essentially terrestrial sovereignty with their colonial rulers in the 1970s, other negotiations were in progress that would affect the majority of their current sovereign territory, which is ocean. These United Nations' negotiations focused on reaching a consensus for an international convention governing access to and control of maritime resources and spaces. This was the third and final convention, lasting from 1973 to 1982.

The 1982 UN Convention on the Law of the Sea (UNCLOS III) substantially extended sovereignty over adjacent waters (United Nations 1982; Brownlie 1995: 87–208; Harris 2004: 381–503). This benefited most modern Pacific nations which consist of island archipelagos surrounded by vast expanses of ocean. The outer limit of territorial seas was set at 12 nautical miles, but coastal states' sovereignty over living and non-living marine resources was extended to 200 miles from shore in the form of exclusive economic zones (EEZs). Coastal states were also given the right to designate what constituted a sustainable catch within their EEZ, as well as who would get access to harvesting stock in excess of this sustainable catch, and the fee they would pay to the coastal state in return for this access (UNCLOS III 1982: Articles 55–9, especially 55–7).

Coastal states were also given rights over the seabed and its subsoil on continental shelves. These are relatively shallow seas that extend out unbroken from the coast. Because of variable geological criteria, they were given fixed legal definitions relating to distance from shore and depth, extending to 350 miles from defined coastlines or 100 miles beyond the 2,600 metre isobeth (UNCLOS III 1982: Articles 76–85; an isobeth is a conceptual line joining points of the same depth). UNCLOS III also provided a detailed conflict resolution structure to resolve competing claims such as where EEZs and continental shelves overlapped, for example. Beyond these sovereign areas, the principle of freedom of the high seas prevailed, with access open to all. However, even here, regulation designed to avoid conflict has occurred. For example, the International Seabed Authority has recognised and registered claims made on much of the eastern Pacific seabed by various applicant nations because of the potential wealth of seabed minerals there, despite most of this region lying in international waters beyond any EEZ (Crocombe 2001: 310).

The last legal concept used in UNCLOS III for extending coastal sovereignty was that of archipelagic rights. Nations with islands considered so closely linked politically, geographically and historically as to form an intrinsically inter-linked entity were given the right to draw their EEZ baseline around the outer edge of their outer islands. All waters within this baseline are deemed to be territorial waters, as long as the ratio of water to land is not greater than nine to one (UNCLOS III 1982: Articles 46–55, especially 47–50; Crocombe 2001: 310).

UNCLOS III makes significant provision for dispute resolution mechanisms. These were needed. The 'universal principles' assumed by many to underlie UNCLOS emerged late in the piece as a compromise based on negotiation between contending perspectives. Historical specifics and legal principles are inter-meshed. The legal principles of the Law of the Sea are partly the result of historically specific disputes bought before judges by contending parties. These cases serve to both test, and clarify or refine legal principles (UNCLOS III 1982: Articles 186–91, 286–96; Harris 2004: 381–503). Three ideas originating from Western historical and cultural traditions underlie the final version of the Law of the Sea: the nation state as the principle unit vested with maritime sovereignty; coastal waters immediately offshore belonging to the nation state, or in the case of narrow passages of water, states, controlling the shorelines closest to that body of near-shore water, and seas further from shore as the common heritage of all humanity, controlled by international rules applicable to all parties rather than the preserve of specific nation states. Through time, these three ideas have come to be seen as universal principles transcending cultures and other specific contexts.

While Pacific Island nations have benefited from UNCLOS, its principles remain rooted in Western legal discourse. UNCLOS advances and protects Pacific Islander and other weaker states' maritime interests by replacing power and size with legal principles. However, it also largely ignores non-western attitudes and practices concerning the sea. For most of Oceania's history, political and social units controlling sea tenure have been much smaller and more localised than the nation state, while frequently used and occasionally contested maritime spaces extended well beyond the three nautical mile average claimed as sovereign seas for the majority of Atlantic World History. The formal legal notion of a territorial sea and the extent of such a space emerged in northern Europe during the seventeenth and eighteenth centuries. Many commentators characterise this process as a debate between advocates of more open seas (*mare liberum*) and closed seas controlled by specific nations (*mare clausum*), in which the former prevailed. The most celebrated advocates are Hugo Grotius for open seas and John Selden for closed seas. However, in reality, both sides varied their arguments to suit the specific cases they were advocating. Grotius argued for open seas when advocating that the Dutch East India Company had the right to seize a Portuguese ship in the Straits of Malacca which the Portuguese claimed exclusive dominion over, including the right to exclude the vessels of other nations. Yet, he argued for closed seas in 1625 when representing the interests of Sweden which was seeking to extend its sovereignty over parts of the Baltic Sea. Similarly, the English argued for closed seas when seeking to protect English fisheries from foreign fishing fleets, yet the opposite when seeking access to the East Indies trade the Dutch had excluded them from (Sanger 1986: 12; Thornton 2004: 17–19, 36, 2006: 127). Both sides were in agreement over the right of coastal nations to control certain activities by foreign vessels in inshore waters. In 1703, the Dutch judicial scholar Van Bynkershoek argued that freedom of the high seas and sovereignty over inshore waters were compatible principles upon which to base maritime law (Schrijver 1995: 190; Sangar 1986: 56). The extent of European coastal states' dominion was more contentious. By the end of the seventeenth century opinion was divided between those linking the width of territorial seas to the range of effective control in the form of the range of shore-based cannon, and those advocating a more arbitrary fixed distance slightly in excess of cannon range. Eventually, the two coalesced as a three mile limit that was widely, but informally, recognised by most Western maritime nations (Schrijver 1995: 190; Sanger 1986: 56).

Variable and contested claims in the half-century preceding UNCLOS III pushed the boundary of territorial seas well beyond three miles. A League of Nations conference in 1930 failed to reconcile differences between the 36 nations attending concerning the width of the territorial sea. Twenty nations supported a three-mile limit, 12 argued for 12 miles, and four advocated a limit of four miles. The 1958 and 1960 UNCLOS meetings also failed to reach agreement, although it was now clear that something beyond three miles would be needed to secure the two-thirds majority required to pass. A joint US–Canadian proposal for a six-mile territorial sea followed by a six-mile fishing zone missed out by just one vote in securing the necessary majority. Iceland unilaterally declared a 12-mile territorial sea in 1958, while certain Latin American, Caribbean, African and Asian states declared even broader territorial seas. By the early 1970s, on the eve of UNCLOS III, claims were being pushed out to 200 miles, either as territorial seas in the case of Chile, or as zones with lesser rights than these for the majority of interested parties. The idea of continental shelf rights first asserted by the US in the late 1940s was also widely supported by the 1970s (Shrijver 1995: 191; Tarte 1998: 77–8).

Pacific Island nations had limited influence on the UNCLOS process. None were independent nations during UNCLOS I and II. Colonial authorities were more concerned with providing technical advice and development assistance within colonies in the 1950s and 1960s than representing their colonial subjects' maritime interests in international forums. Independence was considered a long way off for most (Fry 1979: 52, 63–4; Nero 1997: 359–63). By the time of UNCLOS III many Pacific Islanders were independent and indigenous viewpoints predominated in their regional body – the South Pacific Forum. The forum agreed to a common policy on maritime sovereignty for UNCLOS III centred primarily on supporting the 200-mile EEZ and archipelagic sovereignty principles. In so doing, they conformed to positions that already had widespread support. Also, they did signal their distinct maritime past in raising issues of whether definitions of maritime sovereignty should be primarily based on universal spatial measures, or other cultural and economic criteria. While spatial measures predominate in the final UNCLOS III text, international law still leaves room to argue the Islander case in that a 1951 International Court of Justice ruling on a maritime dispute between Britain and Norway noted that special maritime interests should be taken into account 'if their reality and importance is clearly evidenced by long use'.[7] Much of Oceania was still under the control of the US or France at the end of UNCLOS III in 1982. Although Micronesians under US Trusteeship were given observer status in the negotiations, the non-independent Pacific had little say in proceedings.[8]

The post-colonial Pacific: new legal rights and practical limitations

UNCLOS III did not officially come into force until 1994 when the required number of nations had ratified it. By then, Pacific Island nations had introduced national legislation to apply its measures within their boundaries and the provisions were operating de facto in international fishing agreements relating to the Pacific. The new 200-mile EEZs dramatically increased the territory of Pacific Island nations, particularly archipelagic ones. For example, Fiji's 18,272 square kilometres of land provided an EEZ of 1,290,000 square kilometres, Kiribati's 690 square kilometres of islands translated into an EEZ of 3,550,000 square kilometres, while Federated States of Micronesia's 701 square kilometres of land equated to an EEZ of 2,978,000 square kilometres. Kiribati derives 45 per cent of its revenue from fishing and fishing license fees, while Federated States of Micronesia derive around a quarter of its revenue from these sources (Crocombe 2001: 309; Nero 1997: 369; Gupta and Yala 2000: 367).

The potential maritime benefits of political independence have been eroded by economic realities. Newly independent Pacific Island nations were largely either small or fragmented political and cultural entities that inherited limited modern infrastructure from their former colonial rulers. This restricted their ability to generate income domestically, and meant that much income was absorbed in providing basic facilities and services taken for granted in more developed nations. Offshore fishing fleets from larger and wealthier Pacific Rim nations regularly violated Pacific Island EEZs in the absence of local monitoring. The same lack of resources to monitor offshore waters also meant that Island nations could not develop effective fishing fleets and were forced into fishing access agreements that returned a mere fraction of the value of the catch at market. The alternatives were foregoing this income and watching the offshore fishery erode through unmonitored fishing by non-citizens, or continued over-reliance on foreign aid from former colonisers. Pacific Island government actions were also constrained by the fact that the nations from which the fishing fleets came were often also significant aid donors. Japan, for example, deliberately used fisheries grant aid to secure more generous fishing terms within recipient nations' EEZs. (Tarte 1998: 83; Lobban and Schefter 1997: 274–7; Nero 1997: 368, 377–8; Bardach and Ridings 1985: 43; Gillett 1987: 1). Conditions improved as Island nations agreed to speak as one through the Forum Fisheries Agency, which developed considerable scientific and legal expertise on Pacific fisheries management. Whereas Japan's use of aid to remove restrictive fishing regulations worked well in the early 1980s through essentially lop-sided bilateral agreements with Pacific Island nations, the balance of power changed in the late 1980s. Japan now faced an increasingly united independent Oceania, and significant competition from other players willing to sign more balanced fishing deals. Circumstances particularly changed in favour of Island nations after the US signed a multilateral access agreement with Pacific nations (Tarte 1998: 96).

Island nations still only receive a small fraction of the potential wealth contained in their offshore territorial waters. Modern offshore fishing is both expensive and lucrative. Corporations employ fleets and factory ships, sonar and spotter planes. A tuna fishing vessel can use $5,000 worth of fuel per day. The Pacific tuna fishery produces an estimated billion dollars in value-added sales. Island nations consume little of the catch and probably only receive around 5 per cent of the market value of the reported catch from fishing license fee agreements. After the failure of a number of domestic offshore tuna operations, most Island nations now look to increase their fishery income through developing inshore fisheries.[9] Kiribati, for example, has raised significant revenue in recent years through developing its inshore artisanal fishery, farming seaweed and harvesting *beche-de-mer*, shark fins and reef fish for aquariums. These exports produce significant income for local communities. Pearl cultivation has been a big success in certain atoll communities such as the northern Cook Islands (Crocombe 2001: 309; Thomas 2003: 14–16).

Maritime access for still politically subordinate Pacific Islanders varies significantly from politically and economically marginalised Hawai'ians, to less politically subordinate and better-resourced Māori in New Zealand. Heavy demand for waterfront property and big profits from tourism mean that access to coastal land and power are intimately linked in Hawai'i and are in many ways inimical to formal recognition of Hawai'ian sovereignty. Traditional Hawai'ian near-shore rights are recognised in the legal system, but claimants must prove this in an American court. Meanwhile, state and federal lawyers argue over control of waters further offshore within the 200-mile EEZ. (Daws and Cooper 1985; Murikami 1991: 185–8; Minerbi *et al.* 1993: 125–9). In contrast, New Zealand Māori have a quota of the EEZ fishery set aside for them as part of a policy of compensating and empowering them for past grievances (see Moon 1998; Webster 2002; Waitangi Tribunal 1985).

Even in Aotearoa/New Zealand,[10] however, the minority status of Māori has raised concerns among a number of indigenous commentators that legally empowering principles under the Treaty of Waitangi can and may be eroded. This Treaty was signed between the Crown and Māori chiefs in 1840 prior to the influx of British settlers that made Māori a minority in their own lands by the end of the nineteenth century. Since the early 1980s, the treaty has become the legal basis for legislation requiring consultation with Māori over resource issues as well as claims for compensation by the Crown for lands and resources confiscated.[11] Soon after the Waitangi Tribunal had been set in place to investigate and recommend compensation for historical grievances, the mood of the *Pākehā* (New Zealanders of European origin) majority began to shift from support to concern that the process should be completed as soon as possible and a cap placed on the amount of compensation. By the mid 1990s, the incumbent national government was talking about a full and final settlement to truncate the more exhaustive, time-consuming and open-ended process that was occurring. Matters have come to a head recently with debate over Māori rights to the foreshore versus the English tradition of the foreshore as a public good open to all. When the New Zealand Court of Appeal concluded that Māori should be given the opportunity in court to prove their customary ownership of the foreshore and seabed in June 2003, the government announced that it would introduce legislation to ensure Māori could never hold exclusive title to the foreshore and seabed. This pre-emptive government action to prevent due judicial process seems somewhat of an over-reaction given the reasonable and mutually agreed terms of previous compensation settlements. This action highlights the plight and fragility of gains made by Pacific Islander minorities to reclaim their maritime heritage as peoples of the sea (Webster 2002; Ruru 2004, 2006).

Conclusion: future possibilities

There has been considerable debate over the compatibility of traditional marine tenure and government control using modern scientific fisheries management techniques (see, for example, Johannes 1977: 125–6). Practical solutions rooted in historical practice are the only sustainable way forward in fisheries management. Well intentioned reports that romanticise or overstate indigenous peoples' historical use and understanding of the sea are ultimately counterproductive, as they ignore the mass of solid evidence available in the historical record which is regarded with far more credibility in Western and international courts, and misrepresent the messy and contested reality of human use of the sea.[12]

The battle for maritime sovereignty has moved from the sea to the courtroom. Three legal criteria commonly cited for conferring greater maritime control upon indigenous people find support in Pacific history (see, for example, Johannes and Macfarlane 1990). First, indigenous principles and practices of maritime tenure generally aid conservation. Second, there is clear evidence of continuous use and recognised title, if at times contested, to maritime spaces by families, clans and other communities. Such tenure was as complex and detailed as land tenure before European and Japanese rule, and continued through the colonial era as has been amply demonstrated in documents from claims such as those bought before the Waitangi Tribunal. Where traditional evidence is absent, archaeological excavations trace fisheries back millennia with species identification revealing which near-shore and offshore ecosystems were fished. While few fisheries extended out beyond current 200-mile EEZs, many extended beyond the three- to 12-mile limits of recognized European coastal tenure regimes until the 1950s.[13]

The last criterion is that indigenous practices are compatible with government fisheries management practices. This is the case in many parts of the Pacific where conservation and sustainability are key shared principles. Local community control of local near-shore fisheries as practiced by Pacific Islanders has also worked well as a conservation and management principle in parts of the Pacific Rim not controlled by indigenous peoples such as Japan (Cordell 1984: 315–18). Pacific Island and Pacific Rim marine management systems represent a wide variety of workable schemes and contexts that are all concerned with disputed near-shore access rights. Comparative studies of such disputes and their resolution are needed to broaden awareness of options and put local disputes in context. A series of local regimes and interest groups can and do operate under a broad umbrella of national or international principles, such as conservation of endangered ecosystems and species being paramount over sector or community interests, and open, but differentiated access to the foreshore on the basis of historical and cultural factors.[14]

Coastal Pacific Islanders controlled and exploited a wide variety of inshore and blue water ecosystems. Results varied. Their most enduring and successful systems of fisheries management have been highly localised operations where communities reliant on harvesting the sea also regulate its use (see, for example, Hviding and Baines 1994). This is in keeping with 'tragedy of the commons' theory of resource economics, where resources not owned by anyone are considered particularly vulnerable because no group has an economic interest in preserving them as a sustainable resource. Ecological and social-cultural factors also influence the sustainability of harvests.[15] Much of Oceania's commercially harvested fishery falls within the territorial waters of Pacific Island nations. While concerns have already been raised about the depletion of certain species of tuna in offshore waters by unmonitored multinational fleets, Islanders still retain control of near-shore waters upon which much of the offshore fishery is built. The issue is no longer simply one of indigenous empowerment through increased legal recognition of the diversity of maritime management practices, but rather of ecosystem survival, in which many Islanders are still an intimate part of that ecosystem.

Notes

1 The term Oceania is used here to refer to all Pacific islands within the cultural areas defined as Melanesia, Polynesia and Micronesia. The terms Pacific Islanders or simply Islanders are used to refer to all inhabitants of Oceania with pre-European roots, while Western and European are used interchangeably to refer to all Western cultures that came to the Pacific from the Atlantic world.

2 See particularly Hviding, 1996: chs 5 and 7 and D'Arcy, 2006a: ch. 5. Colonial rule in Oceania generally occurred from 1870 onwards. This section's survey covers the period from 1770 to 1870, for which the documentary record is substantial.

3 See Tobin 1956: 58. Historical sources confirm that this was a long-standing practice. For example, it was mentioned by Kotzebue 1967: vol. 3: 154–5. For similar rights on high islands, see Kamakau 1961: 107; Fornander 1969: 218.

4 See, for example, Lessa 1966: 46, Ushijima 1982: 50–9 and Sudo 1984: 218 on Ulithi; Damm *et al.* 1935: 55 on Puluwat; Cook in Beaglehole 1967: vol. 3: 1, 141 and Newbury 1980: 45, citing LMS Transactions, 1818: 305 for Tahiti; Vason 1810: 136, Martin 1981: 180 and Gifford 1929: 103 for Tonga; and Kamakau 1961: 77, 105, 203 for Hawai'i.

5 See Hommon 1975: 183–197 and Mackenzie 1991: 174 on Hawai'i; and Newbury 1980: 45 on Tahiti.

6 One mile equals 1.609 kilometres, and one nautical mile equals 1.852 kilometres.

7 On special consideration being given to those with especially strong cultural, historical and economic ties to the sea, see Shrijver 1995: 193. The International Court of Justice's 1951 judgment in the Anglo-Norwegian Fisheries Case is discussed in Harris 2004: 388–95. See Doulman 1987: 245–8 and Fry 1979: 168–70 on SPF stance on UNCLOS III.

8 See Nero 1997: 368 and Van Dyke and Nicol 1987: 105–6. A special report on Micronesians and the sea was prepared for the Congress of Micronesia – see Nakayama and Ramp 1974.

9 Despite being published almost 20 years ago, Teiwaki 1988 is still one of the most comprehensive reviews of marine policy options in the independent Pacific. On the difficulties of Pacific Island tuna fishing enterprises, see Jacobs 2002; Hezel and Lightfoot 2005: 8; D'Arcy 2006b: 79.

10 Aotearoa/New Zealand is a term that combines Māori and European terms for the landmass to acknowledge the shared cultural base of the nation.

11 For the history, underlying principles and reports of the Waitangi Tribunal, see www.waitangi-tribunal.govt.nz/ (last accessed Friday, 29 June 2006). For background and analysis of the role and influence of the Waitangi Tribunal in New Zealand society and history, see Lashley 2000; King 1997: 87–102; Kelsey 1995; Walker 1990; Kawharu 1989.

12 Compare, for example, the somewhat vague generalisations in Nakayama and Ramp 1974 to the legal and historical precision of Webster and Ruru, respectively. The latter are much more in keeping with the evidence cited in ICJ judgments outlined in Harris 2004: 388–95. This difference is due, in part, to 30 years of added research enhancing our knowledge on indigenous use of the sea. However, Van Dyke (1994) still cites Nakayama and Ramp's 1974 work, despite the fact that many of their conclusions already required significant modification in light of subsequent research. For example, their claim of indigenous Micronesia-wide empires was contradicted in Goodenough 1986. Such flaws can undermine arguments when exposed to cross examination in the courtroom, see Byrnes 1998.

13 Profiles of millennia of fishing practices and ecosystems targeted can be found in Anderson 1986; Masse 1986; Dye 1990.

14 The Great Barrier Reef Marine Park Authority management plans and planning processes are good examples. They involved deep consultation and cooperation with

wider and more diverse local communities and interest groups, including indigenous peoples. Information on the plan and consultation process can be found at www.gbrmpa.gov.au/corp_site/management/zoning, while further information on specific collaboration with indigenous users of the reef can be found at www.environment.gov.au/indigenous/fact-sheets/gbrmpa.html.

15 See McEvoy 1988 for an excellent account of the influence of 'the tragedy of the commons' idea on fisheries policy, and a convincing argument that this economic theory needs to take account of wider ecological and social factors. See also Dye 1990 on how non-economic factors affect fishing strategies.

Bibliography

Anderson, A. (ed.) (1986) *Traditional Fishing in the Pacific*, Honolulu: Bernice P. Bishop Museum.

Bardach, J.E. and Ridings, P.J. (1985) 'Pacific Tuna: Biology, Economics, and Politics', in E.M. Borgese and N. Ginsburg (eds) *Ocean Yearbook 5*, Chicago: University of Chicago Press.

Barrere, D.B. (ed.) (1976) *The Works of the People of Old: Na Hana a ka Po'e Kahiko*, by Samuel Kamakau, Honolulu: Bernice P. Bishop Museum.

Beaglehole, J.C. (ed.) (1951–1967) *The Journals of Captain James Cook on His Voyages of Discovery* (4 vols), Cambridge: Cambridge University Press.

Brownlie, I. (ed.) (1995) *Basic Documents in International Law* (4th edition), Oxford: Oxford University Press.

Byrnes, G.M. (1998) 'Jackals of the Crown? Historians and the Treaty Claims Process in New Zealand', *The Public Historian* 20(2): 9–23.

Cheyne, A. 'Journal of a Voyage to the Islands of the Western Pacific in the Brigantine "Acis", A. Cheyne Commander', (log I: 28/11/63–14/12/64 and 10/2/65–6/2/66), MS copy in possession of Dorothy Shineberg.

Clunie, F. (1977) *Fijian Weapons and Warfare*, Suva: Fiji Museum.

Cordell, J.C. (1984) 'Defending Customary Inshore Sea Rights', in K. Ruddle and T. Akimichi (eds) *Maritime Institutions in the Western Pacific*, Osaka: National Museum of Ethnology.

Couper, A. (1973) 'Islanders at Sea: Change, and the Maritime Economies of the Pacific' in H. Brookfield (ed.) *The Pacific in Transition: Geographical Perspectives on Adaptation and Change*, Canberra: Australian National University Press.

Crocombe, R. (2001) *The South Pacific*, Suva: University of the South Pacific.

D'Arcy, P. (2006a) *The People of the Sea: Environment, Identity, and History in Oceania*, Honolulu: University of Hawaii Press.

—— (2006b) 'The Role of the Tuna Fishery in the Economy of Federated States of Micronesia', *Pacific Economic Bulletin* 21(3): 75–87.

Damm, H., Hambruch, P. and Sarfert, E. (1935) 'Inseln um Truk (Polowat, Hok, Satowal)' in G. Thilenius (ed.) *Ergebnisse der Sudsee-Expedition 1908–1910*, vol. II, B, VI, ii, 1–288. Hamburg: Friederichsen De Gruyter & Co.

Daws, G. and Cooper, G. (1985) *Land and Power in Hawaii: The Democratic Years*, Honolulu: Benchmark Books.

Doulman, D.J. (ed.) (1987) *Tuna Issues and Perspectives in the Pacific Islands Region*, Honolulu: East-West Center.

Dye, T. (1990) 'The Causes and Consequences of a Decline in the Prehistoric Marquesan Fishing Industry', in D.E. Yen and J.M.J. Mummery (eds) *Pacific Production Systems:*

Approaches to Economic Prehistory, Canberra: Department of Prehistory, RSPAS, Australian National University.

Fornander, A. (1969) *An Account of the Polynesian Race* (2 vols), Rutland, Vermont: Charles E. Tuttle Company.

Fry, G. (1979) 'South Pacific Regionalism: The Development of an Indigenous Commitment', unpublished MA thesis, Australian National University.

Gifford, E.W. (1929) *Tongan Society*, Honolulu: Bernice P. Bishop Museum.

Gillett, R. (1987) *Traditional Tuna Fishing: A study at Satawal, Central Caroline Islands*, Honolulu: Bernice P. Bishop Museum.

Goodenough, W.H. (1986) 'Sky World and this World: The Place of Kachaw in Micronesian Cosmology', *American Anthropologist* 88: 3: 551–68.

Great Barrier Reef Marine Park Authority (n.d.) *Marine Park Zoning*. Available online at www.gbrmpa.gov.au/corp_site/management/zoning (last accessed 29 June 2007).

Great Barrier Reef Marine Park Authority (2001) *Great Barrier Reef Marine Park Authority Working with Indigenous Communities*. Available online at www.environment.gov.au/indigenous/fact-sheets/gbrmpa.html (last accessed 29 June 2007).

Gupta, D. and Yala, C. (2000) 'Fishing, Forestry and Mining' in B.V. Lal and K. Fortune (eds) *The Pacific Islands: An Encyclopedia*, Honolulu: The University of Hawaii Press.

Harris, D.J. (2004) *Cases and Materials on International Law* (6th edition), London: Sweet and Maxwell.

Hau'ofa, E. (1994) 'Our Sea of Islands', *The Contemporary Pacific* 6(1): 148–61.

Hezel, F.X. and Lightfoot, C. (2005) 'Myths of the FSM Economy' *Micronesian Counselor* 59: 1–20.

Hommon, R.J. (1975) *Use and Control of Hawaiian Inter-island Channels – Polynesian Hawaii: A.D. 1400–1794*, Honolulu: Office of the Governor of Hawaii.

Howard, A. (1995) 'Rotuman Seafaring in Historical Perspective' in R. Feinberg (ed.) *Seafaring in the Contemporary Pacific Islands: Studies in Continuity and Change*, DeKalb, Illinois: Northern Illinois University Press.

Hviding, E. (1996) *Guardians of Marovo Lagoon: Practice, Place, and Politics in Maritime Melanesia*, Honolulu: University of Hawaii Press.

Hviding, E. and Baines, G.B.K. (1994) 'Community-based Fisheries Management Tradition and the Challenges of Development in Marovo, Solomon Islands', *Development and Change*, 25, 13–39.

Imthurn, E. and Wharton, L.C. (eds) (1925) *The Journal of William Lockerby*, London: Hakluyt Society.

Jacobs, M. (2002) 'Spoiled Tuna: A Fishing Industry Gone Bad', *Micronesian Counselor* 40: 1–15.

Johannes, R.E. and Macfarlane, J.W. (1990) 'Assessing Customary Marine Tenure Systems in the Context of Marine Resource Management: A Torres Strait Example' in K. Ruddle and R.E. Johannes (eds) *Traditional Marine Resource Management in the Pacific Basin: An Anthology*, Jakarta: UNESCO.

Johannes, R.E. (1977) 'Traditional Law of the Sea in Micronesia', *Micronesica* 13(2): 121–7.

Kamakau, S.M. (1961) *Ruling Chiefs of Hawaii*, Honolulu: Kamehameha Schools Press.

Kawharu, I.H. (1989) *Māori and Pākehā Perspectives on the Treaty of Waitangi*, Auckland: Oxford University Press.

Kelsey, J. (1995) *The New Zealand Experiment*, Auckland: Auckland University Press.

King, M. (1997) *Nga Iwi o te Motu: 1000 Years of Māori History*, Auckland: Reed.

Kotzebue, O. (1967) *A Voyage of Discovery into the South Sea and Behring's Straits, in*

Search of a North-east Passage, Undertaken in the Years 1815, 16, 17, and 18 in the Ship Rurick (3 vols), Amsterdam: N. Israel and New York: Da Capo Press.

Kubary, J.S. (1896) *Ethnograpische Beitrage zur Kenntnis des Karolinen – archipels*, Leiden: P.W.M. Trap.

Lashley, M.E. (2000) 'Implementing Treaty Settlements via Indigenous Institutions: Social Justice and Detribalization in New Zealand', *The Contemporary Pacific* 12(1): 1–55.

Lessa, W.A. (1966) *Ulithi: A Micronesian Design for Living*, New York: Holt, Reinhart and Wilson.

Lewis, D. (1978) *The Voyaging Stars: Secrets of the Pacific Island Navigators*, Sydney: Collins.

Lobban, C.S. and Schefter, M. (1997) *Tropical Pacific Island Environments*, Guam: University of Guam Press.

McEvoy, A.F. (1988) 'Toward an Interactive Theory of Nature and Culture: Ecology, Production and Cognition in the California Fishing Industry', in D. Worster (ed.) *The Ends of the Earth: Perspectives on Modern Environmental History*, Cambridge: Cambridge University Press.

Mackenzie, M.K. (1991) *Native Hawaiian Rights Handbook*, Honolulu: Native Hawaiian Legal Corporation.

Marck, J.C. (1986) 'Micronesian Dialects and the Overnight Voyage', *Journal of the Polynesian Society* 95(1): 253–8.

Martin, J. (1981) *Tonga Islands, William Mariner's Account* (2 vols, 4th edition), Tonga: Vava'u Press.

Masse, B.W. (1986) 'A Millennium of Fishing in the Palau Islands, Micronesia' in A. Anderson (ed.) *Traditional Fishing in the Pacific*, Honolulu: Bernice P. Bishop Museum.

Minerbi, L., McGregor, D. and Matsuoka, J. (eds) (1993) *Native Hawaiian and Local Cultural Assessment Project: Phase 1 Problems/Assets Identification*, Honolulu: University of Hawaii Press.

Moon, P. (1998) 'The Creation of the "Sealord Deal"', *Journal of the Polynesian Society* 107(2): 145–74.

Murikami, A. (1991) 'Konohiki Fishing Rights and Marine Resources' in M.K. MacKenzie (ed.) *Native Hawaiian Rights Handbook*, Honolulu: Native Hawaiian Legal Corporation.

Nakayama, M. and Ramp, F.L. (1974) *Micronesian Navigation and Island Empires and Traditional Concepts of Ownership of the Sea*. Saipan: Study for the Joint Committee on the Law of the Sea Conference, 5th Congress of Micronesia, 14 January 1974.

Nason, J.D. (1975) 'The Effects of Social Change on Marine Technology in a Pacific Atoll Community', in R.W. Casteel and G.I. Quimby (eds) *Maritime Adaptations of the Pacific*, The Hague: Mouton, 5–38.

Nero, K. (1997) 'The Material World Remade' in D. Denoon (ed.) *The Cambridge History of the Pacific Islanders*, Cambridge: Cambridge University Press.

Newbury, C. (1980) *Tahiti Nui: Change and Survival in French Polynesia 1767–1945*, Honolulu: The University Press of Hawaii.

Oliver, D.L. (1974) *Ancient Tahitian Society* (3 vols), Honolulu: University of Hawaii Press.

Parmentier, R.J. (1987) *The Sacred Remains: Myth, History, and Polity in Belau*, Chicago: The University of Chicago Press.

Payoyo, P.B. (ed.) (1994) *Ocean Governance: Sustainable Development of the Seas*,

Tokyo: United Nations University Press. Available online at www.unu.edu/unupress/unupbooks/uu15oe/uu15oe00.htm#Contents (last accessed 29 June 2007).

Purcell, D. (1976) 'The Economics of Exploitation: The Japanese in the Mariana, Caroline and Marshall Islands, 1915–1940', *The Journal of Pacific History* 11, 189–211.

Rappaport, M. (1996) 'Between Two Laws: Tenure Regimes in the Pearl Islands', *The Contemporary Pacific* 8(1): 33–49.

Ruru, J. (2004) 'A Politically Fuelled Tsunami: The Foreshore/Seabed Controversy in Aotearoa Me Te Wai Pounamu/New Zealand', *Journal of the Polynesian Society* 113: 57–72.

—— (2006) 'What Could Have Been: The Common Law Doctrine of Native Title in Land Under Water in Australia and Aotearoa/New Zealand', *Monash University Law Review* 32(1): 116–44.

Sanger, C. (1986) *Ordering the Oceans: The Making of the Law of the Sea*, London: Zed Books.

Schrijver, N.J. (1995) 'Sovereignty over Natural Resources: Balancing Rights and Duties in an Interdependent World,' PhD. Thesis, University of Groningen. Available online at http://irs.ub.rug.nl/ppn/128220244 (last accessed 29 June 2007).

Sudo, K. (1984) 'Social Organisation and Types of Sea Tenure in Micronesia' in K. Ruddle and T. Akimichi (eds) *Maritime Institutions in the Western Pacific*, Osaka: National Museum of Ethnology.

Tarte, S. (1998) *Japan's Aid Diplomacy and the Pacific Islands*, Canberra: National Centre for Development Studies.

Teiwaki, R. (1988) *Management of Marine Resources in Kiribati*, Suva: University of the South Pacific.

Thomas, F.R. (2003) 'Fisheries Development in Kiribati: Sustainability Issues in a "MIRAB" Economy', *Pacific Studies* 26(1–2): 1–36.

Thorton, H. (2004) 'Hugo Grotius and the Freedom of the Seas', *International Journal of Maritime History* 16(2): 17–38.

—— (2006) 'John Selden's Response to Hugo Grotius: The Argument for Closed Seas', *International Journal of Maritime History* 18(2): 105–27.

Thrum, T.G. (ed.) (1919) *Collection of Hawaiian Antiquities and Folk-lore* (6 vols), by Abraham Fornander, Honolulu: Bernice P. Bishop Museum.

Tobin, A. (1956) *Land Tenure in the Marshall Islands* (Revised Edition), Washington DC: The Pacific Science Board.

United Nations (1982) The full 1982 UNCLOS III text is available online at www.un.org/Depts/los/convention_agreements/texts/unclos/closindx.htm (last accessed 29 June 2007).

United Nations (1992) *The Law of the Sea: Exclusive Economic Zone, Legislative History of Articles 56, 58 and 59 of the United Nations Convention on the Law of the Sea*, New York: Division for Ocean Affairs and the Law of the Sea, United Nations.

Ushijima, I. (1982) 'The Control of Reefs and Lagoons: Some Aspects of the Political Structure of Ulithi Atoll', in M. Aoyagi (ed.) *Islanders and their Outside World: A Report of The Cultural Anthropological Research in the Caroline Islands of Micronesia in 1980–1981*, Tokyo: Committee for Micronesian Research, St. Paul's (Rikkyo) University.

Van Dyke, J. (1994) 'The Role of Indigenous Peoples in Ocean Governance' in P.B. Payoyo (ed.) *Ocean Governance: Sustainable Development of the Seas*, Tokyo: United Nations University Press. Available online at www.unu.edu/unupress/unupbooks/uu15oe/ uu15oe09.htm#the%20role%20of%20indigenous%20peoples%20in%20ocean%20governance (last accessed 29 June 2007).

Van Dyke, J. and Nicol, C. (1987) 'U.S. Tuna Policy: A Reluctant Acceptance of the International Norm' in D.J. Doulman (ed.) *Tuna Issues and Perspectives in the Pacific Islands Region*, Honolulu: East-West Center.

Vason, G. (1810) *An Authentic Narrative of Four Year's Residence at Tongataboo*, London: Longman, Hurst, Rees, Orme.

Waitangi Tribunal (1985) *Report of the Waitangi Tribunal on the Muriwhenua Fishing Claim, Wai-22*, Wellington: Department of Justice.

—— (n.d.) Available online at www.waitangi-tribunal.govt.nz/.

Walker, R. (1990) *Ka Whawhai Tonu Matou: Struggle Without End*, Auckland: Penguin.

Webster, S. (2002) 'Maori Retribalization and Treaty Rights to the New Zealand Fisheries', *The Contemporary Pacific* 14(2): 341–76.

Yanaihara, T. (1938) *Pacific Islands under Japanese Mandate*, London: Oxford University Press.

3 Ocean, empire and nation

Japanese fisheries politics

Kate Barclay

Introduction

Water has been as important as land in Japanese senses of self and belonging in relation to place.[1] Scholar Amino Yoshihiko has proposed that ways of life revolving around the sea were at least as influential as wet rice agriculture in the historical development of Japanese cultures, and that Japanese people should be understood as being 'sea folk' (*kaimin*) (Amino 1994). Other scholars who have contributed to this field include Tanabe Satoru, who wrote of 'sea people' (*kaijin*), and proposes that the coastal peoples of Japan shared a common culture with coastal peoples in areas we now call China, Korea and Taiwan (Tanabe 1990; Habara 1949). This *kaijin* culture was based on shared experiences of lives lived on or near the sea, involving fishing, travel, trade and piracy. Marcia Yanemoto (1999) has written of Japanese imaginaries of the world in the Tokugawa era (1608–1868) through to the early modern era being made up of a 'complex web of regional and global connections' across the seas.

This chapter focuses on the modern era, showing how Japanese ideas of maritime sovereign rights evolved through imperial expansion, defeat in war, Japan's postwar re-emergence as a world fishing power, development of the United Nations Law of the Sea, and finally, Japan's declining status as a fishing power. The Japanese empire was in many ways a naval and fishing empire. Using the protection afforded by Japan's military, Japanese fishing interests came to see the Asia Pacific region as their territory in terms of resource exploitation. Defeat in war did not rupture this sense of entitlement. Rather, entitlement to fisheries resources was seen as belonging to those with a history of using those resources, as opposed to being a sovereign right within the waters 200 nautical miles out from coastlines, which was the version of entitlement that came to be internationally accepted through the Law of the Sea in the 1970s and 1980s. Understanding this history helps explain Japan's position in contemporary international fisheries negotiations. The second half of the chapter then explores the implied role of the ocean in contemporary Japanese identities through economic and cultural nationalism in representations of fisheries and fish food culture.

History of Japanese distant-water fisheries

Japan's modern industrial fishing industries started during the Meiji era (1868–1912). The Meiji government had a mission to match European powers of the time by modernizing, building military strength and building a colonial empire. Overseas fishing activities were part of the empire building exercise and part of the improvement and expansion of food production and distribution necessary for an urbanizing industrializing economy, especially since parts of Japan were susceptible to food shortages (Peattie 1984; Fujinami 1987). Fisheries were so important the Meiji government supported them in various ways within the framework of the Fisheries Promotion Act of 1897. Government support for fisheries included initiatives such as the Fisheries Training Institute (opened 1889, now the Tokyo University of Marine Science and Technology), as well as financial support for technological developments in shipbuilding, such as installing engines (1903), refrigeration equipment (1907) and radios (1918) (Fujinami 1987).

Japanese fleets were fishing around the Korean coastline from the start of the Meiji era. Japanese fishing effort intensified as Japan moved towards colonizing Korea, so that by the early 1900s Japanese interests dominated fishing in Korea, and Korea was supplying a significant portion of Japan's seafood (Koh 1998). Fisheries were also a key part of Japanese colonial settlement in Pacific territories taken from Germany in the Treaty of Versailles. Families with limited economic opportunities at home, especially from Okinawa, went to these colonies, often on fishing vessels, and many continued working in fisheries in the colonies, while others branched out into trading stores and other small businesses (Hanlon 1998; Tomiyama 2002; Wakabayashi 1993).

Along with most of the rest of Japan's infrastructure, Japan's fishing fleets were decimated at the end of World War II. In part because of the important role played by fisheries in Japan's empire, Japanese fishing fleets were restricted to waters close to Japan. Then there were food shortages in the immediate postwar years. The empire had provided a large proportion of Japan's food supply, so Japan had not only to recover domestic food production but also to replace colonial production. In order to boost food production the Allied occupying forces and the Japanese government again supported fisheries to rebuild fleets and port infrastructure. Fisheries, including whaling, played a major role in this (Bestor 2004: 177). Restrictions on Japanese fishing fleets' travels were lifted by the Allied occupying force in 1952, so Japanese fishing fleets once again roamed the waters of the globe. This re-expansion was promoted in the government slogan 'from coastal to offshore, from offshore to distant waters' (Bergin and Haward 1996: 13; Fujinami 1987: 58).

The Japanese postwar economic recovery was consolidated in the 1960s, and fisheries production increased dramatically. Up until 1950 tuna production had remained under 10,000 tons, then in 1960 it was over 50,000 tons and from then on mostly stayed over 40,000 tons (Fujinami 1987).[2] Quantity ceased to be a pressing national food security issue and consumers started to demand high quality, high value products. At the same time developments in freezing technology on fishing vessels and refrigerated transport on land enabled widespread supply of chilled or frozen fresh seafood (in the past only locally caught, canned, cured or dried seafood were feasible).

Up until the 1970s the oceans were open slather in terms of resource rights.[3] Territorial waters extended only a few nautical miles from coastlines, and beyond that the ocean was available to anyone with vessels that could fish those waters. The Japanese and US fleets were dominant in international waters during the 1960s and 1970s. Then, in the spirit of the New International Economic Order, when newly independent former colonies were optimistic of the economic opportunities they could make from their natural resources, countries started declaring exclusive economic zones (EEZs) 200 nautical miles out from their coastlines. Japan and the USA fiercely opposed this move by coastal states to extend their sovereign rights over waters to which they had previously had free access (Schurman 1998). Especially in the case of tuna, a highly migratory species, the Japanese perspective was that no state could claim rights to a resource that was in one EEZ one day then in another EEZ the next. Japan argued that rights to migratory marine resources such as tuna should lie in the history of using those resources, rather than in a territorial zone.

The weight of international opinion, however, was against Japan and the USA. Two hundred-mile EEZs were enshrined in practice and the United Nations Law of the Sea by the 1980s. This was seen by the Japanese government and fishing industry as a grave injustice and a great setback to their fisheries. The advent of the *nihyaku kairi jidai* (200-nautical miles era) warranted a whole chapter in the *Fifty Year History of the Kagoshima Prefecture Tuna and Skipjack Fisheries Cooperative* (2000), discussing the difficulties faced at that time such as the oil shocks as well as the advent of EEZs. One captain was quoted as saying that, since fish were caught close to land, with the 200-nautical mile rule they might as well just give up (Kagoshima 2000: 359).

Japan's international fisheries politics from the 1970s were shaped by the need to secure access to what had ceased to be open access marine resources through the advent of EEZs. Postwar distant-water fishing was no longer part of a military expansion, but it retained a sense of being a Japanese political presence overseas, mainly through economic ties and aid diplomacy (Tarte 1998). In the 1970s the favored way to secure fisheries access was to establish joint ventures with newly independent coastal states. This way Japanese fishing companies were in economic partnership for technology transfer and employment with Pacific Islands countries, and through the joint venture being classified as a local company avoided paying access fees, which would imply acceptance of the legitimacy of EEZs. More than a dozen such joint ventures were established around the Pacific from the 1960s to 1980s. Fisheries aid and later on the payment of large access fees for the Japanese fleet were other modes of Japanese international fisheries politics in the second half of the twentieth century.

Japanese government representatives and fishing industry people do not seriously expect that the 200-nautical mile EEZ rule can be wound back, but neither have they quite accepted it as a normal part of business. Their representations of EEZs and other issues relating to international fishing access indicate that they see EEZs as an unjust obstacle to business, and that any further developments in allocating oceanic fishing rights on the basis of national ownership of certain zones of ocean should be vigorously opposed. This is visible in Japanese negotiations on fisheries management for the Western and Central Pacific Ocean (WCPO).

The management of fisheries targeting species that migrate through or live across more than one EEZ must by necessity be conducted in the international arena. Under the United Nations Law of the Sea this has come to be done through regional fisheries management organizations (RFMOs). The RFMO for the WCPO is the Western and Central Pacific Fisheries Commission (WCPFC 2006). This came into existence in 2004, after its foundational Convention was ratified by a sufficient number of signatories, subsequent to several years' negotiation through a series of multilateral high level conferences and preparatory conferences. Fishing rights have not yet been allocated in the WCPFC, but throughout the negotiations leading up to the Convention and all Commission meetings so far there have been disputes about the basis on which rights might be allocated, and Japan has been a vocal participant in these disputes. The island states of the Pacific have argued for an allocation of fisheries rights based on zones, with rights to fish on the high seas to be divided up among fishing states and rights to fish in EEZs to be divided up among coastal states. Japan has argued instead that the allocation of fishing rights should be based on catch history (the amount of fish the fleet of each country has caught in the past) rather than the location where the fish was caught. This pattern of allocation would wind back the rights island states have asserted over catches in their EEZs (Anderson 2002). Agreeing on an allocation of fishing rights will be difficult in any case (with nearly 30 countries involved in the process) and Japan's position adds to the difficulty. Allocation of fishing rights is a necessary step to implementing effective fisheries management for the region, so Japan's sense of national rights over the ocean is playing an important role in a fishery that is ecologically and economically of global significance.

Fish in Japanese politics

Although Japan was no longer in danger of famine by the 1960s, oceanic fisheries remained domestically politically important to the end of the twentieth century. This is visible in the membership of what was the premier fisheries promotion organization, the Dai Nippon Suisan Kai (Great Japan Fisheries Association, 1998). Another organization, the Federation of Japan Tuna Fisheries Cooperative Associations (shortened to Japan Tuna in English and *Nikkatsuren* in Japanese) took over as the leading body for distant-water tuna fisheries in the 1960s, but the Dai Nippon Suisan Kai remained important through its exceedingly high connections to government. The Honorary President of the Dai Nippon Suisan Kai, until his death in 2004, was former Prime Minister Suzuki

Zenko.[4] Members of the imperial family have always been involved with the organization. Membership of the committees for this organization also includes the heads of all key sectors related to fishing, such as trading companies, fisheries cooperatives and fish markets. The high ranking membership of the Dai Nippon Suisan Kai both reflected the importance of fisheries in Japan and helped ensure fisheries stayed a priority at the highest levels of government.

One reason fisheries have been politically important is that rural areas have been disproportionately electorally important in Japan. This is both because of a historical concern with food security and because rural electorates are weighted more heavily than urban electorates. These rural electorates have been the heartland of the Liberal Democratic Party, which has been in power almost continuously since 1955.[5] Rural areas receive a range of government benefits from preferential tax treatment, to lower electricity charges, to public works for infrastructure development (George Mulgan 2000). Many distant-water fishing companies are based in rural areas, such as Kushikino in Kagoshima Prefecture, and Kesennuma in Miyagi Prefecture (see Figure 3.1).

The political clout of oceanic fisheries is reflected in the extensive government support they have received. By the 1980s fisheries had become very competitive, and the relatively high cost fleets of the USA and Japan lost their dominance to lower cost fleets from Taiwan, Korea and Southeast Asia.

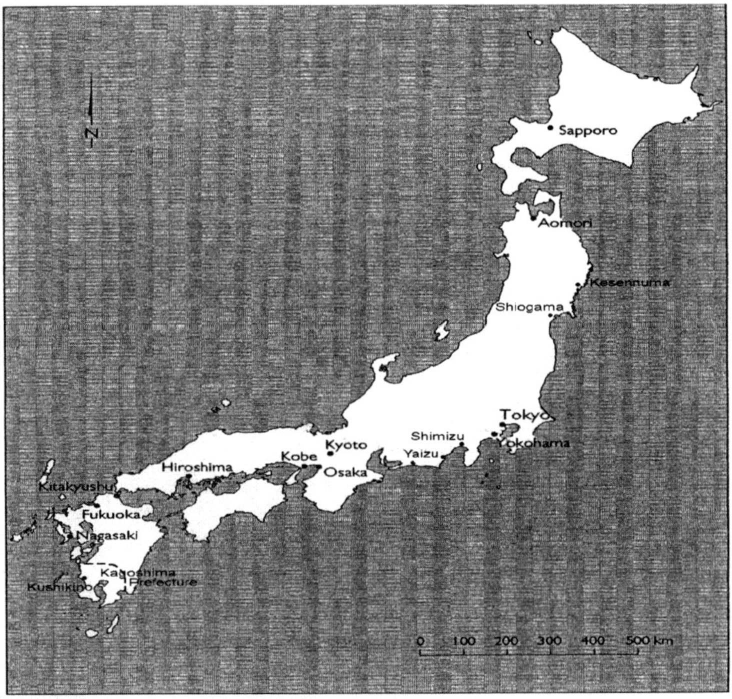

Figure 3.1 Map of Japan.

Competition from lower cost fleets (while Japanese immigration regulations restricted Japanese distant-water fleets from cutting their labor costs by hiring non-Japanese) as well as increasing fuel costs and increased fishing ground access costs due to EEZs all contributed to Japan's decline as a major fishing power. Because distant-water fisheries (mainly tuna) were politically important, national government support was provided in the form of price support schemes, low interest loans, fleet reconstruction schemes (to update technology) and structural adjustment (Campbell and Nicholl 1994; Fujinami 1987; Bergin and Harward 1996). Economists Campbell and Nicholl (1994) found that in 1987 the total subsidies to the tuna industry from the Japan Fisheries Agency (¥269 billion, US$1.8 billion) exceeded the losses incurred by the tuna fleet that year. They also found that during the 1980s as a whole the Japanese distant-water tuna fleet was operating at a loss to the extent that 'it is difficult to believe the industry could have continued without such assistance'.

Fisheries-related nationalism

It is well known that the political influence wielded by the rice growing lobby in Japan has been bolstered by a nationalist ideology that links food security, national identity bound up with eating certain kinds of food, and the economic health of rural communities (see Francks 2006; George Mulgan 2000). Oceanic fisheries have also shored up political support through this ideology, being rurally based, through contributing to the seafood that makes up a large part of Japanese diets, and through the iconic importance of the tunas used in sashimi and sushi cuisine for contemporary Japanese cultural identities.

Ever since Japan entered into the modernization race with the Western powers in the late 1800s, the belief that Japan is a resource poor country has influenced political and economic decisions. Food shortages, especially those after World War II, have been used to support the argument that Japan should have self-sufficiency in basic foodstuffs. An opinion poll by the Prime Minister's Office in 2000 found that 78 percent of Japanese were concerned about the stability of food supplies in the future and 95 percent called for the government to ensure national food security (MAFF 2003). The mass media disseminates the discourse of dependency on imports, helping to keep fears about food security alive (Bestor 1999: 167), even though famine seems a highly unlikely scenario in contemporary Japan. Food production has a special place in Japan's political landscape, and fisheries, like rice, are a key part of Japanese imaginaries of food production.

As part of a project looking at southern bluefin tuna industries, co-researcher Koh Sunhui and I interviewed members of the non-government consumers' organization, Shōdanren, for their views on sashimi tuna.[6] The Shōdanren members said Japanese consumers tend to prefer domestically produced food because they believe that it is more likely to be healthy and safe to eat than food produced overseas. They also said Japanese consumers believe some goods, such as sashimi tuna, are better quality when produced by Japanese than by non-Japanese. Anthropologist Theodore Bestor (1999: 168–9) has noted that seafood products labeled '*kokusan*' ('made in Japan') claim higher prices and prestige than imported seafoods. The Shōdanren interviewees said Japanese consumers are willing to pay up to 50 percent more for domestic rather than imported food. They also raised the issue of Japan's low rate of food self-sufficiency, saying they felt the current rate of 40 percent domestic food production was too low, and that Japanese consumers felt that a rate of '80 something percent' self-sufficiency in food was the right level.

The Shōdanren discussion of food self-sufficiency ended with a strong statement from one of the interviewees saying that globalization was going too far and that she felt it reasonable that 'Japanese citizens' should defend their food self-sufficiency. The word she used for 'citizen' in this outburst was '*kokumin*', literally 'nation-people'. Another word she could have used was 'consumer' (*shōhisha*), or another word for 'citizen' '*shimin*' (literally 'city-people'), which is often used for 'citizen' in a civil society sense, such as in 'citizens' movements' (*shimin undō*). Her choice of the word 'kokumin' shows the consumer nationalism undercurrent pervading the food security and food self-sufficiency debates in Japan.[7]

Patricia Maclachlan (2004) has theorized a *kokumin* aspect of Japanese consumer identity, arguing that historical developments during the twentieth century caused Japanese consumers to be politically different to consumers in the English-speaking world. Before and during World War II part of the difference was that consumption was seen by many Japanese as shameful waste, because of an ethic of personal frugality in order to be able to devote resources to the national endeavor. Then in the postwar period, with famines and chaos as Japan rebuilt, consumers sided with producers in a joint effort to achieve national food self-sufficiency. Consumers thus developed a 'survivor' identity that was teamed on the same side as, rather than in opposition to, food producers. This postwar survivor consumer identity again connoted a sense of pulling together for the nation. Maclachlan notes that the 'survivor' *kokumin* aspect to Japanese consumer identity has meant consumers' movements have done apparently paradoxical things, like supported agricultural protectionism, which meant they paid several times the world price for rice.

The Tokyo-based consumers' group Women's Forum for Fish (WFF, in Japanese *Ūmanzu Fuōramu Sakana*) also represents fisheries issues with a *kokumin* aspect to consumer identity like that of the interviewee from Shōdanren. Shiraishi Yuriko started the WFF organization in 1993 after realizing the extent of Japan's reliance on seafood imports.[8] She felt Japanese consumers should be better educated about this important part of their diet. Shiraishi's consumer identity resonates with that detailed by Maclachlan (2004) when she noted that *kokumin* identity was 'rarely evoked in movement discourse' (because it is an explicitly nationalist term which sits uneasily with progressive social movements in postwar Japan) but is nonetheless visible in activities and attitudes. In written material Shiraishi uses the word *shōhisha* (consumer), not *kokumin* (Shiraishi 2004). In her spoken representations, however, she does use the word *kokumin*.[9] Economic and cultural nationalisms are evident in various representations she makes about fisheries issues, interwoven with internationalism.

Shiraishi allies consumers not only with Japanese producers, but with producers the world over who supply the Japanese market. She wants to establish dialogue with seafood producers everywhere in order to educate Japanese consumers. She calls for an alliance between fishing industries, governments, traders and consumers against illegal fishing, which endangers stocks and undermines fisheries operating in accordance with international and national measures to protect stocks (Shiraishi 1999a, 1999b). This aspect of Shiraishi's consumer activism is internationalist.

Shiraishi also calls for an alliance of 'fish food culture' (*gyoshoku bunka*) countries of Asia against the hegemony of the 'meat food culture' countries of Europe and North America. Describing Japan as having a fish food culture versus the meat food culture of the 'West' is a way of asserting Japanese national identity (Hirata 2004; Bestor 1999). Fisheries production is important in Japan not only because of concerns about food security, but also because it is seen as part of Japan's cultural heritage (Bestor 2004: 167). Food is a prominent part of culture at all levels in Japanese society and is used as a marker of cultural identity, both for regional differences within Japan and between Japanese and foreigners (Bestor 1999). Fish food culture – the arts of fishing, preparing and consuming fish – is seen by many as an essential part of Japaneseness. So in evoking the idea of fish food culture, Shiraishi is engaging in a kind of cultural nationalism. Economic nationalism is evident in Shiraishi's assertion that increasing world population will put pressure on food stocks such that there will be a 'fish war' (*osakana sensō*) in the twenty-first century. She deplores the fact that Japanese consumers feel no sense of danger that half of their seafood is imported and predicts that soon it will not be possible to buy fish from other countries (Shiraishi 2004).

Bureaucrats governing distant-water tuna fisheries usually represent the issues similarly to the consumer activists quoted above. Komatsu Masayuki has been a key figure in Japanese distant-water fisheries governance over the last decade. A senior bureaucrat with the Ministry of Agriculture, Forestry and Fisheries (MAFF), he has been the Japanese Head of Delegation in international tuna management commissions and also been a vocal presence at meetings of the International Whaling Commission meetings. Komatsu is more outspoken than many of his colleagues but it is fair to say he represents the prevailing public policy philosophy of the Japanese government regarding fisheries production.[10] According to Komatsu:

> Japan cannot continue simply relying on imported food. Can we afford as a country to be dependent on others, such as the United States or Australia, for our basic foods? Will we always have enough precious dollars to import what we need? It is the answers to these questions that should tell you why I firmly believe that we need to become more self-sufficient for reason of our national health and at the most basic level, to guarantee the supply of food to our people.[11]

Komatsu's representation is nationalist in that his 'us' and 'our' signify Japan, not some transnational alliance of fish consumers or producers.[12] In Komatsu's vision, Japanese fisheries must be supported for the sake of the Japanese nation. He has said that 'Japan does not need globalization', and that importing 'too much' tuna is 'bad for Japan'.[13] Other MAFF officials also assert that national interest should be balanced against globalization. In response to calls for further trade liberalization under the World Trade Organization, MAFF has said 'further radical reforms will ... deteriorate food self-sufficiency and multifunctional benefits. This must be a huge loss for *the Japanese* and their *national* economy' (MAFF 2003, italics added).

Conclusion

The history of fisheries over the last century shows the central position of the ocean in Japan's political landscape. Japan's empire was made up of watery as well as earthy territory, and movement in the watery world was restricted under the postwar occupation. Japanese senses of having a right to be in and appropriate resources from the world's oceans, based on its history of having done so, however, remained essentially unchanged. Consequently, the Japanese government and fishing interests were outraged by the development of EEZs and remain opposed to the notion that fishing rights are based on national ownership of bodies of ocean. This background is useful for understanding contemporary Japanese international relations on fisheries issues. The domestic political importance of oceanic fisheries in Japan is similar to that of rice farming in Japan. Continuation of Japanese oceanic fisheries is understood as being important for the nation, for reasons of food security as well as cultural identity.

Notes

1 This chapter is based, in part, on collaborative research with Dr Koh Sunhui funded by the Australian Research Council and the Japan Society for the Promotion of Science 2001–2004. It also utilizes research carried out as an AusAID Postdoctoral Fellow at the Crawford School at the Australian National University in 2005. Parts of the empirical material and analysis of nationalism in Japanese fisheries contained in this chapter are also contained in a paper that evolved through incarnations as proceedings from a workshop, a book chapter, a working paper and a journal article, see Barclay and Koh 2005, 2006, 2008.

2 These figures are for the large species of tuna such as bluefin, yellowfin, bigeye and albacore, not skipjack.

3 While the oceans were commons, probably because of the difficulty of establishing and protecting resource rights over oceans until modern shipping and surveillance technology was developed, coastal zones were not open access. Histories and anthropologies of coastal fishing communities have shown that sophisticated regimes of resource rights usually operated in coastal zones.

4 Suzuki had originally studied fisheries at college, and then worked in organizations connected to the fishing industry until entering politics in 1947. He was the Minister of Agriculture Forestry and Fisheries for several years in the 1970s, before becoming Prime Minister in 1980.

5 Rural areas are in decline, however, mostly from depopulation. For this reason among others they are less politically important than they were.
6 *Zenkoku Shōhisha Dantai Renraku Kai*, usually abbreviated to *Shōdanren*, or 'Consumers Japan' in English. Interview in *Chiyoda-ku*, Tokyo, May 2003.
7 As McVeigh (2004) has pointed out, labeling social features in Japan 'nationalist' can be very contentious because of undesirable associations with Imperial Japan's militarist ultranationalism, and contemporary sentiments along these lines held by small numbers of *uyoku* right wing groups. The nationalisms described in this paper are neither militarist nor ultranationalist, but are the 'banal' forms of nationalism discussed by Billig (1999) that are endemic in the contemporary normative system of nation-states. I am not trying to make the case that Japan is any more nationalist than other countries, rather I aim to identify the roles played by everyday forms of cultural, economic and consumer nationalisms.
8 According to MAFF (2003), Japan imports 60 percent of its food supplies, measured in caloric intake. In the 1970s Japan was the world's largest seafood exporter. By 2001 Japan had become the worlds largest seafood importer, with 23 percent in value and 14 percent in volume of world production (JIFRS 2004).
9 Shiraishi's spoken representation was observed when she spoke in a panel at the biennial conference of the International Institute for Fisheries Economics and Trade in Tokyo, July 2004.
10 According to Hirata (2004), opinion on whaling in MAFF is not unified and the Ministry of Foreign Affairs (MoFA) often disagrees with MAFF stances taken on whaling, but the pro-whaling group, lead by Komatsu, is dominant and their agenda prevails. Komatsu's position vis-à-vis MAFF and MoFA on tuna issues is similar.
11 Komatsu as quoted (and translated) by Roger Smith in his chapter 'Japanese Whaling Policy and Food Security' from his doctoral thesis in International Relations, St Anthony's College, Oxford University, 2007.
12 This style generates political capital in that domestic contesting voices can be devalued because they seem to be against the nation. Hirata (2004: 194) notes the political device of framing issues as 'us' versus 'them' in the whaling dispute has helped marginalize domestic anti-whaling voices.
13 These comments were made by Komatsu in a panel discussion at the biennial conference of the International Institute for Fisheries Economics and Trade in Tokyo, July 2004.

Bibliography

Amino, Y. (1994) *Nihon shakai saikō: Kaimin to rettō bunka* (A Reconsideration of Japanese Society: Sea People and Archipelago Culture), Tokyo: Shōgakkan.

Anderson, K. (2002) 'Tuna Politics in Oceania: The Effectiveness of Collective Diplomacy', unpublished doctoral thesis, Department of International Relations, Research School of Pacific and Asian Studies, The Australian National University, Canberra.

Barclay, K. and Koh, S. (2005) 'Neoliberalism in Japan's Tuna Fisheries? Government Intervention and Reform in the Distant Water Longline Industry', Working Paper in International and Development Economics 05–2, Canberra: Australian National University, (available at www.crawford.anu.edu.au/degrees/idec/working_papers/IDEC05–2.pdf).

—— (2006) 'Marketization of Japanese Governance? Case Study of Long Line Tuna Fisheries' in J. Goodman (ed.) *Regionalization, Marketization and Political Change in the Pacific Rim*, Guadalajara: University of Guadalajara Press.

—— (2008) 'Neoliberalism in Japan's Tuna Fisheries? A History of Government Intervention in a Food Producing Sector', *Japan Forum* 20(2): 139–70.

Bergin, A. and Harward, M. (1996) *Japan's Tuna Fishing Industry: A Setting Sun or a New Dawn?* New York: Nova Science.

Bestor, T. (1999) 'Constructing Sushi: Culture, Cuisine and Commodification in a Japanese Market', in S. Orphett Long (ed.) *Lives in Motion: Composing Circles of Self and Community in Japan*, Ithaca, NY: Cornell University Press.

—— (2004) *Tsukiji: The Fish Market at the Center of the World*, Berkeley, CA: University of California Press.

Billig, M. (1999) *Banal Nationalism*, London: Sage.

Campbell, H.F. and Nicholl, R.B. (1994) 'The economics of the Japanese tuna fleet, 1979–80 to 1988–89', in H.F. Campbell and A.D. Owen (eds) *The Economics of Papua New Guinea's Tuna Fisheries*, Canberra: Australian Council for International Agricultural Research (ACIAR).

Dai Nippon Suisan Kai (Great Japan Fisheries Association) (1998) (available at www.suisankai.or.jp/ accessed 22 March 2005).

Francks, P. (2006) *Rural Economic Development in Japan: From the Nineteenth Century to the Pacific War*, London: Routledge.

Fujinami, N. (1987) 'Development of Japan's Tuna Fisheries', in D. Doulman (ed.) *Tuna Issues and Perspectives in the Pacific Islands Region*, Honolulu, HI: East–West Center.

George Mulgan, A. (2000) *The Politics of Agriculture in Japan*, London: Routledge.

Habara, Y. (1949) *Nihon kodai gyogyō keizai-shi* (An Economic History of the Ancient Japanese Fishing Industry), Tokyo: Kaizōsha.

Hanlon, D. (1998) *Remaking Micronesia: Discourses over Development in a Pacific Territory, 1994–1982*, Honolulu, HI: University of Hawai'i Press.

Hirata, K. (2004) 'Beached Whales: Examining Japan's Rejection of an International Norm', *Social Science Japan Journal*, 7(2): 177–97.

Japan International Fisheries Research Society (JIFRS) (2004) *Japan and Her Fisheries*, Tokyo: Overseas Fishery Cooperation Foundation (OFCF).

Kagoshima Prefecture Tuna and Skipjack Fisheries Cooperative Fifty Years History Editorial Committee (Kagoshima) (2000) (eds) *Kagoshima Ken Maguro Katsuo Gyogyō Kyōdō Kumiai Sōritsu Goju Shūnen Shi* (Fifty Year History of the Kagoshima Prefecture Tuna and Skipjack Fisheries Cooperative), Tokyo: Suisan Shinshio Sha.

Koh, S. (1998) *20 Seiki no Tai Nichi Saishuu Tou Jin: Sono Seikatsu Katei to Ishiki* (Jeju Islanders Living in Japan in the Twentieth Century: Life Cycles and Consciousness), Tokyo: Akashi Shoten.

Maclachlan, P.L. (2004) 'From Subjects to Citizens: Japan's Evolving Consumer Identity', *Japanese Studies*, 24(1): 115–34.

McVeigh, T. (2004) *Nationalisms of Japan: Managing and Mystifying Identity*, Lanham, MD: Rowman and Littlefield.

Ministry of Agriculture, Forestry and Fisheries (MAFF) (2003) 'Why Agriculture needs Different Treatment in Trade Rules? Japan's Policy Reform and WTO Negotiations', Fact Sheet No. 1, Ministry of Agriculture, Forestry and Fisheries, (available at www.maff.go.jp/eindex.html accessed 22 March 2005).

Peattie, M.R. (1984) 'The *Nan'yō*: Japan in the South Pacific, 1885–1945', in R.H. Myers and M.R. Peattie (eds) *The Japanese Colonial Empire, 1895–1945*, Princeton, NJ: Princeton University Press.

Schurman, R.A. (1998), 'Tuna Dreams: Resource Nationalism and the Pacific Islands' Tuna Industry', *Development and Change*, 29: 107–36.

Shiraishi, Y. (1999a) 'We're all on this planet together – those of us who eat tuna and those of us who don't. Now let's think about the future of the ocean and tuna', *All About Fish – Gyo!*, 1. Available from Women's Forum for Fish (WWF) Secretariat, 3–12–15 Ginza, Chuo-ku, Tokyo 104–0061, Japan.

—— (1999b) 'The Fish We Eat: What Tuna Means to Us', *All About Fish: Gyo!*, 8–21. Available from Women's Forum for Fish (WWF) Secretariat, 3–12–15 Ginza, Chuo-ku, Tokyo 104–0061, Japan.

—— (2004) 'Nōchikusuisan ga ittai to natta kankyō hozen – yutaka umidzukuri wo mezashite (Environmental Sustainability by a United Agriculture and Fisheries: Aiming for Creation of Fertile Seas)', Agriculture, Forestry and Fisheries Section, Takamatsu City Hall, Kagawa Prefecture, homepage for the 24th National Meeting for *Yutaka Umizukuri* (available at www.city.takamatsu.kagawa.jp/sangyou/suisan/index.files/home.files/umizu/gif/040123.htm accessed 22 March 2005).

Tanabe, S. (1990) *Nihon ama dentō no kenkyū*. (A Study of the Japanese *Ama* Tradition), Tokyo: Hōsei Daigaku Shuppankyoku.

Tarte, S. (1998) *Japan's Aid Diplomacy and the Pacific Islands*, Canberra: Asia Pacific Press.

Tomiyama, I. (2002) 'The "Japanese" of Micronesia: Okinawans in the Nanyō Islands', in R. Nakasone (ed.), *Okinawan Diaspora*, Honolulu, HI: University of Hawai'i Press.

Wakabayashi, Y. (1993) 'Nanpō katsuo gyogyō no chiiki teki haikei to tenkai katei: Okinawa ken Irabu chō ni kansuru chiiki monogurafu', Matsuyama Shinonome Women's College, Annals of the Faculty of Humanities 1 (August).

Western and Central Pacific Fisheries Commission (WCPFC) (2006) Website www.wcpfc.int/index.htm (accessed 13 February 2007).

Yanemoto, M. (1999) 'Maps and Metaphors of the "Small Eastern Sea" in Tokugawa Japan (1603–1868)', *Geographical Review*, 89(2).

4 Water futures and their influence on sovereignty in the Marshall Islands

Dirk H.R. Spennemann

Introduction

Several chapters in this book have explored the human responses to living near shorelines which form the boundaries between the sea and the land, between fresh and saltwater environments. There are, however, areas where the sea prevails both in expanse and in day-to-day presence, while the land is marginal and human life is precariously balanced. Human life on the small islets that make up the atolls in the world's oceans is dependent on the presence of potable fresh water, while at the same time it is imperilled by the ever present threat of the sea inundating the low-lying islands. In response to these threats, island societies have developed response mechanisms that ensure, to the extent feasible, human and societal survival.

Life on coral atolls can be very precarious. The sand cay islets are low-lying (in the main less than 2 m above high water) and small. Only the larger islands (over 500 m by 1,000 m) are suitable for permanent human habitation, as they possess a fragile lens of freshwater floating on top of a saltwater base. It is this lens of groundwater that allows for a variety of plant life, and it is this source of fresh water that allows humans to exist on the island. Environmental disasters, such as typhoons with waves of over 10 m washing across an entire islet, can swamp the groundwater lens with saltwater, causing salinisation and thus imperilling human survival.

This chapter describes the situation on the Marshall Islands, a small atoll nation comprising 29 atolls and five islands, located in the northwest equatorial Pacific, about 3,790 km west of Honolulu, 2,700 km north of Fiji and 1,500 km east of Ponape. With the exception of the two northwestern atolls, Enewetak and Ujelang, the Marshall Islands are arranged in two island chains running roughly NNW to SSE: the western Ralik Chain and the eastern Ratak Chain. Unlike the high volcanic islands of Hawaii or Fiji, the atolls of the Marshall Islands are a series of low-lying sand cays with a maximum natural elevation not exceeding 3 m.

As will be shown, in order to reduce the consequences of environmental disasters, traditionally the Marshallese chiefs had land holdings scattered over several islands of the same atoll, as well as land rights and, importantly, rights to

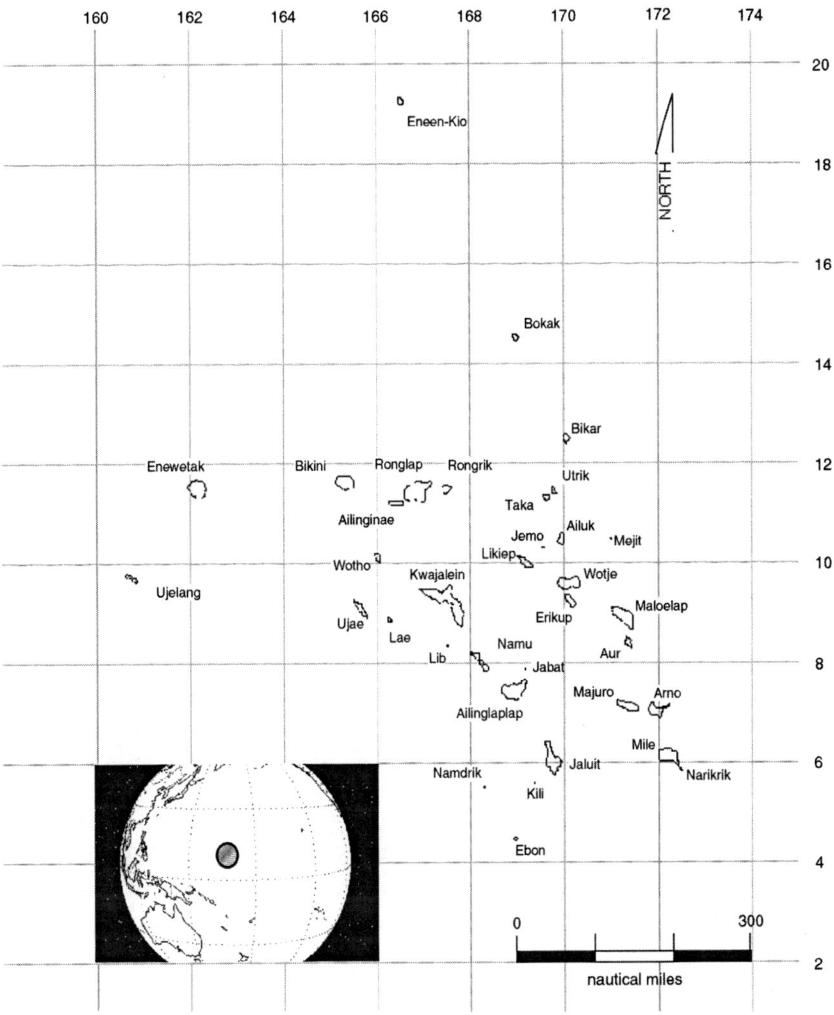

Figure 4.1 Index map of the Marshall Islands showing the atolls mentioned in the text.

resources, on other atolls. In times of disaster there were thus other resources to call upon. That level of connectivity allowed Marshallese society to thrive on the marginal land they inhabited. With the spectre of rising sea levels looming, the environmental challenges are now more pressing than ever before. As their traditional predecessors before them, the current leaders are faced with challenges to ensure the survival of the population under their charge.

Environmental parameters

While the climatological patterns may be subject to change due to global climate change and associated phenomena such as sea-level rise and changes to typhoon patterns, the underlying geophysical parameters remain the same. As they circumscribe the conditions of past, present and future life on the atolls of the Marshall Islands, they need to be briefly addressed here.

Geomorphology

The principal agent supporting life on atolls is the small freshwater lens on each of the islets that stud the atoll rim. To understand the nature of the lens, some geomorphology is required. Live coral originally formed barrier reefs around raised islands. As the island's core gradually submerged, the coral continued to grow, effectively forming rings of coral in the sea. The shape of the atoll reflects the original shape of the barrier reef. The atolls can be as small as Taka Atoll, with only 0.6 km^2 combined land area, or as large as Kwajalein Atoll, the world's largest atoll with a lagoon area of 2,174 km^2 but only 16.4 km^2 combined landmass (Bryan 1971). The atolls rise steeply from the ocean floor, often over 1,500 m, and slope gently into the lagoon, which is commonly not any deeper than 40–80 m. Water exchange between the lagoon and the sea is maintained through passes, as well as across the reef platform at high tide. The only parts of an atoll that are permanently above mean high seawater level are the sand cays or islets, made up from erosion products of the reef, predominantly calciferous sand and coral rubble. The particle size of the material decreases from the ocean side to the lagoon side. In addition, there is variation between the islets of an atoll depending on the location of the islet in relation to prevailing wave action. Islets on the leeward side of the atoll tend to be larger and have finer sediments, while islets exposed to the swell, and hence more likely to be water-washed during strong storms, tend to have more coarse-grained sediments.

Freshwater lenses

Because of the total lack of physical elevation and hence orographic rainfall patterns, the precipitation in the Marshall Islands is solely governed by the general Pacific-wide climatic belts as well as by highly localised micro-climatic rainfall over the lagoons. On the regional scale, there is a distinct precipitation gradient running from the equatorial zone in the south to the north. The further north the atoll is located, the less precipitation can be expected. Thus Jaluit, located at 5°47'N has a precipitation of almost 4,000 mm per annum, while Wake, located at 19°28'N has only a precipitation of less than 1,000 mm per annum (Williamson and Sabath 1982; Spennemann 2006a). Intense tropical storms of short duration contribute much of the total rainfall, and the incidence of the storms themselves is quite variable from one year to the next for any particular island or atoll. Any rain that is deposited on the atoll is dependent on the trajectory and nature of the clouds. In many instances, especially during the drier season, rain-bearing clouds may be seen to pass over a particular stretch of land, but may miss another completely or discharge into the lagoon. Unless rain falls on an islet it is of no use to the land ecosystem.

The flat landscape, permeability of the underlying rock and the composition of soils and reef-derived sediments prevent the occurrence of streams or creeks. Therefore, after the wetting loss (the amount of moisture needed to wet the surfaces of plants and roofs etc. to such a degree that additional moisture will run off) all of the rainfall dropping on a given islet will percolate through the sand and settle into the ground. As rainwater has a lower specific gravity than saltwater, the rainwater will in effect 'float' on top of the saltwater (Ghyben–Herzberg principle; Drabbe and Badon Ghijben 1889; Herzberg 1901). Moreover, because of weight, it will gradually depress the surface of the saltwater, creating a lens-shaped region of fresh water. As the lens grows, some of the lens will run out at the edges of the islet. As rain falls on the islet, the lens will become thicker, with the interface with the seawater being gradual. As there is no wave action inside the islet's core, the integrity of the lens is maintained. Limited mixing of the salt and fresh water will occur at the boundaries of the lens, caused by water-level fluctuations as a function of tidal movements or as convective forces due to capillary action. The underlying substrate is not homogenous however, as it is made up of the old reef platform with various coral heads, intermixed with now consolidated but formerly loose sediment that accumulated between the coral. Thus the 'storage capacity' of different substrates will differ (Arnow 1954; Cox 1951; Anthony *et al.* 1989; Wheatcraft and Buddemeier 1981). The shape of the island determines the thickness of the lens. Ignoring any variations in the coral limestone substrate, the thickest possible lens would result from a circular island. As a real island's shape on the atolls is either oblong or triangular of some description, the greatest thickness of the lens is predetermined by the width of the island.

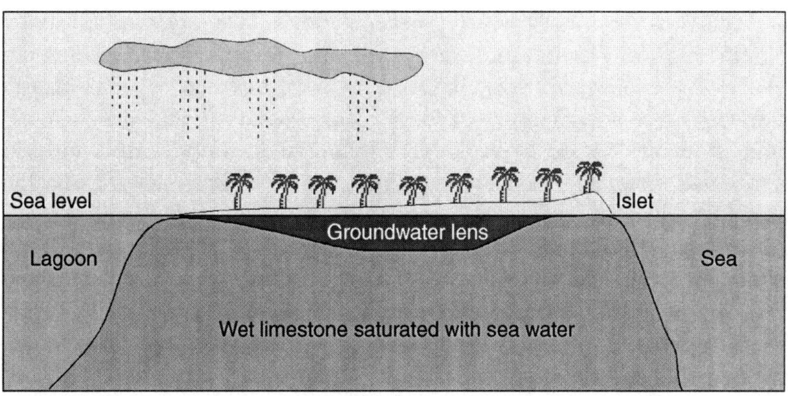

Figure 4.2 Concept of the freshwater lens.

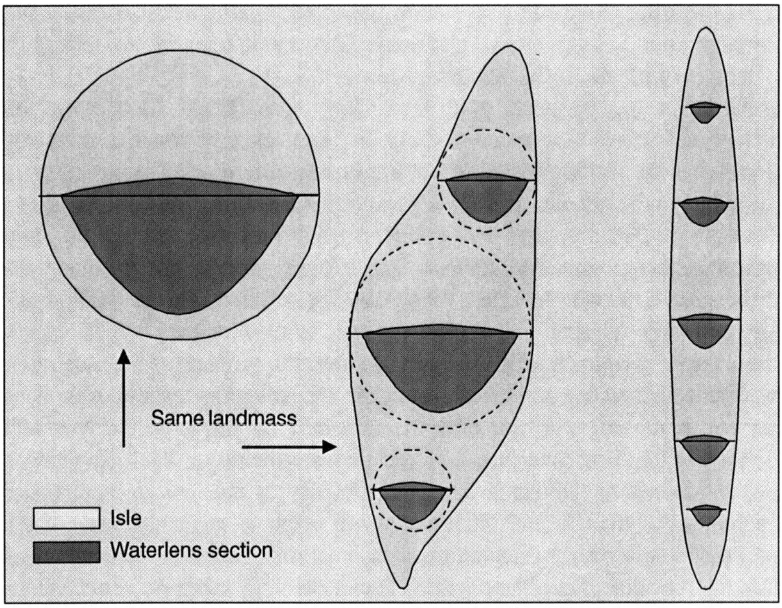

Figure 4.3 Conceptual relationships between island size, island shape and water lens.

Vegetation patterns

The freshwater lens provides a stable water supply for any vegetation growing on the islet. On small and very low-lying islets the vegetation is limited to hardy shrubs that can withstand both the salt spray from the ocean and can thrive on a supply of brackish water. On the larger islets, the freshwater lenses allow other vegetation to grow, such as breadfruit (*Artocarpus altilis*) which are dependent on non-saline water. The gradation of the soil/sand substrate, availability of fresh water, wind, wave action and the concomitant salt spray cause the vegetation on the sand cays of the coral atolls to occur in clearly defined zones, reaching from the lagoon side to the ocean side of the island. The area of greatest productivity is in the centre where a thick fertile soil can build up from decaying plant matter which, coupled with easily accessible permanent freshwater sources, i.e. the freshwater lens, allows many trees, particularly breadfruit trees, to grow well (summarised from Fosberg 1990; Spennemann 1990a, 2006a). The vegetation zonation on any given island depends on the island's location on the atoll, with leeward islands, away from the swell and strong salt spray, being generally more conducive to complex vegetation patterns than windward islands. Moreover, as stated, the latitude of the atoll determines the overall rainfall, which in turn has implications on the viability of vegetation.

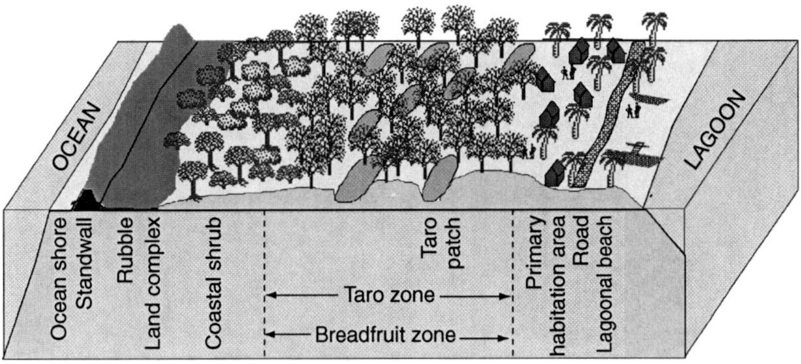

Figure 4.4 Schematic representation of the vegetation zonation across a leeward atoll islet in the central and southern Marshalls (source: Spennemann 1990a with modifications).

Traditional responses

These environmental parameters lead to a number of traditional responses, mainly in terms of settlement patterns and land ownership, which combined with the precariousness of existence, have had implications for the social structure of the Marshallese community.

Settlement patterns and land ownership

The low-lying sand islands of the coral atolls are exposed to environmental hazards and changing conditions. Therefore, the atoll environment faced by the prehistoric, early historic and also the present-day settlers of the Marshall Islands, defines very clearly the way their settlements, their horticultural (agricultural) sites and their ritual sites, such as cemeteries, are arranged on any island of a given atoll. The environmental parameters to be considered are:

- availability of freshwater;
- availability of gardenable/arable land;
- availability of a protected anchorage for boats;
- availability of a protected area for housing.

Given the zonation of the vegetation on any given island, the traditional land divisions, the *wato*, were laid out as strips of land running from the ocean side of the islet to its lagoon side, thereby ensuring that each household had access to all environmental zones. Figure 4.5 shows the modern pattern at the left, and the reconstructed prehistoric patterns at the right (after Spennemann 1990a). The *wato* on larger islets, especially on the environmentally favoured southern atolls,

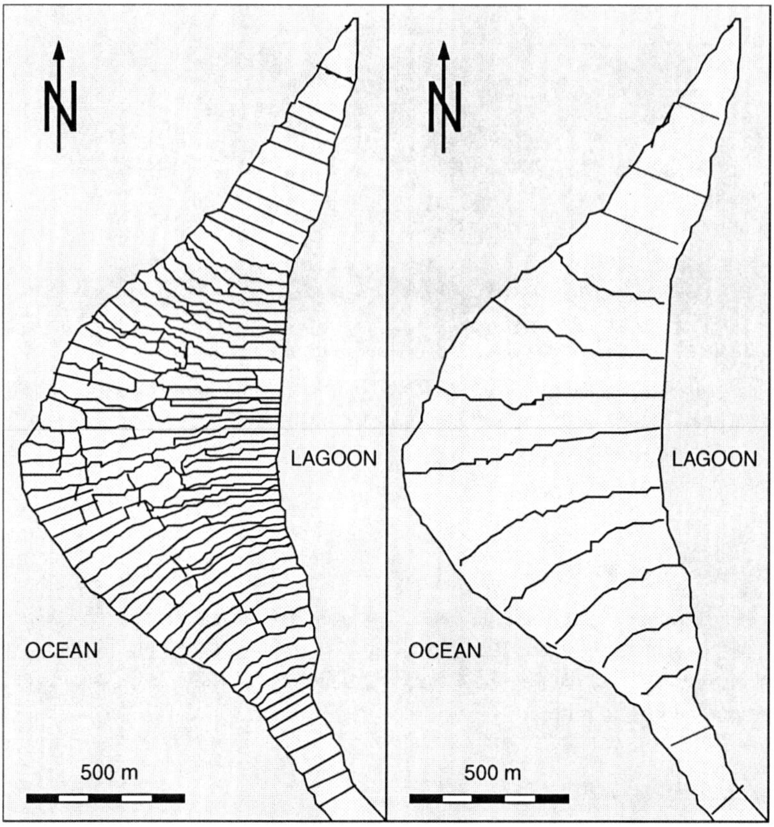

Figure 4.5 Land allotments on Majuro Islet ('Laura'), Majuro Atoll. Left: allotments as they appear today. Right: reconstructed size and appearance of allotments based on a reversal of the fission sequence (source: Spennemann 1990a).

are narrower than on the smaller islets of the same atolls. On the drier, and thus less favourable, northern atolls the *wato* are wider.

The prehistoric settlement pattern is almost entirely defined by these environmental constraints. Archaeological and historical site surveys found that the settlement on a major southern atoll, such as Majuro, favours larger islands. The coral gravel spreads, indicating house sites, were concentrated on the larger islands and, where a more detailed analysis was possible, it was found that the settlements were located on both sides of the breadfruit zone, with the main settlements on the lagoon side. The habitation sites would begin some 30–50 m inland from the present lagoon edge, well above the storm high tide mark and behind a small natural strand wall. Going inland, these gravel spreads would gradually change to shell middens, indicating cooking facilities and associated rubbish dumps on the inland, the 'backward' side, of the houses. Inland of these rubbish heaps an area of burials is encountered, located between the houses and the gardening centre. In the fertile middle of the island the breadfruit trees and a dense zone of taro patches are found. Going towards the ocean side one would encounter another, narrower zone of habitation and then would get into a dense salt resistant shrub and broadleaf forest fringing the ocean shore. In this zone some burials can also be expected (Spennemann 1992, 1999).

The settlement patterns described for a fertile, ideal atoll islet in the southern Marshalls is open for modifications in other parts of the Marshall Islands. A decreasing variety in plant life, and correlated with this a decreasing availability of food, are directly related to decreasing rainfall intensity the further north an atoll is located. On Ailuk Atoll, for example, the climate is too dry for breadfruit trees (*Artocarpus altilis*) to exist. The food available to the people on that atoll is restricted to coconuts (*Cocos nucifera*), pandanus and arrowroot (*Tacca leontopetaloides*). Further north, such as on Bikar, the climate is too dry for coconut palms and pandanus to exist. It is not surprising that Bikar was apparently never settled on a permanent basis. As productive and habitable land was in limited supply, the Marshallese population had to ensure that the limited resources were not over-exploited. While some natural resources, such as fish, turtles and seabirds, could be managed through seasonal and social taboos (Tobin 1952), terrestrial resources had to be managed through a regime of population control that only allowed two children per couple (of common people) (Spennemann 1995).

Precariousness of existence

The single most destructive climatological phenomenon affecting atolls are typhoons ('cyclones' south of the equator). These high-speed circular wind systems are created around a central area of low air pressure. Spawned as tropical depressions in areas of warm seawater, located at the interface between two opposing air currents, these systems can pick up wind speed, and thus strength, if the required movement of air in the central column is sustained over a long period, and if a strong jet stream overhead creates a sucking motion. Tropical storms of gale force have sustained wind speeds (for ten minutes or more) of 88 km/h and can develop into typhoons with minimum sustained wind speeds of 117 km/h. Sustained wind speeds of close to 200 km/h are not uncommon among 'super typhoons'.

Tropical storms and typhoons are *the* most frightening natural phenomenon, especially for those living on a coral atoll where the maximum elevation is rarely more than 2 m above sea level. The waves associated with such events can be 10 m and higher, on occasion compounded by tidal fluctuations. The damage to the islands varies. Low-lying islands and islets of the coral atolls, however, suffer both from wind effects and from inundation. Often the entire islet is awash. Not only does the inundation with salt water contaminate the fragile freshwater lens within the islets, the wave action also suspends much of the top soil, washing it away and filling the taro patches in the centre of the islets with salt water and sediment.

Typhoons have been a fact of life for the people in Micronesia since the time of their initial settlement thousands of years ago. The precariousness of (semi-) traditional life on an atoll is best illustrated by describing the impact of a particular typhoon that struck the southern Marshalls on 30 June 1905 and that is well documented in the German colonial records (Spennemann 2004b). On 30 June 1905 a strong typhoon passed over the southern Marshall Islands, severely affecting Nadikdik (Knox) (6°20'N 172°10'E), Mile, Arno, Majuro and Jaluit atolls. Other atolls, namely Aur (8°12'N 171°06'E), Maloelap (8°40'N 171°00' E), Ailinglapalap, Ebon and Ujelang, were also affected but to a lesser degree. Over 227 Marshallese lost their lives on that day on the affected atolls, most of them on Nadikdik and Mile. Many more people were injured. Hardest hit was Nadikdik Atoll, located just to the southwest of Mile. This atoll was completely washed over, all inhabited islands were completely reduced to the bare reef platform and the human population of that atoll (70 people) completely extinguished save for two boys who, clinging to an uprooted breadfruit tree, survived a 24-hour drift voyage to the southern coast of Mile (Jeschke 1905). Following the destruction of all food stocks and fruit on the trees, approximately another 90 people died during the subsequent months due to starvation. Immediately following the event, the lagoon of Mile, and to a lesser extent that of Jaluit, were reported to be congested with floating debris: trees, bushes, houses, broken canoes, wooden utensils and corpses. The concentration of drift material in the waters of the Marshalls during July and August 1905 was so high that it constituted a serious shipping hazard, increasing the difficulty of the very limited relief operations. The flooding of several islets by salt water caused dieback of fruit trees as well as the contamination of the freshwater lens (see Spennemann 2004b for further details).

Social structure

Given the precariousness of human existence on a single atoll, it is not surprising that the Marshallese designed social structures that mitigated such impacts both within an atoll and between atolls. Marshallese society is matrilineal and matrilocal (Erdland 1909, 1912, 1914; Krämer 1906). The status and resource rights of the parents influenced the status and rights of the children, with the mother's rights and status being stronger. The Marshallese social structure at the time of contact, as presented by Erdland (1914: 99ff.), had four main tiers of increasing land ownership:

- *kajur*, commoners, effectively serfs, with rights to (some of) the resources on a single allotment of land but no control over land management decisions;
- *ledikdik*, commoners who because of capacity had been appointed as 'advisers' to the chiefs and given ownership rights to a single allotment of land by a *buirak* or *irooj* as a feudal holding in perpetuity and inheritable by the next generation;

- *buirak*, of chiefly lineage but subordinate to the *irooj*, with absolute rights to more than one allotment of land, usually on the same islet, but certainly on the same atoll, and rights to produce and resources from other allotments;
- *irooj*, high ranking chiefs, with absolute rights to more than one allotment of land, usually on the same atoll (on occasion on more than one atoll) and who exercised rights to produce and resources from allotments on other atolls.

The allotments were bounded by other allotments and the shorelines. Traditional rights extended as far into the lagoon or ocean as the chief could physically stand to fish (Erdland 1914). Given the fact that the shape of an islet was subject to continual change caused by the processes of erosion and accretion, such a stipulation makes a great deal of sense. If and when two islets merged, the boundary line was drawn at the locality of the actual merger.

The German colonial administration (1886–1914) intentionally, directly and indirectly, consolidated the hierarchical structure and the power position of the *irooj*. On the one hand, it prohibited warfare as a legitimate means of altering the balance of power, while it also introduced a head tax in 1888 (Sonnenschein 1888a, 1888c; Biermann 1889, 1890) with consequences to the hierarchy. Levied on every Marshallese subject, the tax could be forcibly collected if those levied attempted to default (Sonnenschein 1888b). Whereas, traditionally, the *irooj* had only a share of the food and other produce, as well as a share of his people's labour, the introduction of the head tax, payable in copra, the main commercial export article of the Marshall Islands, led to the development of a formal payment of the *irooj*'s share in copra. As the German authorities collected the tax as well as purchased any other copra from the *irooj* rather than directly from individuals, the power position of the *irooj* was strengthened and essentially formalised. As a result of these and other more subtle colonial changes, the traditional tenure structure collapsed into three levels (Tobin 1952, 1958):

- *dri-jerbal*, or workers, with ownership rights to aspects of a single allotment of land;
- *alap*, or 'land manager', who has rights to more than one allotment of land, usually on the same islet, but certainly on the same atoll; and
- *irooj*, who had rights on one or more entire atolls, as well as rights to resources on other atolls.

In practical terms, the increased movement from the outer islands to the population centres since the 1970s has created a new fourth level: those people who have no traditional rights whatsoever to the land allotment they reside on, but who are tolerated as squatters subject to the approval and good will of the *irooj*.

As the strength of the socio-political position of an *irooj* depended on his capacity to provide for his commoners, whom he needed in order to be able to wage war, an *irooj* was reliant on the productivity of the island and its people. The traditional societal structure with land ownership scattered over several islets of an atoll and resource rights to islets on other atolls, ensured that *irooj*, and to a lesser degree *buirak*, had access to a range of natural resources. This was an effective strategy for both physical and social survival in a fluctuating environment. Because rainfall intensity varies not only between but also *within* atolls, the productivity of some of the land allotments was patchy, even without taking into account climatic extremes such as typhoons or drought. During times of devastation wrought by typhoons or extended drought, the spread of such land holdings was especially important as it ensured that carbohydrate food stuffs were available for redistribution to the starving community members (a typhoon devastated community cannot live on fish alone).

Connectivity

Traditional inter-atoll obligations are on record for the early contact period as well as for the early German colonial period, with islanders providing a share of produce to the higher-ranking chief. This redistribution of wealth, and the flow of important items to the highest ranking chief, have been observed from early European contact times onwards (cf. redistribution of iron from Wotje to Aur; Chamisso 1836; Kotzebue 1832; Spennemann 2004a). It could take on substantial dimensions. For example, the German, Otto Eisenhardt (1888), stranded on Ailuk Atoll in 1871, reported that once a year most of the islanders would sail to another atoll, some 150 nautical miles distant (most likely Wotje Atoll) to pay their obligations in the form of food, especially arrowroot starch (Spennemann 1992) and dried pandanus paste (Krämer and Nevermann 1938). Typhoon food shortages have always been a problem in the atolls, and traditionally in times of starvation people would 'cash in' on inter-atoll alliances and would move part of the population to other atolls. We know, for example, that the typhoon of 1857, which seems to have devastated Ebon Atoll, resulted in severe starvation and some 800 people out of a total of 1,300 moved temporarily from Ebon to Jaluit Atoll (Krämer and Nevermann 1938: 30). Similarly, after the typhoon of 1905, people moved from Mile to Arno and coconuts, pandanus and breadfruit were sent from Arno and Majuro to Mile (Spennemann, forthcoming).

These contacts and reciprocal obligations did not operate randomly throughout the Marshall Islands. Rather, any connectivity was derived from the productivity of the atoll, the proximity of the atolls to each other, and the sailing conditions prevailing. Based on a variety of data, ranging from historic accounts, linguistic analyses, epidemiological data and biogeographical information, the connectivity of the atolls of the Marshall Islands can be speculatively reconstructed for the contact period and the first half of the nineteenth century (Spennemann 2005). The majority of the communications occurred *within* each of the two chains, with inter-chain communications very rare, except at the southern end. In part this is a factor of the greater population density on the southern atolls.

Modern challenges

The traditional responses to environmental conditions have faced a range of challenges in the post-Second World War period. The introduction of Christianity terminated the traditional method of population control (Spennemann 1995). Natural demographic growth saw the population of the Marshall Islands swell from about 8,700 in 1880 to 9,800 in 1945. Improved healthcare systems and natural demographic gains accelerated population growth to 20,500 in 1970 and an estimated 67,800 in 2007 (Gorenflo and Levin 1994; Spennemann 2000; CIA 2007). While much of the population growth on the outer atolls has been absorbed by internal migration to the capital, Majuro, as well as Ebeye Island on Kwajalein Atoll, where employment opportunities are perceived to exist, a substantial number of residents migrated overseas, particularly to Guam, Hawai'i and several states of the mainland USA (Ogden 1994; Gorenflo and Levin 1989; Allen 1997; Hess *et al.* 2001; Spennemann 2006b).

Internal connectivity and settlement patterns today

The centralised colonial governments which consolidated the position of the *irooj* on the one hand, and the paternalistic stance the colonial administrations took towards the Marshallese (for an exception see Spennemann 1998), relieved the *irooj* of most of their traditional responsibilities to provide for their people in times of distress. Modern aid and emergency relief supplies, provided first by the colonial German administration (cf. Spennemann 2004b for a partial history) and today, even after independence, by the US Federal Emergency Management Agency, have obviated the need for such inter-atoll connectivity.

Artefacts of history, such as locating the US World War II naval and air base on the western end of Majuro Atoll and the subsequent siting of the US Trust Territory administration in the existing infrastructure, have meant that human settlement spread to areas traditionally only sparsely settled because of their low productivity and their exposure to typhoon events (Spennemann 1996). Moreover, modern-day food imports, as well as sophisticated tapping of the freshwater lens, combined with desalination plants on some atolls, have allowed the population living on the atolls of the Marshall Islands to swell to more than ten times the traditional carrying capacity (Spennemann 1999) despite the abovementioned out-migration. This has had implications on settlement patterns and land use (Spennemann 1990b), which have led to further and increasingly dense settlement on (traditionally) even more marginal land (Spennemann 1990b). This is particularly the case on Majuro, the current capital, and on Kwajalein, a major US missile testing base, where more than 9,000 Marshallese live on neighbouring Ebeye and a group of other very small islands with a combined land mass of less than 0.4 km^2 (SOPAC 2001).

While there is no longer an urgent need to maintain traditional settlement and connectivity patterns, the land rights generated by traditional custom, however, remain and have adapted to new economic circumstances. Current day *irooj*, for example, request, and obtain, their share of rental payments (from businesses, for example) as well as shares of atoll-based incomes such as those derived from compensation for the lease of some islands of Kwajalein Atoll to the US military. By reciprocal action, commoners can call on the *irooj* for permission to squat on *irooj*-controlled lands on Majuro and Kwajalein.

Global climatic change and sea-level rise

A new level of complexity is now introduced through the potential impact of global climatic change and corresponding sea-level rise. Studies of global climatic change predict a probable rise in world sea levels between 0.18 m and 0.59 m by the end of the twenty-first century (IPCC 2007a, 2007b). Worst-case scenarios, such as the collapse and melting of the West Antarctic Ice Sheet, could see a sea level rise of up to 6 m (Tol *et al.* 2006). What are the implications of this for atoll nations such as the Marshall Islands?

Despite media coverage to that effect, the projected rise in sea levels does not imply that the islands will drown. Indeed, dramatic sea level rises have occurred in the past, such as at the start of the Holocene some 8,000 years ago, and the sea level has been higher than at present some 4,000 years ago (Buddemeier *et al.* 1975; Tracy and Ladd 1974). At these times, the coral growth eventually caught up with the sea level rise and new islets were formed from coral-based erosion products. Thus, the question to be addressed here is not whether the islands will survive in the *long term*, but whether the corals can keep up with the projected rise in sea level (Hughes *et al.* 2003) and whether (through wave action) sufficient amounts of sand can be generated that will maintain the existence of the islets as we know them in the *short term*. If the corals cannot keep up, then the islets will temporarily disappear with the sediment washed into the lagoon.

The disappearance of some or all islands will clearly have serious implications on the construction of sovereignty as we define it today (Barnett and Adger 2003). At present, the territoriality of a country requires that a habitable spot of natural land is permanently above water. As long as a country maintains natural areas above sea level, it will have a sovereignty and territorial existence in international law. The Montevideo Convention on the Rights and Duties of States (26 December 1933: §1) provides that 'the state as a person of international law should possess the following qualifications: (a) a permanent population; (b) a defined territory; (c) government; and (d) capacity to enter into relations with the other states'. Artificial structures, such as the Second World War anti-aircraft platforms outside the territorial waters of the United Kingdom, or oil drilling or production platforms, for example, do not qualify as they do not have natural territory nor are they recognised by other states. In the case of coastal nations, the external points of the territory also define the territorial waters and the size of the 200-nautical mile Exclusive Economic Zone (EEZ) (United Nations Convention on the Law of the Sea of 10 December 1982). If, in the case of the Marshall Islands, some of the atoll were to temporarily disappear, then by implication, the EEZ would also shrink. At present, international law is unclear as to how to deal with a situation where an island might temporarily disappear and then re-emerge. Examples where this has happened, such as Fonualei Volcano in Tonga (e.g. Spennemann 2004c), are fully within the country's EEZ – and thus their disappearance has had no territorial implications.

Even if the islets survive more or less in their present form, any factors that affect the make-up of the island will have implications on the suitability of the island for human habitation because the size of the groundwater lens is directly related to the size and shape of the islet. With any rise in sea level, there will be lag between the actual rise of the sea level relative to the island and the commencement of coral growth. The lag is caused by the fact that corals have already reached their maximum growth height; that the reef platforms are covered intertidally with solar-heated water; and that corals do not like to grow in water with high temperatures. During this transitional period the shape and thickness of the groundwater lens will change and the storage capacity of the lens will be reduced (e.g. Bobba 1998; Titus 1990; Roy and Connell 1991; Burns 2000).

In addition to the straight rise in sea levels, atoll populations will also have to contend with changes in climatic patterns. The increased global temperatures will influence sea surface temperatures (IPCC 2007a), which are directly related to the spawning of tropical depressions and which have a direct influence on the strength and maintenance of typhoons. Even comparatively small changes in sea surface temperatures, such as those during El Niño events, have serious implications not only on the frequency of typhoons affecting the Marshall Islands (Spennemann and Marschner 1996), but also on typhoon intensity and on the availability of rainfall outside the typhoon season (Burns 2002; UNFCCC 2005). These typhoon systems are not only destructive of infrastructure and human habitation but, through storm waves and raised sea levels during the event, typhoons also affect the physical integrity of the low-lying islets. The study of historic typhoon events in the region (Spennemann 2004b) has demonstrated that islets can be temporarily submerged during such events or, on rarer occasions, be totally washed off the reef platform. Temporary inundation of the islet will lead to the contamination of the freshwater lens with saltwater.

Both the reduction of the freshwater lens due to the time lag between actual rise of the sea level relative to the island and the commencement of coral growth, as well as the potential inundation of the lens due to typhoon-induced storm surges, will have a direct impact on the availability of potable water on the atolls of the Marshall Islands. Any shortcomings thus generated can be overcome through technological means, such as desalinisation plants. Mitigation through technological means, however, is not possible for the environmental changes to vegetation that will occur as well. Even though the younger population of the Marshall Islands, like other islands of Micronesia, has increasingly come to rely on, and to prefer, Western-style foods over traditional ones (O'Neill and Spennemann 2006, 2008), there is still a considerable interest in the maintenance of traditional food options among the adult generation.

Towards future solutions

The current leaders of the Republic of the Marshall Islands (RMI) are faced with three discrete, yet interlinked problems posed by the effects of global climatic change and the associated sea level rise: (i) the ability of citizens to relocate and reside in other countries without being compelled to surrender their nationality; (ii) the ability to maintain a resident population on the home atolls, even if the conditions for habitation might be deteriorating and the quality of life might be reduced; and, finally, (iii) the ability to maintain sovereignty over the current territory and EEZ of the RMI, even if some or all atolls were to be temporarily submerged, in order to maintain the existence of the nation state of the Republic of the Marshall Islands and its rights to terrestrial (as limited as they are) and marine resources.

The ability of citizens to relocate and reside in other countries

The immediate past leaders of the RMI have ensured this right through appropriate negotiations in the 1980s. Following the termination of the Trust Territory of the Pacific Islands, the Marshallese population, like that of Chuuk, Kosrae, Pohnpei and Yap (now Federated States of Micronesia – FSM), rejected the option of full independence and chose a close affiliation with the USA, which provided for independence in all aspects bar military matters (CFA RMI 1986). In return for granting the USA the right to decide on defence matters within the territorial boundaries of the RMI – and through additional compacts also within the FSM (CFA FSM 1982) and the Republic of Palau (CFA Palau 1993) – the RMI obtained substantial financial and other support from the USA. In addition, the signing of the Compact of Free Association between the USA and the RMI in 1986 (effective 1989) (CFA RMI 1986) gave Marshallese citizens the right to reside in the USA and its territories. The Compact was renewed in 2001 (effective 2003) with a series of additional accountability provisions (CFA RMI 2003).

Despite comments that the new Compact is restrictive and reduces independence (Underwood 2003), the Compact status ensures that RMI citizens can travel freely to and reside in the USA. These expatriate communities are both an asset, as they provide revenue through remittances sent back to families on the home atolls (e.g. Odgen 1994; Connell and Conway 2000), and a source of potential problems, as the expatriate Marshallese are a source of external influences (O'Neill and Spennemann submitted) exerted through on-line discussion forums and chat rooms, and increasingly also through cheap Voice-over-Internet Protocol telephone calls (Spennemann 2006b). The leaders of the RMI can ill-afford to lose the migration option in view of the size of the population on the atolls and the current population growth rate (2.21 per cent; CIA 2007) which shows no sign of slowing down despite a range of programmes. If, in the light of projections of sea level rise, the conditions for habitation in the atolls of the RMI worsen, the reliance on out-migration will increase, which is likely to require the RMI to be more compliant with the wishes of the USA than is already the case.

The ability to maintain a resident population on the home atolls

The solution to this issue is purely a matter of the RMI's economic ability to pay for the technological options required to support a population (desalination plants, shoreline protection, infrastructure upgrades) and for the resident population to pay for the food products and other consumer goods required. The economy of the RMI is at present reliant on subsidies paid by the USA under the provisions of the Compact, and to a lesser degree on aid monies provided by various nations (such as the People's Republic of China and by Taiwan), as well as on loans extended by international organisations such as the Asian Development Bank. Given this dependency on the USA, the RMI can again ill afford to alienate its Compact partner and will be required, as indicated before, to be more compliant with the wishes of the USA than is already the case

The ability to maintain sovereignty over the current territory and EEZ of the RMI

The biggest challenge for the leaders of the RMI will be the ability to maintain sovereignty over the current territory and EEZ of the RMI, even if some or all atolls were to be temporarily submerged. At present, a nation state requires a territory, and that territory cannot be an artificial structure such as an oil platform. Given the lack of territorial recognition other traditional immigrant countries such as Australia or the United States of America give to the self-determination and autonomy of their own Indigenous populations, it is highly unlikely that either of those countries would be prepared to cede part of their land mass to the RMI to establish its own nation state on (formerly) Australian or American soil. Thus, solutions have to be found that ensure that the existence of a nation state and its territory can be enshrined in perpetuity based on that nation states' appearance at a given cut off date, irrespective of whether that nation state will remain above water or not. Given that this is a global problem, the solution will have to be found in the global arena of the United Nations. An alternative approach is the de-coupling of sovereignty with territoriality. This approach has been advocated by a range of ethnic groups that see states as an obstacle to their own claims to sovereignty (Richmond 2002).

In that quest, however, the RMI are not alone: other atoll nations, such as much of the Federated States of Micronesia, Tuvalu, Kiribati, the Cook Islands, the Maldives and the Seychelles, as well as several Caribbean nations, such as the Bahamas, are in the same predicament. While it can be argued that none of these nations have much political influence on a world scale, there are, however, also other global players that have a vested interest in a positive outcome to the matter. For example, France currently controls a large area of the South Pacific through its EEZ based on the coral atolls of the Marquesas and Tuamotus. In the Indian Ocean, France controls a sizeable EEZ through the isolated atolls of Bassas da India and Europa (between Madagascar and Mozambique) and Tromelin (northeast of Madagascar). The United Kingdom controls a large and scattered EEZ through its British Indian Ocean Territory, made up from the Chagos Archipelago (including Diego Garcia), and India controls a substantial additional EEZ through its atoll groups of the Lakshadweep (Lakkadives). Even the USA is a major player, through its possessions of Midway, Wake, Johnston, Jarvis, Palmyra, Howland and Baker in the Pacific, all with their own EEZs. Finally, we need to include Japan, which through its possession of Minami Torishima (Marcus Island) has an isolated 200-nautical mile EEZ to the southeast of the Bonin Islands.

While in all these cases the potential sea level rise does not threaten the existence of the British, French or Indian nation states, it does affect substantially its economic area, and in particular the rights to the mineral resources on the ocean floor as well as the ever-decreasing fish stocks. It can be speculated that an increasing demand on the Earth's resources will make the exploration and exploitation of submarine minerals a viable option. In that case, the legal protection of these resources will gain prominence, especially among naturally resource-poor nations such as Japan, France and the United Kingdom.

Outlook

Just as the environmental situation and precarious nature of human settlement faced by the Marshallese of traditional times required their chiefs to develop unique solutions, so do the new challenges require the current leaders of the Republic of the Marshall Islands to find innovative solutions. While the traditional responses to safeguard the survival of an atoll's population lay in the development of a system of distributed land and resource rights and a network of reciprocal rights and obligations across several atolls, the current and future problems will require the leaders to develop a system of rights *beyond* the territorial confines of the current nation state of the RMI.

Bibliography

Allen, L.A. (1997) 'Enid Atoll: A Marshallese Migrant Community in the Midwestern United States', unpublished PhD thesis, University of Iowa.

Anthony, S.S., Peterson, F.L., Mackenzie, F.T. and Hamlin, S.N. (1989) 'Geohydrology of the Laura Fresh-water Lens, Majuro Atoll: A Hydrogeochemical Approach', *Geological Society of America Bulletin* 101: 1066–75.

Arnow, T. (1954) 'The Hydrology of the Northern Marshall Islands', *Atoll Research Bulletin* 30, Washington, DC: Pacific Science Board, National Research Council.

Barnett, J. (2001) 'Adapting to Climate Change in Pacific Island Countries: The Problem of Uncertainty', *World Development* 29(6): 977–93.

—— and Adger, W.N. (2003) 'Climate Dangers and Atoll Countries', *Climatic Change* 61(3): 1473–80.

Biermann, M. (1889) *Verordnung [des Kaiserlichen Landeshauptmannes] betreffend die Erhebung von persönlichen Steuern. Jaluit, 15 October 1889*, Ms. German Colonial Records, Bundesarchiv Berlin.

—— (1890) *Verordnung [des Kaiserlichen Landeshauptmannes] betreffend die Erhe-*

bung von persönlichen Steuern. Jaluit, 17 April 1890, in G. Riebow, *Die Deutsche Kolonialgesetzgebung. Sammlung der auf die deutschen Schutzgebiete bezüglichen Gesetze, Verordnungen, Erlasse und internationalen Vereinbarungen, mit Anmerkungen und Sachregister. Erster Theil bis zum Jahr 1892*, Berlin: D. Reimer.

Bobba, A.G. (1998) 'Application of a Numerical Model to Predict Freshwater Depth in Islands due to Climate Change: Agatti Island, India', *Journal of Environmental Hydrology* 6: 1–13.

Bryan, E.H. (1971). *Guide to Place Names in the Trust Territory of the Pacific Islands (the Marshall, Caroline and Mariana Islands)*, Honolulu, HI: Bishop Museum, Pacific Science Information Center.

Buddemeier, R.W., Smith, S.V. and Kinzie, R.A. (1975) 'Holocene Windward Reef Flat History, Enewetak Atoll', *Bulletin of the Geological Society of America* 86: 1581–4.

Burns, W.C.G. (2000) 'The Impact of Climate Change on Pacific Island Developing Countries in the 21st Century', in A. Gillespie and W.C.G. Burns (eds) *Climate Change in the South Pacific: Impacts and Responses in Australia, New Zealand, and Small Island States*, Dordrecht: Kluwer Academic.

—— (2002) 'Pacific Island Developing Country Water Resources and Climate Change', in P. Gleick (ed.) *The World's Water 2002–2003: The Biennial Report on Freshwater Resources*. Washington, DC: Island Press.

Central Intelligence Agency (CIA) (2007) *The Marshall Islands. The World Fact Book 2007*, Washington, DC: Central Intelligence Agency. Available online at www.cia.gov/cia/publications/factbook/geos/rm.html (accessed 1 May 2007).

CFA FSM (1982) *Compact of Free Association between the Government of the United States and the Government of the Federated States of Micronesia (1982).*

CFA Palau (1993) *Compact of Free Association between the Government of the United States and the Government of the Republic of Palau (1993).*

CFA RMI (1986) *Compact of Free Association between the Government of the United States of America and the Government of the Republic of the Marshall Islands*, Signed 14 January 1986 (P.L. 99–239).

—— (2003) *Compact of Free Association, as Amended, between the Government of the United States of America and the Government of the Republic of the Marshall Islands*, Signed 30 April 2003.

Chamisso, A. von (1836) *Reise um die Welt mit der Romanzoffischen Entdeckungs-Expedition in den Jahren 1815–1818 auf der Brigg Rurik, Kapitain Otto v. Kozebue. Adalbert von Chamisso's Werke*, Leipzig: Weidmann'sche Buchhandlung.

Connell, J. and Conway, D. (2000) 'Migration and Remittances in Island Microstates: a Comparative Perspective on the South Pacific and the Caribbean', *International Journal of Urban and Regional Research* 24(1): 52–78.

Cox, D.C. (1951) *The Hydrology of Arno Atoll, Marshall Islands*, Atoll Research Bulletin 8, Washington, DC: Pacific Science Board, National Research Council.

Drabbe, J. and Badon Ghijben (Ghyben), W. (1889) 'Nota in verband met de voorgenomen putboring nabij', *Tijdschrift van het Koninklijk Instituut van Ingenieurs Verhandelingen* 1888/1889: 8–22.

Eisenhart, O. (1888) 'Acht Monate unter den Eingeborenen auf Ailu (Marshall-Gruppe)', *Aus allen Welttheilen* 19: 207–8, 223–6, 250–2.

Erdland, A. (1909) 'Die Stellung der Frauen in den Häuptlingsfamilien der Marshall Inseln', *Anthropos* 4: 106–12.

—— (1912) 'Die Eingeborenen der Marshall Inseln im Verkehr mit ihren Häuptlingen', *Anthropos* 7: 559–65.

—— (1914) *Die Marshall Insulaner. Leben und Sitte, Sinn und Religion eines Südseevolkes*, Anthropos Ethnologische Bibliothek, Bd. 2, Heft 1. Münster in Westfalen: Aschendorffsche Verlagsbuchhandlung.

Fosberg, F.R. (1990) 'A Review of the Natural History of the Marshall Islands', *Atoll Research Bulletin* 330, Washington: Smithsonian Institution.

Gorenflo, L.J. and Levin, M.J. (1989) 'The Demographic Evolution of Ebeye', *Pacific Studies* 12: 91–128.

—— (1994) 'The Evolution of Regional Demography in the Marshall Islands', *Pacific Studies* 17: 93–157.

Herzberg, A. (1901) 'Die Wasserversorgung einiger Nordseebäder' *Journal für Gasbeleuchtung und Wasserversorgung* 44: 815–19; 842–4.

Hess, J., Nero, K.L. and Burton, M.L. (2001) 'Creating Options: Forming a Marshallese Community in Orange County, California', *The Contemporary Pacific* 13(1): 89–121.

Hughes, T.P., Baird, A.H., Bellwood, D.R., Card, M., Connolly, S.R., Folke, C., Grosberg, R., Hoegh-Guldberg, O., Jackson, J.B.C., Kleypas, J., Lough, J.M., Marshall, P., Nyström, M., Palumbi, S.R., Pandolfi, J.M., Rosen, B. and Roughgarden, J. (2003) 'Climate Change, Human Impacts, and the Resilience of Coral Reefs', *Science* 301(5635): 929–33.

IPCC (2007a) *Summary for Policymakers. Contribution of Working Group I (the Physical Basis of Climate Change) to the Fourth Assessment Report of the Intergovernmental Panel on Climate Change*, Geneva: Intergovernmental Panel on Climate Change.

—— (2007b) *Climate Change 2007: Impacts, Adaptation and Vulnerability Working Group II Contribution to the Intergovernmental Panel on Climate Change Fourth Assessment Report. Summary for Policymakers*, Geneva: Intergovernmental Panel on Climate Change.

Jeschke, C. (1905) 'Bericht über den Orkan in den Marschall-Inseln am 30. Juni 1905', *Petermanns Mitteilungen* 51: 248–9.

Kotzebue, O. von (1832) *Neue Reise um die Welt in den Jahren 1823, 24, 25 und 26*, 2 vols, Weimar: Wilhelm Hoffmann and St. Petersburg: J. Brief.

Krämer, A. (1906) *Hawaii, Ostmikronesien und Samoa*, Stuttgart: Schweizerbartsche Verlagsbuchhandlung.

—— and Nevermann, H. (1938) 'Ralik-Ratak (Marschall Inseln)', in G. Thilenius (ed.) *Ergebnisse der Südsee-Expedition 1908–1910. II. Ethnographie, B: Mikronesien. Vol. 11*, Hamburg: Friedrichsen and de Gruyter.

Lee, A.G. (2003) '3-D Numerical Modeling of Freshwater. Proceedings, Tough Symposium 2003', Lawrence Berkeley National Laboratory, Berkeley, California, 12–14 May 2003.

Ogden, M. (1994) 'MIRAB and the Marshall Islands', *Isla: A Journal of Micronesian Studies* 2(2): 237–72.

O'Neill, J. and Spennemann, D.H.R. (2006) 'Cultural Traditions: The Realities for Elementary School Children in Micronesia', *Micronesian Educator* 11(1): 1–26.

—— (2008, in press) 'Education and Cultural Change: A View from Micronesia', *International Journal of Educational Development.*

—— (submitted) 'Absentee Stakeholders-Expatriate Micronesian Values and Views on Cultural Heritage', *Pacific Studies* (Suva) (under review).

Richmond, O.P. (2002) 'States of Sovereignty, Sovereign States, and Ethnic Claims for International Status', *Review of International Studies* 28: 381–402.

Riebow, G. (1893). *Die Deutsche Kolonialgesetzgebung. Sammlung der auf die deutschen Schutzgebiete bezüglichen Gesetze, Verordnungen, Erlasse und interna-*

tionalen Vereinbarungen, mit Anmerkungen und Sachregister. Erster Theil bis zum Jahr 1892, Berlin: D. Reimer.

RMI (2006) *National Development Policy Implications Resulting from the 2006 RMI Community Survey. October 2006*. Majuro: Republic of the Marshall Islands Economic Policy, Planning and Statistics Office, Office of the President, Republic of the Marshall Islands.

Roy, P. and Connell, J. (1991) 'Climate Change and the Future of Atoll States', *Journal of Coastal Research* 7(4): 1057–64.

Sonnenschein, F. (1888a) *Verordnung, betreffend die Erhebung von persönlichen Steuern. Jaluit, 28 June 1888*, Ms. on file, German Colonial Records, Bundesarchiv Berlin.

—— (1888b) 'Verordnung betreffend die zwangweise Eintreibung rückständiger Steuern. Jaluit, 11 Dezember 1888', in G. Riebow, *Die Deutsche Kolonialgesetzgebung. Sammlung der auf die deutschen Schutzgebiete bezüglichen Gesetze, Verordnungen, Erlasse und internationalen Vereinbarungen, mit Anmerkungen und Sachregister. Erster Theil bis zum Jahr 1892*, Berlin: D. Reimer.

—— (1888c) 'Verordnung [des Kaiserlichen Kommissars] betreffend die Art der Steuererhebung. Jaluit, 28 September 1888', in G. Riebow, *Die Deutsche Kolonialgesetzgebung. Sammlung der auf die deutschen Schutzgebiete bezüglichen Gesetze, Verordnungen, Erlasse und internationalen Vereinbarungen, mit Anmerkungen und Sachregister. Erster Theil bis zum Jahr 1892*. Berlin: D. Reimer.

SOPAC (2001) *Water Resources Unit. Report of Visit to Ebeye, Kwajalein, Marshall Islands 22–24 October 2001*. SOPAC Preliminary Report 134. Suva: SOPAC.

Spennemann, D.H.R. (1990a) *Cultural Resource Management Plan for Majuro Atoll, Republic of the Marshall Islands*, 2 vols. Report prepared in fulfilment of US Department of Interior, Office of Territorial and International Affairs Technical Assistance Grant MAR-42. Report submitted to the Historic Preservation Office, Majuro, Republic of the Marshall Islands, August 1990, printed 1992.

—— (1990b) *Predictive Model of the Expansion of Habitation Areas on Majuro Atoll Until the Year 2010 and Its Implications for Historic Preservation*. Report presented to the Historic Preservation Office, Majuro, Republic of the Marshall Islands. Report OTIA-TAG-MAR-42–10/90. Alele Museum, Majuro Atoll, Republic of the Marshall Islands.

—— (1992) 'Makmõk. Notes on the Occurrence, Utilisation, and Importance of Polynesian Arrowroot (Tacca leontopetaloides) in the Marshall Islands', Republic of the Marshall Islands Ministry of Internal Affairs/Ministry of Social Services, Occasional Paper No. 1, Majuro, Marshall Islands: Ministries of Internal Affairs and Social Services.

—— (1993) 'Toorlok Bok (Predictions of Environmental, Economical, Social and Cultural Impacts of a Potential Rise in Relative Sea-level on the Atolls of the Marshall Islands, Micronesia', in S. Burgin (ed.) *Climate Change: Implications for Natural Resource Conservation*, University of Western Sydney, Hawkesbury Occasional Papers in Biological Sciences 1, Richmond, NSW: University of Western Sydney, Hawkesbury.

—— (1995) 'Population Control Measures in Traditional Marshallese Culture and their Implications for Today', *Asian Culture (Asian-Pacific Culture) Quarterly* 23(1): 19–30.

—— (1996) 'Dreading the Next Wave: Non-traditional Settlement Patterns and Typhoon Threats on Contemporary Majuro, Marshall Islands', *Environmental Management* 20(3): 337–48.

—— (1998) *An Officer, Yes; but a Gentleman? A Biographical Sketch of Eugen Brandeis, Military Adviser, Imperial Judge and Administrator in the German Colonial Service*, South Pacific Island Studies Monographs Vol. 21, Sydney: Centre of South Pacific Studies, University of New South Wales.

—— (1999) 'No Room for the DEAD. BURIAL PRACTICES in a Constrained Environment', *Anthropos* 94(1): 35–56.

—— (2000) 'Historic Demographic Information for the Marshall Islands – Period from 1891 to 1914'. Available online at http://micronesia.csu.edu.au/Marshalls/html/demography/1891.html (last accessed 23 April 2008).

—— (2004a) 'Chamissos Blick auf die Südsee und die Rezeption der "Reise um die Welt" im Südpazifischen Raum', in *Mit den augen des Frenden. Adelbert von Chamisso – Dichter, Naturwissenschaffender, Weltreisender.* Berlin: Gesellschaft für interregionalen Kulturaustauch. V.

—— (2004b) *Typhoons in Micronesia. A History of Tropical Cyclones and their Effects until 1914.* Saipan, Commonwealth of the Northern Mariana Islands: Division of Historic Preservation.

—— (2004c) 'The June 1846 Eruption of Fonualei Volcano, Tonga. An Historical Analysis', *Johnstone Centre Report* No. 196. Albury, NSW: Johnstone Centre, Charles Sturt University.

—— (2005) 'Traditional and Nineteenth-century Communication Patterns in the Marshall Islands', *Micronesian Journal of the Humanities and Social Sciences* 4(1): 25–51.

—— (2006a) 'Freshwater Lens, Settlement Patterns, Resource Use and Connectivity in the Marshall Islands', *Transforming Cultures* 1(2): 44–63.

—— (2006b) 'Digital Futures in Micronesia: Cultural Management and the Role of the Micronesian Expatriate Communities in Hawaii and in the Mainland USA', *Micronesian Journal for the Humanities and Social Sciences* 5(1/2): 580–95.

—— (forthcoming) 'From Disaster to Disaster ... The efforts of the German Colonial Administration in Micronesia to Mitigate the Effects of the Typhoons of 1905 and 1907'.

—— and Marschner, I.G. (1996) 'Association between ENSO and Typhoons in the Marshall Islands', *Disasters* 19(3): 194–7.

Titus, J.G. (1990) 'Greenhouse Effect, Sea Level Rise and Land Use', *Land Use Policy*, 72: 138–53.

Tobin, J.E. (1952) 'Land Tenure in the Marshall Islands', *Atoll Research Bulletin* 11. Washington, DC: Pacific Science Board, National Research Council.

—— (1958) *Land Tenure Patterns in the Trust Territory of the Pacific Islands. Volume 1. Land Tenure in the Marshall Islands*, Guam, HI: Office of the Staff Anthropologist, Territory of the Pacific Islands.

Tol, R.S.J., Bohn, M., Downing, T.E., Guillerminet, M.-L., Hizsnyik, E., Kasperson, R., Lonsdale, K., Mays, C., Nicholls, R.J., Olsthoorn, A.A., Pfeifle, G., Poumadere, M., Toth, F.L., Vafeidis, A.T., Van der Werff, P.E. and Yetkiner, I.H. (2006) 'Adaptation to Five Metres of Sea Level Rise', *Journal of Risk Research* 9(5): 467–82.

Tracey, J.I. and Ladd, H.S. (1974) 'Quaternary History of Eniwetok and Bikini Atolls, Marshall Islands', *Proceedings of the Second International Coral Reef Symposium* 2: 537–550.

Underwood, A. (2003) 'The Amended U.S. Compacts of Free Association with the Federated States of Micronesia and the Republic of the Marshall Islands: Less Free, More Compact', *East-West Center Working Papers, Pacific Islands Development Series* No. 16. Honolulu, HI: East–West Center.

UNFCCC (2005) *Climate Change, Small Island Developing States*. Bonn: United Nations Framework Convention on Climate Change Secretariat.

Wheatcraft, S.W. and Buddemeier, R.W. (1981) 'Atoll Island Hydrology', *Ground Water* 19(3): 311–20.

Wilkinson, C.R. (1996) 'Global Change and Coral Reefs: Impacts on Reefs, Economies and Human Cultures', *Global Change Biology* 2: 547–9.

Williamson, I. and Sabath, M.D. (1982) 'Island Population, Land Area and Climate: A Case Study of the Marshall Islands', *Human Ecology* 10(1): 71–84.

5 'The Fisherman's Lot'

Popular responses to the Indian Ocean in economic and ecological crisis

Devleena Ghosh and Stephen Muecke

Oh Bhagirathi[1], was this the fisherman's lot?...
No fish hauled in any net
At the rise of the morning star
Fishermen call to each other
Come on brothers, let's all go and fish.

(Bhatiali song)[2]

This traditional song is a poignant expression of the everyday life-world of traditional fishermen all over the globe. It encapsulates the profession: an enterprise that is both individual and collaborative; that requires intense labour; that depends on both nature and ecology. And today the call to go fishing depends on various levels of technology, from the petrol or diesel outboard motor to the advanced mechanisation of the trawler. Fisherfolk deal with similar problems all over the world, whether they fish in fresh or saltwater, across physical or geopolitical boundaries and within an increasingly fragile ecology. This article will trace some aspects of the changing labour practices and environment contexts in the present day lives of fisherfolk in the Mumbai and Goa area. It will demonstrate the imbrication of the activity of fishing with the changing ecologies of the coast and the modernisation of India's economy, specifically through industrialisation and tourism. It will also explore the experiences of two communities of artisanal fishing people on India's western coast, their craft and their lives in the challenging conditions of globalisation.

Between 2003 and 2006, the authors conducted fieldwork among fisherfolk in the Mumbai and Goa area who spoke about the impact of changing work and ecological practices in their present day lives. The Koli are the indigenous people of Mumbai. They have had to fight repeatedly for space on the highly competitive commercial harbourside of Mumbai, suburbs such as Colaba and Cuff Parade. Though they occupy a substantial area in Colaba, which they won in 1977, they find themselves coming under increasing pressure. The *ramponkar*, or fishing communities, in Goa are less than 600 kilometres down the coast from Mumbai and face similar challenges from mechanisation and commercialisation, but also different pressures from monoculture and tourism.

To understand these local views, the essay will first sketch in the broader changes in the global fishing industry and then discuss the way coastal industries have developed in India before returning to hear how these two artisanal communities deal with the new conditions for their lives and livelihoods.

Fresh and saltwater is an iconic presence in coastal Indian literature. The 1956 Malayalam novel, *Chemmeen* (Prawn), written by Thakazhi Sivasankara Pillai is a powerful story about the intertwining of individual and family responsibility and desires. The Kerala fishing community believes that a fisherman can only return safely from the sea if his wife is faithful to him while he is away. This is enmeshed with the myth of the 'sea-mother', the destroyer and preserver of the community. Other books written in the first half of the twentieth century, such as Tarashankar Bandyopadhyaya's *Hanshuli Banker Upakatha*, (Legends of Hanshuli Bank), Manik Bandyopadhyaya's *Padma Nadir Majhi* (The Boatman of the Padma River) and *Titas ekti Nadir Nam* (Titas is the Name of a River) by Aditya Mallabarman, himself a member of a fishing community, portray, vividly and unforgettably, the lives of people who eked out their livelihood from the great rivers of East Bengal. *Padma Nadir Majhi* depicts the advent of capitalist intervention in the small business enterprises of fishing while *Titas ekti Nadir Nam* is an extremely powerful and poignant evocation of the fate of a riparian community when a river dies.

Global fishing and fisherfolk

James Acheson, in his comprehensive article on the anthropology of fishing, points out the heterogeneous and uncertain environment, both physical and social, in which the activity takes place. Both seas and rivers can be dangerous and alien, places that 'man [*sic*] enters only with the support of artificial devices (i.e. boats, canoes, platforms,... and other technologies) and then only when weather and sea conditions allow'. Inclement weather, accidents and mechanical failure enhance this danger, and Acheson emphasises that 'fishing devices are not simply transferences of land hunting devices'. Marine ecozones may contain a large number of species with different habits and capture techniques and periodical availability so that fisherfolk need to know a variety of fishing techniques. Finally, catches can fluctuate greatly and even traditional fisherfolk may affect fishing stocks. Fisherfolk thus work in the liminal area between land and sea and their fishing activities are often affected by diffuse and uncertain notions of sovereignty over coastal waters and marine boundaries (Acheson 1981: 276).

In particular, all fisherfolk have been affected by one of the major environmental crises over the last decades, the exhaustibility of the world's oceans. It is now incontestable that marine resources are not unlimited and, although renewable, not infinite and need to be sustainably managed. The fisheries of India are among the top ten in the world, producing over two and a half million tonnes annually at the beginning of this century (Chacko 1998: 60). Specifically, in the Indian Ocean region, overfishing has compromised the natural process of renewal, resulting in biological disaster. As far back as 1997, the Food and

Agricultural Organization warned that almost 70 per cent of the world's marine stocks required urgent conservation and rehabilitation and recommended sustainable management measures (Ansari *et al.* 2008). Recently, newspaper reports have recorded significant apprehension that rising acidity levels in oceans will have a devastating impact on marine life (*Sydney Morning Herald* 2008).

The improvement in efficiency of fishing technologies means that even small-scale fisherfolk are able to increase their catch size and fish during traditional fallow periods when fish stocks used to recuperate. Experts, such as Hutchings (2000), claim that when fish stocks collapse, only a few species actually make a complete recovery. The west coast of India is particularly susceptible to this process as it produces approximately 73 per cent of the total marine fish catch of India (Madhupratap *et al.* 2001). Goa, for example, has a littoral of about 105 kilometres with an actively fished area of about 20,000 square kilometres. Fish curry and rice is generally considered affordable and is the staple dish of Goan people. However, fishing has moved from being a sustainable food source to a valuable export commodity and a major contributor to India's balance of payments. It is now a capital-intensive industry with traditional fishing producing only 25 per cent of fish caught while the mechanised sector produces the rest (Ansari *et al.* 2008).

Fishing industry and commercial 'development' in India

The first post-independence venture into the mechanisation of fishing was an Indo-Norwegian mechanised fishing venture in 1953. Claude Alvares, in his activist sourcebook on Goan ecology, *Fish Curry and Rice*, tends to be forceful in his support of local/traditional practices. According to him:

> The stated motive was to improve the standard of living of the population in general (by increasing the fish catch and thereby the protein available to the people for consumption) and the economic condition of the poor fisherfolk in particular. The methods imported sought to increase not only production but also productivity by the use of modern equipment and technology. The hidden motive seems to have been the desire of the West to create a market for its fishing equipment and technology.
>
> (Alvares 2002: 174)

A branch of the Indo-Norwegian project operated in Kerala, an Indian state further south, with a long coastline, a major fishing industry and a militant political tradition. This Keralan branch of the Indo-Norwegian business was riven with tension. There was clearly little consultation with fishermen and other stakeholders and scant attention paid to the diversity of the fishing communities. For example, a sales and distribution cooperative that was set up was initially boycotted and later flooded with fish, consequently going bankrupt (Klausen 1964: 10). The Catholic community in Kerala was better able to adapt to the changes initiated by the Indo-Norwegian project in terms of new technology and took up night fishing, unlike the Hindu Arayas who sold the motor boats they received from the project to the Catholic community and went back to their traditional ways of fishing with canoes. Klausen concludes that the social costs of mechanised fishing were far greater for the Arayas who prioritised the retention of their community and cultural practices over the adoption of an incompatible techno-economic system (Klausen 1964: 12–13). He demonstrates that the intervention of the Indo-Norwegian project in bringing mechanised fishing to Kerala benefited the wealthier communities of fishermen at the expense of poorer ones.

Development as mechanisation

By the 1970s, the ideology of mechanisation was firmly enshrined in Indian development policy – the five-year plan. The government still aimed to improve the general health of the littoral populations by increasing their protein intake and, to this end, continued to encourage the increase of fish catches specifically through mechanisation. Robert Newman argues that this decision was based on a Western model of development and modernisation that focussed on production rather than distribution. Loans on generous terms were offered to people who wanted to operate mechanised trawlers; however these loans were still beyond the reach of ordinary fishermen. Hence, the trawlers were bought by local capitalists or 'moneyed unwanted elements' rather than traditional fishermen. Neither did the supply of protein available to poor Indians increase. In fact, the mechanisation and the consequent increase in fish and prawn harvesting led to a burgeoning canning and export industry worth millions of rupees (Newman 1984: 441).

In 1991 India introduced a new deep sea fishing policy. Huge foreign trawlers, working under the guise of joint ventures, paying massive fees to the government, were given licenses for Indian waters. There are some 25,000 such vessels around the world. They have depleted all the oceans and are a threat to over 100,000,000 people in low-income countries who depend on fisheries for their livelihood. Ten million fisherfolk went on all-India strikes and the government was forced to change its deep sea policy and, from 1996, temporarily stopped granting new licenses. For probably the first time, a fishing community changed the policies of globalisation through protest (Kurien 1995). A high level committee, the Murari Committee, was set up to review deep sea fishing policy. Among other things, this committee recommended reservation for Indian vessels below 20 metres length of up to 100 nautical miles from the seaboard on the west coast and 50 nautical miles on the east coast and the island groups (Mathew 2003).

However, in some cases, the victories were short-lived. In November 2002, the Agriculture Ministry issued new guidelines for deep sea fishing which contradicted the Murari Committee recommendations regarding foreign owned trawlers and their entry into the Indian economic zone. In fact, the guidelines were similar to the provisions rescinded six years before. The government failed to institute any vessel quotas or licence fees appropriate to the value of the catch or any requirement to employ Indian labour or dock in Indian ports. It reinstated a system biased in favour of foreign deep sea fishing vessel operators registered as Indian companies (Mathew 2003).

How do those who use the coast, fresh and saltwater, for their livelihood counteract the hyper-modern song of 'larger, faster, wealthier'? There are alternatives. A cooperative of tribal fishermen in Maharashtra has prospered after they formed the Tawa Fishermen's Co-operative, which ensures the sustainable use of natural resources, handles the marketing of the catch and the supply of boats and nets. This is a unique experiment in co-operative fishing created, ironically, by the building of a dam on a tributary of the Narmada River in the 1970s. The dam created a reservoir that spread over 21,000 hectares and submerged 44 Gond and Korku tribal villages. Attempts were made to resettle some of these people in Gujarat but it was not successful. After a struggle under the leadership of the Kisan Adivasi Sangathan, these tribal people were given a compensation of 75 to 150 rupees per acre of land and rights to fish in the reservoir. This co-operative is a commendable example of community management of natural resources and co-operative sustainable development. It has totally eliminated middlemen and created employment opportunities for many tribal people. The annual fish production has doubled since 1999–2000, providing livelihoods for around 500 fishermen (twice the earlier number). Fish production has been increased without depleting resources or over-fishing. Monofilament yarn fishing nets have been banned and conservation rules are diligently observed, with a closed season of two months beginning from 16 June every year (Prasad 2001). There is also an increasing body of data supporting the ban of monsoon fishing, a traditional practice, since this is the season when most fish breed. In spite of outright hostility from the government in Goa, the High Court of India admitted and later upheld a Public Interest Litigation suit to institute the monsoon fishing ban from 1 June to 15 August (Alvares 2002: 177).

Development as monoculture

Holly Hapke has described how, similarly, the macroeconomic pressures on Kerala fishing cultures meant that local fisheries left behind the era of 'fish production by the people for the people'. An international market for prawn emerged at roughly the same time as rich, untapped prawn resources were discovered off the coast of Kerala, and 'the devaluation of the rupee and the associated crisis in foreign exchange reserves faced by the country as a whole [which] compelled the government of India to promote any activity that could earn foreign exchange' (Hapke 2001: 225).

Mechanisation led to conflict with local fisherfolk, who had a powerful political response at the same time as some of them got into the trawling business. In terms of the management of coastal cultures, mechanisation was aimed at establishing a monoculture: a massive technology harvesting one product. Fine-tuned interchanges between coast and hinterland were not relevant, unlike the Goan system of *khazan* farming, which is an example of an ecologically sustainable activity that takes into account the needs of humans, the land and the oceans.

The Kerala attempt to develop a monoculture on the marine zone where freshwater meets ocean exposes the interdependence of economies and ecologies. It allows the stories of the seas or rivers to be grounded in local places, rather than floating free in the abstracted realm of reform policy as dictated by corporate globalism. The Oxford economist, Partha Dasgupta, helps us to unpack the value of narrative and location. 'Economists ... have moved steadily away from seeing location as a determinant of human experience. Indeed, economic progress is seen as a release from location's grip on our lives' (Dasgupta 2005: 21).

Dasgupta continues,

> Economic statisticians interpret wealth narrowly. Wealth should include not only manufactured capital (roads and buildings, machinery and equipment, cables and ports) and what is nowadays called human capital (knowledge and skills), but also natural capital (oil and minerals, fisheries, forests and, more broadly, ecosystems). I use the term 'inclusive investment' for this broader definition of wealth and contrast it with the narrower scope of 'recorded investment'.
>
> (Dasgupta 2003: 6).

Thus, according to Dasgupta, those who destroy mangroves in order to create shrimp farms, or cut down forests in the uplands or watersheds to export timber, should be required to compensate fishermen dependent on the mangroves, or people in the lowlands whose fields and fisheries are protected by the upland forests. Economic development in the guise of growth in per capita GNP of improvement in the Human Development Index can come in tandem with the decline in the wealth of some of society's poorest members. Rural communities in poor countries recognised the local connectedness of nature's services long ago and devised mechanisms to cope with the problems created by it. A pond or a woodland is a system of organic and inorganic material, offering multiple services. This feature of ponds and woodlands makes them unsuitable for division into private property (Dasgupta 2003: 6).

Dasgupta, by adding another variable ('nature's services') to the formula for an *inclusive* calculation of wealth, comes up with a result which contradicts the misplaced optimism about the rise of wealth in developing economies. India, for example, is supposed to be growing at a healthy rate of GNP per head, but on the inclusive calculation the average Indian is getting poorer at a rate of 0.5 per cent (Dasgupta 2003: 7). We scarcely need to add that the warming of the Indian Ocean, with its effects on reefs and fish, has produced an immediate reduction in natural capital. In this context, we would then note that, compared to mechanised fishing, traditional artisanal fishing has the advantage of hiring more people, creating negligible bycatch (waste) and producing a higher return of fish caught per unit of money invested and fuel consumed (Chacko 1998: 60).

The logic of natural capital is one of complexity and interconnectedness, which contradicts the grid pattern of ownership of parcels of land, where the free services or common wealth provided by nature, as in a stream flowing through a number of properties, or the bounty of the sea, do not enter into the calculations of economists. In this context, the macro-economic story contradicts the local stories about the love of homeland, travellers' tales about the beauty of place and fishermen's songs about the intangible experiences of fishing. Each story is told about some good (value), crafting a narrative of a place that is in some sense algebraic, a set of calculations working towards a positive outcome, that values production and place.

In the Goan system of *khazan* farming, there are fine-tuned interchanges between coast and hinterland, an ecologically sustainable agricultural practice that works with human, oceanic and local ecologies. Intricate systems of dykes, made of locally available cheap and recyclable materials such as mud, straw, mangrove litter and so on, protect these saline flood plains in tidal estuaries from ocean and river tides. There are different systems of regulating tidal inflow and outflow depending on how many crops are farmed annually and, when drained, these plains become the perfect soil for the production of a kind of salt resistant paddy. Some *khazan* lands are used for rice cultivation during the monsoon and for pisciculture for the rest of the year.

The major importance of these *khazan* lands is their great adaptability for both agriculture and pisciculture as economic, social and other factors demand. These lands also serve as emergency storm water receptacles. 'If this land is destroyed or filled up, flooding (in the surrounding area) is bound to occur.' (Alvares 2002: 100)

Fishing in Goa

> The sea was both essential to life and casual in taking it. It was unpredictable and had to be appeased. Fishermen believed that the sea was owed for the catch: symbolic heads, coconuts, had always been sacrificed. And it was owed a life for the lives it spared; by custom, the drowning were not rescued, for fear that the rescuer would one day be drowned himself.
>
> (Tomory 2006: 52)

Fish harvesting in Goa increased from 17,000 tonnes in 1963 (Sardessai 1999) to over 56,000 tonnes in 1990, a positive growth of 118 per cent in that period. Between 1963 and 1999, Goa's average annual marine fish production (at about 6 per cent) grew at twice the rate as that of all of India (3.5 per cent) (Ansari *et al.* 2008). Trawler fishing is now a major industry bolstered by the political patronage of trawler owners, little or no environmental protection and 'a growing capitalist penetration of a traditional economy and increasing ties to a world-wide system of markets' (Newman 1984: 442). The ordinary Goan fisherman has little to show for the growing fish economy with its plenitude of export dollars. The trawlers do not keep outside the ten mile limit set by the government, thereby destroying traditional fishing grounds, while pollution from the canneries has poisoned rivers. Claude Alvares concludes that mechanisation has been disastrous, quoting an assessment from the CMFRI (Central Marine Fisheries Research Institute): 'The return per unit of investment of non-powered boats has been found to be twice that of the powered boats and the former generate almost seven times more direct employment opportunities than the mechanised boats' (Alvares 2002: 174).

When prawn farming became lucrative, many of the *khazans* were inundated for aquaculture which was considered a low capital investment/high yield venture. But the ecological costs were immense: increase in soil salinity, polluted groundwater and rotting coconut plantations. Since rehabilitating *khazans* is expensive, they were then abandoned when they were no longer useful for aquaculture.

Thus the ecology of the *khazan* lands depends on a sensitive and fragile balance between people, animals, land, plants and water. This balance is enabled by traditional knowledges such as those of climate, tidal cycles, soil properties. These knowledges can be enhanced but not replaced by modern technology and science because phenomena like *khazans* are not comprised of individual units but are 'integrated systems specific to each estuarine region, floodplain and river basin' (Alvares 2002: 101). The liminal area of the coast can be seen as a palimpsest, inscribed and reinscribed by the people who husband it for its harvest.

The most important question to ask those who would scienticise and economise the coast, is why aquacultures like shrimp farms exist. They do so because a particular variety of fish like shrimp, cuttlefish or salmon is so depleted that it is no longer available in the ocean. But it is a monoculture unlike the natural multiculture of the ocean, depending on high use of pesticides and other chemicals that pollute the coast, and both fresh drinking and salt seawater. Then the paddyfields, which are meant for the people's basic needs, are converted to aquaculture and, as a consequence, the mangroves, the breeding ground for many species, begin to disappear. On the west coast of India, around 200,000 hectares of coastal land have been converted into shrimp farms. This means that millions of coastal people and fishing communities living on these lands have been displaced.

Talking to fisherfolk: the river at Baradi and the beach at Goa

> Whenever there is a storm
> The trees on all sides bend in the wind
> They come together in prayer
> No one can see these things
> Not the people on the land
> Except the fisherfolk on their boats
> Open to everything
>
> (A fishing song sung by the *ramponkars* of Baradi, Goa)

For fisherfolk in Mumbai and Goa, the notion of belonging, at work and at home, is no longer purely economic, geographic (a notion of place) or historical (a sense of connection) but cross-cut by a variety of global forces. Imbricating commerce with culture allows us to focus on the unfixed and changing construction of space and reflect on how those who made a living from the sea functioned across that fluid terrain, appropriating the accoutrements of different contexts as they needed them. The narratives of our interlocutors mirrored this complex, amphibian relationship between the land and the ocean.

The fisherfolk or *ramponkar* community at the river in Baradi, in Goa, spoke to us of the decreasing catch and their precarious livelihoods. The fragility of the catch was further compromised by tourism activities. As we spoke, we watched several tourist boats, laden with disposable incomes, sail by on the way to participate in 'watersports'. 'Much less. The fish is much less. They are putting chemicals no? Everything in rivers, food, lime, plastic.' AG, who had two fishing canoes (each costs between 30,000 and 40,000 rupees) made huge wave like motion with his hands. 'The motorboats coming down this river, making waves, huge waves! How can we fish?' As if to demonstrate the truth of this statement, we watched a small fishing canoe draw into the bank – steered by a woman with a rather tipsy man sitting next to her. They had spent all night on the water and had, for their pains, a small wicker basket of fish. This fall in catch size means that these fisherfolk cannot afford to observe the monsoon ban. Their children are no longer taking up the profession, often leaving to go into the other common Goan profession – the seafarer.

The community reiterated the importance of fish and fishing in their lived tradition, emphasising that for Goans, fish curry and rice is a staple and defines the way in which ordinary Goans view the quotidian: 'There is rice in the fields and fish in the waters. If we care for the water, the fish will take care of us.' All fishermen, whatever their religion, Catholic, Muslim or Hindu, reduced the risk and danger of the sea through ritual and magic. When the traditional fallow season for fishing finished after the monsoon, Catholic fishing communities in Candolim practiced rituals such as blessing their fleet of fishing boats while Hindu communities performed *puja* and the breaking of coconuts. TC commented, 'First I pray, then I put the net. All fishermen do that'. He also recounted with glee a story about a priest who had tried, with temporary success, to stop Catholic fishing communities from performing the Hindu rituals of their ancestors. When he was transferred to another parish, the fishermen just went back to their old rituals to secure safe return from fishing and good catches. Some of these rituals lost their potency when trawlers began to flout the monsoon ban and the safety of fishing increased through the development of technology, institutions and communications.

AC, a retired fisherman, gave us a vivid description of the *rampons* (large nets manoeuvred by groups of fisherfolk, 50 to 1,000 strong) that could be seen in Candolim before the advent of large tourist ventures. They had a unique way of conserving fish by suspending their nets, often 12-kilometres long, with large catches of fish in the sea itself. They only took as much catch as they could sell and were able to keep the fish alive for up to 15 days. Then a five-star hotel was built on empty land that the fisher community considered haunted. The developers blatantly flouted the regulations of the Environmental Protection Act that mandated that at least 200 metres on beaches should be left free of development to prevent the destruction of the natural protection afforded by sand dunes and mangrove forests. According to AC, the advent of tourism in the 1980s as well as mechanised fishing and Gulf labour destroyed traditional fishing in his area completely. *Ramponkars* returning from the Arabian Gulf now owned 70 per cent of mechanised boats or trawlers. Mechanised fishing, said BL, who is employed on a trawler, forced both fishermen and their families to play roles that are not standard in their cultural milieu. The men had to organise their work and sustenance effectively; women had to bring up families and run households with their men gone for regular periods. Since women usually take the fish to market, they have also to juggle this with other domestic duties. When BL went home after long hours of work on crowded trawlers in an all-male environment, away from his family for days, his children felt shy with him. Being away so much made him a stranger to his own family (Sampson 2005).

Many fishermen, who found their livelihood depleted, moved into the tourist industry in various guises. Some started small cafes in beach shacks, others worked in tourist establishments and still others started housing tourists in their homes. Eventually, many former fisherfolk rented out their whole house and lived outside in shacks, also hiring out any small space for retail outlets, earning enough money in the six months of the tourist season for the whole year. Ironically there is a tragic marriage between the labour arrangements in this informal sector of tourism and postmodern consumer preferences. Labour law enforcement in the informal sector is minimal and the workers usually work very long hours. Modern tourists find the combination of 24-hour personal service, friendly, concerned and helpful, very seductive. They are not served by aloof uniformed attendants but shack boys with their personal touch – the lift on the back of the scooter, the chat with the cup of tea, the flower on the breakfast tray – and they find this extremely attractive.

Many older people are convinced that the younger generation is 'losing' its traditions through the penetration of package tour culture such as parties, drugs and 'free' sex into Goan society. JA, a retired seafarer, tells us, 'When you have tourists in your house, their culture lives in your house too'. AS, an academic at the University of Goa, confirmed that these fears exist. A Goan *teatre* or play, called *Sweet Poison*, describes tourism as a Trojan Horse bringing drugs into Goa. In the last few years, said AS, more people have died from drug-related trade disputes than from overdoses. And, more unusually, the sex trade in the international tourism sector appears to be focused on what local Goans call 'beach boys' – young men of the fishing community who service older female tourists, performing the services of escort, sexual partner and, sometimes, boyfriend. 'Local men are much more available on the beaches than local women.'

The boom in Goan tourism is driven by charter tourism at ridiculously low prices. This is made possible, AS informed us, because non-resident Indians own the resorts, such as the one in which we were staying, on a rent-back scheme. These flatettes are hired out to tourists at competitive low prices during the high season to repay the loans. The attraction for non-resident Indians is a consolidation of their Goan identity as well as the advantage of a property near the beach.

AS conceded that the economic situation for fisherfolk has somewhat improved along with better infrastructure such as roads, electricity and the telephone. But the boom in tourism has created an inflation of property prices. There was tension in the community as people now had to pay large amounts of 'key money' to rent shacks on the beach. In addition, a catastrophic shortage of water loomed as well as breakdown in road infrastructure, garbage disposal and pollution.

Mumbai: the Koli – tradition and modernity

> The Fishermen were here first. Before Mountbatten's ticktock ... the East India Company built its Fort ... at the dawn of time, when Bombay was a dumbbell-shaped island tapering, at the centre, to a narrow shining strand beyond which could be seen the finest and largest natural harbour in Asia ... in short, before reclamation – turned the Seven Isles into a long peninsula like an outstretched, grasping hand, reaching westwards into the Arabian Sea; in this primeval world before clock towers, the fishermen – who were called Kolis – sailed in Arab dhows, spreading red sails against the setting sun. They caught pomfret and crabs, and made fish-lovers of us all ... And where are they now, the first inhabitants?... Where the prayers of the pomfret folk, the devotions of crab-catchers?... Of all the first inhabitants, the Koli fishermen have come off worst of all ... But there are still Arab dhows, every evening, spreading their sails against the sunset.
>
> (Salman Rushdie, *Midnight's Children*)

At Macchimaar in Mumbai, fishing boats lined up like buses at a depot on the shore. Middens of fish scales, oyster shells, plastic bags were interspersed with shrines to fishing goddesses, lines flapping with drying fish and the ubiquitous groups of boys playing cricket. In fact, Mumbai takes its name from a Koli goddess, Mumbadevi.

Later we spoke to the leader of the Fisherman's Action Forum in Cuff Parade, Colaba, in his neat three-room house, while he hospitably plied us with whisky, fried fish and sweets. DT has a fleet of mechanised boats with crew that spends days on the water, casting nets. In Maharashtra, he says, there are 10,000 mechanised boats of which 3,000 are trawlers, employing 700,000 or 800,000 people. There are only 10,000 non-mechanised fishing boats ('small fishermen' who fish at night and 'move by the wind'). They fish in the waters closer to the shore, unlike the bigger mechanised boats and trawlers, using new types of more effective nets, such as the white 'disco' net which shimmers in the water, but their living has been increasingly threatened by the environmental depredations caused by mechanised fishing.

DT proudly recounted the story of the Koli fishermen's struggle to remain in their ancestral lands on the fishing portside at Colaba, land that is among the most expensive real estate in the world, let alone in Mumbai. They claimed and reoccupied the land in 1977 ('we had to struggle a lot, demonstrations, protest marches, we captured the land'). There are 2,000 households in this settlement with 10,000 people. DT says,

> We have to struggle with the government for everything, we've been asking for a lighthouse – a simple thing that will save the lives of hundreds of fishermen. And our Fishermen's Action Forum provides support and insurance for fisherfolk who are lost at sea or lose their boats and their families. The government gives us nothing, not even water or electricity.

The Koli operate within the current commercial fishing environment but they draw on their traditional culture to assert their rights to do so. DT retells one of these stories:

> The gods and the demons churned the primeval ocean seeking nectar and immortality but poison came first, blue and iridescent, threatening to destroy the world. The great God Shiva swallowed the poison but it burnt him, turning him blue with agony. He immersed himself in the sea for relief but the fish in the sea began to nibble at him. Angered, he spattered drops of sea water on the beach and they turned into people. 'You will eat these creatures that have the temerity to try and eat me,' he commanded, 'and you will make your living from them.' And that is how the Kolis came to the shores of the Arabian Sea.

This origin myth encapsulates their deep traditions and active present as people who are consummate negotiators. The intimate experiences of broad social and economic practices that we have described contain much of the most compelling and memorable moments of their social life. They do not construct themselves in either/or categories, either in a nativist longing for a golden traditional past, or in a global representational economy of the new capitalist culture of modernity, but in an ongoing context of counterpolitics and interventions, in the constant reinterpretation of the past and the translation of the present through historical landscapes, domestic spaces, the impact of ideals and the weight of history.

There is increasing pressures on Koli communities from pollution, declining fish stocks and increasing costs. For example, DT explains that fisherfolk cannot fish within three kilometres of the 117 offshore oil and gas rigs set up by the Indian Oil and Natural Gas Company, yet these are the areas, perhaps because of the topography, where fish is most plentiful. There is evidence that pollution in creeks in Bandra and Mahim has leached the oxygen out of the water so that there is no marine life and no possibility of monsoon fishing for fisherfolk in the period where deep sea fishing is prohibited. The state government has also established industrial areas all along the coast where factories discharge untreated effluents into the sea. This means that the shellfish that breed near the shore have been decimated and subsistence fishermen working in these areas have lost their livelihoods. KMK, the leader of the fishing community on Madh Island, points out that pollution has driven fish stocks further away from the shores, into the area frequented by trawlers and out of reach of small fishermen. DT laughed and warned us not to eat fish and prawns from particular areas in the industrial development zones because they were completely contaminated. Warhaft (2001: 217) also details the continuing struggle of the Kolis against the encroachment of tourism facilities on the waterfront – five star hotels, commercial complexes and holiday resorts as well as other major infrastructure projects such as airports and port facilities for vessels and trawlers.

Conclusion

The fisherfolk of Goa and Mumbai who are still independent operators (that is not employed on or owning trawlers) are aware of the environmental damages that have occurred from the capitalisation of fishing. They told us that they recognised that mechanisation had many merits, such as larger boats that can fish farther offshore, better supplies of fish, a quicker turnaround for the market and the ability to make more trips in rougher seas. On the other hand, mechanisation also involved bigger investment, operational and repair costs, exploitation by commission agents, middlemen and moneylenders, frequent and heavy repair costs for machines such as outboard engines and exorbitant costs of fuel. What most of these fisher people would like is a *via media* between low-cost motorised fishing methods and artisanal fishing (Chacko 1998: 62).

Fishing cultures should not be romanticised as the true sites for some kind of radical re-enchantment. Rather, the fishing communities we discuss have struggled to escape the dictates of local stringencies and adapt to the contingent character of the present. The possibilities of these communities have to do with their potential to resist both the allurements of nativism and those of capitalist modernisation. The fisher people in Goa and Mumbai co-exist with the rest of their compatriots, plying their trade on the most popular tourist beaches, presenting perfect material for tourist photographs with their traditional and picturesque wooden boats, their strong and wiry physique and their silhouettes etched against the sea. Yet they are not suspended in time, like flies in amber. Fishing is a pragmatic activity to them, their trade. They display enormous adaptability in the face of capitalist modernisation and a significant ability to cope with change. Their capability to negotiate the borders between land and water, tradition and cultural change, old and new, the intermeshings of family, community and the collective with the individual is a poignant and vivid indication of the wider productive and social processes of labour and class which they inhabit.

Interviews were conducted by Devleena Ghosh and Stephen Muecke in Goa and Mumbai at various times between 2003 and 2006.

Notes

1 Another name for the River Ganga in India.
2 Folk songs sung by Bengali fisherfolk and boatmen.

Bibliography

Acheson, J.M. (1981) 'Anthropology of Fishing', *Annual Review of Anthropology* 10: 275–316.

Alvares, C. (ed.) (2002) *Fish Curry and Rice: A Sourcebook on Goa, Its Ecology and Life-style*, Goa: The Goa Foundation.

Ansari, Z.A., Achuthankutty, C.T. and Dalai, S.G. 'Overexploitation of fishery resources, with particular reference to Goa', NIO, http://209.85.141.104/search?q=cache:pALQyTP2JBUJ:drs.nio.org/drs/bitstream/2264/201/1/MD_GEChange_2006_285.pdf+fisheries+%2B+goa&hl=en&ct=clnk&cd=1&gl=au (accessed 15 May 2008).

Chacko, T. (1998) 'Artisanal Fishing along the Alleppey Coast, Southwest India', *Human Organization* Spring 57: 1.

Dasgupta, P. (2003) 'Arrested Development', *Australian Financial Review*, Friday 14 December, pp. 6–7.

—— (2005) 'Bottlenecks', *London Review of Books* 27(10), 19 May.

Hapke, H.M. (2001) 'Petty Traders, Gender, and Development in a South Indian Fishery', *Economic Geography* July, 77 (3).

Hutchings, J.A. (2000) 'Collapse and Recovery of Marine Fishes', *Nature*, 406: 882–5.

Klausen, A.M. (1964) 'Technical Assistance and Social Conflict: A Case Study from the Indo-Norwegian Fishing Project in Kerala, South India', *Journal of Peace Research* 1(1): 5–18.

Kurien, J. (1995) 'Joint Action against Joint Ventures: Resistance to Multinationals in Indian Waters', *The Ecologist* 25(2–3) (March–June).

Madhupratap, M., Nair, K.N.V., Gopalakrishnan, T.C., Haridas, P., Nair, K.K.C., Venugopal, P. and Gauns, M. (2001) 'Arabian Sea Oceanography and Fisheries of the West Coast of India', *Current Science* 81: 355–61.

Mathew, S. (2003) *Hinduonnet*, www.hinduonnet.com/thehindu/biz/2003/01/06/stories/2003010600150200.htm (accessed 27 April 2008).

Newman, R. (1984) 'Goa: The Transformation of an Indian Region', *Pacific Affairs* 57(3) Autumn: 429–49.

—— (1981) 'Green Revolution – Blue Revolution: The Predicament of India's Traditional Fishermen', *South Asia* IV(1) June.

Nieuwenhuys, O. (1989) 'Invisible Nets: Women and Children in Kerala's Fishing', *MAST* II(2): 174–94.

Norr, K.F. (1980) 'The Organisation of Coastal Fishing in Tamilnadu', in A. Spoehr, (ed.) *Maritime Adaptations, Essays on Contemporary Fishing Communities, Contributions from Ethnology*, Pittsburgh: University of Pittsburgh Press.

Pokrant, R. and Reeves, P. (2001) 'Putting Globalisaton in Its Place: Globalisation, Liberalisation and Export-Oriented Aquaculture in West Bengal and Bangladesh', *South Asia* XXIV(1): 159–84.

Prasad, A. (2001) *Frontline*, 18(25) December: 8–21, www.hinduonnet.com/fline/fl1825/18250440.htm (accessed 27 April 2008).

'Rapid Rise in Ocean Acidity Brings Fears for Marine Life' (2008) *Sydney Morning Herald*, 28 May, www.smh.com.au/text/articles/2008/05/27/1211654031589.html (accessed 28 May 2008).

Reeves, P. (n.d.) '"Development", "Modernisation" and Artisanal Fisherfolk: Recent Indian Experience with Special Reference to Kerala', Typescript Xerox.

Reeves, P., Pope, A., McGuire, J. and Pokrant, R. (1996) 'The Koli and the British at Bombay: The Structure of their Relations to the Mid-Nineteenth Century', in M.N. Pearson and I. Bruce Watson (eds) 'Asia and Europe: Commerce, Colonialism and Cultures: Essays in Honour of Sinnappah Arasaratnam', in *South Asia* [Special Issue] XIX, November: 97–120.

Sampson, H. (2005) 'Left High and Dry? The Lives of Women Married to Seafarers in Goa and Mumbai', *Ethnography* 6(1): 61–85.

Sardessai, U.D. (1999) 'Status of Fisheries Development in Goa', *Fishing Chime* 19: 47–8.

Tomory, D. (2006) 'The Chaishop Years', in Jerry Pinto (ed.) *Reflected in Water: Writings on Goa*, New Delhi: Penguin.

Warhaft, S. (2001) 'No Parking at the Bunder: Fisher People and Survival in Capitalist Mumbai', *South Asia* XXIV(2): 213–23.

6 Boundaries, scale and power in South Asia

Douglas Hill

Introduction

Disputes over water are central to the political economy of development in South Asia. This chapter looks at the way that the allocation of water is mediated by different kinds of state-society relations in India, Bangladesh and Pakistan by examining common property resource management issues from three different spatial scales: international, intra-national and intra-community. By doing so, we can begin to appreciate the complexity of problems in the management of water and the likely trends throughout the region. We do this by examining the contestations over rivers, canals, dams and groundwater. The role of agricultural change in contributing to the intensification of water usage in the rural areas is emphasised. Despite some diversification into non-agricultural activities in the rural areas and limited industrialisation in the urban areas, 70–80 per cent of the region's fresh water is utilised for agriculture at the present juncture (Haq 2003).

At the broadest level, the management and utilisation of water resources in the riparian regions of South Asia is pivotal to the geopolitics of the region. Ongoing trans-border disagreements related to rivers and canals frame the relationship between the countries of both the Indus River Basin (India and Pakistan) and the Ganges–Brahmaputra–Meghna River Basin (India, Bangladesh and Nepal; hereafter referred to as the Ganges Basin). These resources have been regulated to some extent through bilateral treaties between the relevant nations in each basin but suspicions between the nation-states remain. In addition to these international conflicts, there are also contestations occurring at different spatial scales within each nation. The development process is different in each country and this has impacted upon the way that these domestic disputes over water resource usage are framed.

This chapter examines the structural and political characteristics of each economy, which includes an examination of different agrarian class structures and their relationship to the state and the urban classes. The chapter examines intra-national disputes in two interrelated senses. The first is the competition between provincial states within a nation over water resources, which often involves dams seen as emblematic of the pattern of development in each country. The second is the social cleavages affecting the division of resources within each society. These intra-national disputes take different forms in each of the countries examined, depending on the balance of state-society relations. The paper's last level of analysis is intra-community. Local clashes over the management of water resources, particularly groundwater, are an increasing trend in each of these countries. Indeed unequal access to water remains one of the most significant factors in perpetuating uneven development, resource scarcity and poverty. These distributional conflicts have geographical, class and gender dimensions. The intra-community scale is undoubtedly of growing importance, with greater demands on water at the local level. The chapter notes that at each of these levels, there are emerging coordination problems, which will present ecological and social dilemmas in the future. Significantly, however, the political strength of emergent movements from the rural areas militates against an appropriate response to this.

Dimensions of the Indus and Ganges River Basins

The two major river basins in the northern parts of South Asia are the Ganges Basin and the Indus Basin. These, respectively, cover the eastern and western sections of the subcontinent. The significant rivers of these two basins – the Indus, Ganges and Brahmaputra – all originate near the Mount Kailash range in Tibet. Thereafter, the Indus flows to the west, eventually running into the Arabian Sea. The Ganges and Brahmaputra flow down to the south and east, respectively. Both of these latter rivers eventually link together and discharge into the Bay of Bengal.

Both of these basins are historically significant as the bases of great civilisations. The Ganges Basin is one of the largest in the world, inhabited by a population of at least 600 million people (Bandyopadhyay 1995). Nevertheless, it is also comparatively one of the most under-utilised systems in the world. Its catchment area includes five countries (Bangladesh, Bhutan, India, Nepal and China), although the majority of the downstream sections of the basin are within Bangladesh and India. The Gangetic delta is also fed by the Indian states of Uttaranchal (part of Uttar Pradesh until 2000) and Sikkim (an independent nation-state until 1973) as well as the independent nation-states of Nepal and Bhutan.

The Indus Basin is ostensibly a much simpler geopolitical situation than the Ganges Basin, since it only involves two countries. In Pakistan, the alluvial plains of the Indus basin cover approximately 25 per cent of the land area of Pakistan, with Punjab and Sindh the most agriculturally important provinces (World Commission on Dams 2000). In India, the basin includes only 9.8 per cent of the total geographical area of the country. On the Indian side, the upper part of the basin includes the mountainous states of Jammu and Kashmir and Himachal Pradesh. The lower part of the basin includes the plains area of the fertile and productive states of Punjab and Haryana, the semi-arid Rajasthan and the Union Territory of Chandigarh.

International contestations over water: India–Pakistan and India–Bangladesh

Given the importance of these basins, it is unsurprising that boundaries drawn across them – thus dividing their resources – have been the source of significant controversy. In this sense, the region's defining event was the partition of British India at Independence in 1947. After war-weary Britain acceded to demands for the independence of its former colonies, the two basins were divided between India and two geographically separate halves of Pakistan. East Pakistan, later to become Bangladesh, was surrounded by upper riparian parts of India's north-eastern states, while the delta flowed into the Bay of Bengal in both (Pakistani) East and (Indian) West Bengal. In the western part of the sub-continent, the resulting partition of India and Pakistan was achieved by drawing a boundary across the Indus Basin, so that the upper riparian territory was claimed by India, while the Indus flows into the sea entirely within Pakistani territory.

Up until partition, there had been a far greater investment in the infrastructure of the western part of British India, and so the Indus basin has historically been an important component of the agricultural systems of both western India and Pakistan. After the canal developments in the 1860s, an enormous population expansion occurred in the (then undivided) Punjab and the region continued to benefit from the building of canals in the nineteenth and early twentieth centuries. The centralisation of the canal system was important for the political structures it helped create and then perpetuate, with the colonial bureaucratic state and large landholders as the major beneficiaries (Ali 2004).

The boundaries drawn up at partition left Pakistan, as the lower riparian, in a vulnerable position, since the irrigation canal supplies in Punjab, Pakistan's most fertile area, had their source in Indian territory. In April 1948 India closed the canals on the eastern rivers of Ravi and Sutlej, only agreeing to reopen them after the Inter-Dominion Agreement of May 1948, where it claimed the entire water of the eastern rivers (Gazdar 2005). This was only an interim agreement and the Indus Water Treaty (IWT) was finally negotiated between India and Pakistan in 1960. This gave India the eastern rivers (Ravi, Beas and Sutlej) and Pakistan the western rivers (Jhelum, Chenab and the Indus itself).

There is a commonly held belief that the Indus Water Treaty is a significant example of bilateral cooperation between two nations that otherwise remain largely mired in seemingly intractable conflicts. Advocates of this position note that the Treaty was not abrogated even during the 1965 war between the two nations. However, this largely ignores the historical contingencies that were so important in constraining Pakistan's initial scope of action (Gazdar 2005). The agreement between India and Pakistan was largely brokered with the assistance of the World Bank and although there was the appearance of concession, India was able to achieve its objectives.

The Indus Basin Project was the compensation Pakistan received for its loss of access to the eastern rivers. This led to the building of new storage reservoirs, barrages and inter-river link canals and the remodelling of three existing link canals (World Commission on Dams 2000). The most visible results included dams at Tarbela (the world's largest earth filled dam), Mangla and Chashma (Haq 2003: 59). The main purpose of this infrastructure was irrigation, with power as a secondary objective. The Indus Basin Project was financed via the Indus Basin Development Fund (IBDF), which included contributions from the World Bank, bilateral donors and a fixed contribution from India (World Commission on Dams 1999).

In recognition of the fact that India is the upper riparian country for the western rivers which were allocated to Pakistan, there are restrictions placed on its capacity to modify the flow of these rivers, so that Pakistan's lower riparian rights are not impeded. One of these provisions is that India is able to build storage facilities on rivers that flow into Pakistan only if these are of limited capacity. This provision has consistently been tested by India as it has sought to expand the number of projects it has in the upper reaches of the western rivers. In recent months another dispute has arisen over the building of the Baglihar barrage on the Chenab River in the Indian state of Jammu and Kashmir. The barrage, on which construction began in 1999, is scheduled to be finished in 2007. It is contentious because Pakistan believes the barrage is in violation of the Indus Water Treaty and India's international obligations under the *Convention on the Protection and Use of Transboundary Watercourses and International Lakes* signed at Helsinki in March 1992. According to these treaties the Chenab is supposed to be primarily for use by Pakistan. Pakistan asked the World Bank to appoint a neutral arbiter, but the Bank was unable to broker a solution satisfactory to both parties despite repeated meetings (*Hindu Businessline* 2005a, 2005b; Noorani 2002). The issue continues to be a background tension in the evolving relationship between India and Pakistan. Despite the objections of Pakistan and contention over the legality or otherwise of the project, it is clear that India intends to complete the barrage. Thus, while there were early indications that the Baglihar may not be used to full potential, the Indian government has renewed its commitment to the project in its 2006–07 Budget, which includes a Rs2.3 billion outlay for Baglihar as part of a more broad ranging allocation aimed at enhancing power development in the troubled Indian state of Jammu and Kashmir (*Hindustan Times* 2006a, 2006b).

India–Bangladesh

Despite the fact that there are several countries involved in the Ganges Basin, the management of these water resources has been negotiated bilaterally, with India negotiating with Nepal and Bangladesh as separate parties. Here, geopolitical considerations limiting the cooperation between countries have historically been at least as important in limiting the usage of water resources as the hydrological properties of the rivers within this basin (Brichieri-Colombi and Bradnock 2003). Although Bangladesh and India share 54 common rivers, the main dispute between India and Pakistan/Bangladesh in the Ganges Basin has been over the building of the Farakka Barrage, which diverts water from the Ganges into the Hoogli River on the Indian side of the border. The Farakka Barrage was first conceived of in 1950 by then Prime Minister Nehru, who supposedly regarded the building of the barrage as having few ill-effects on Bangladesh (then East Pakistan). India's rationale then, as now, was that it needed diversion of water to the Hoogli River in order to flush out siltation and keep the port of Calcutta operational (Hossain 1998).

When Pakistan drew India's attention to the reports of these plans to build the barrage, in October 1951, India dismissed the claims by saying that the possibility of building a barrage at Farakka was only under investigation. Meetings on the issue began between the two countries in 1960, with India officially beginning construction in January 1961. Meetings continued until 1970 without any real progress being achieved. A measure of India's attitude towards the sharing of these waters is evidenced by the fact that it was not until 1970 that it was acknowledged that usage of the Ganges was an international issue.

By 1970 India had completed construction of the barrage but still had some technical problems. Talks were suspended when the East Bengali political forces under the Awami League began agitations that would escalate into Bangladesh's War of Independence. Bangladesh's independence from Pakistan, with considerable assistance from India, signalled an era of goodwill between India and Bangladesh, with the signing of the Treaty of Friendship and Cooperation, which was to be valid for 25 years. In May 1972 the two countries established a Joint Rivers Commission, which would be the final arbiter of matters if the process fails through the negotiations of lower levels, such as secretaries. However, the ambit of the Commission specifically excluded the issue of Ganges development, which was to be addressed at the Prime Ministerial level.

It was not until May 1974 that the two Prime Ministers met and agreed to try to find a mutually agreeable solution, which was to be achieved by turning the issue over to the Joint Rivers Commission. In April 1975 both sides agreed to a trial period of operation of the barrage. When this trial period ended, after 41 days, India continued to divert water without seeking fresh permission from any level of Bangladeshi government. Thereafter, the continuing round of meetings achieved little, until Bangladesh formally lodged a complaint with the United Nations in 1976. The United Nations urged the two parties to find a solution. The Ganges Water Agreement, signed in November 1977, was for a period of five years. When this time elapsed, no new agreement was reached until 1985, with a Memorandum of Understanding for sharing water in the lean season. This was valid until 1988 and after this no new agreement was signed until the Ganges Water Sharing Treaty in December 1996. The main provisions of the Treaty concerned a formula for the distribution of water during the lean season between January 1 and March 31 each year. Bangladesh was assured a guaranteed flow of 35,000 cusec. The agreement should guarantee an adequate flow of water to the southwestern districts of Bangladesh, where much of the country's agriculture, aquaculture and industries are located, and prevent salination of the Sunderbans mangrove delta.

Despite these agreements, the water-sharing arrangements have remained controversial. This is particularly the case in Bangladesh, where these bilateral agreements have become a rallying point for nationalist campaigns against India, particularly by the Bangladesh Nationalist Party (BNP). The Hindu populist Bharatiya Janata Party (BJP) has conducted similar campaigns in India over what it sees as the compromises of national interest (Wright 2002; Anwar 1996). Significantly, while both of these parties have been vociferous in their demands against current water-sharing arrangements when in opposition, when in government, neither have shown any interest in abrogating the treaty.

The critics of the current arrangements in Bangladesh view the terms of water-sharing as inequitable and symptomatic of the broader relationship between the two countries. From this perspective, India has aggressively asserted its own interest to the detriment of Bangladesh, to the extent that almost every negative development in rural Bangladesh is linked to the Farakka Barrage. The Indian perspective, in contrast, asserts that Bangladesh has been unwilling to compromise and has expected that its share of water resources will always remain undiminished.

After the division of resources had been settled, the issue then moved to strategies to augment storage, since it was recognised that the current arrangements could not guarantee sufficient water for both sides. Bangladesh's solution was to involve Nepal, since its vast, snow-fed seasonal resources were seen as largely wasted for want of appropriate storage facilities. However, India consistently refused to involve Nepal. Indeed, water-sharing negotiations are conspicuously absent from discussions at the South Asian Association for Regional Cooperation (SAARC), the regional body that would otherwise have seemed an obvious forum for such multilateral coordination.

Intra-national contestations: the political economy of development in India, Pakistan and Bangladesh

Discussion about bilateral issues between countries can only take us so far in understanding the complexity of issues inherent in water-sharing, since the compulsions for these international disputes have domestic roots embedded in the prevailing structure of development. In all the countries examined, internal political forces conditioning the nature of the development strategy have been important in the usage of water. There are strong historical reasons for this.

In India, the state at independence was not strong enough to undertake planned industrialisation and so assisted the domestic bourgeoisie via a mixed economy. This strategy politically necessitated an alliance with rich farmers, who dominated provincial-level politics. The various class interests of these dominant groups, along with those who had participated in the mass-movement for independence, were accommodated within the Indian National Congress. The strength of the large landholders conditioned the shape of post-independence development policy. In this sense, land reform, as a central component of an alternative agricultural strategy, was never seriously considered, despite rhetorical commitment to the contrary (Corbridge and Harriss 2000). The resultant 'passive revolution' continues to condition the contours of

India's development strategy (Chakrabarti and Cullenberg 2003; Kaviraj 1998). Pranab Bardhan has captured the dominant consensus on the class biases of the development process with his description of the three 'dominant proprietary classes' of industrialists, rich farmers and intelligentsia or bureaucracy (Bardhan 1984).

Issues of federalism have complicated these matters. In the constitution, the initial division of powers pertaining to water disputes envisaged a two-fold approach, which reflects the division of powers between centre and state in the Union and State lists. First, in Entry 56 of the Union list, the centre was given the power to develop trans-boundary waters. Second, in Entry 17 of the State list, each state was given the power to develop waters within its boundaries. Since this time, distribution of water resources has become an important area of political contestation between different states. The *Inter State Water Disputes Act* (1956), amended in 2002, provides a mechanism for the formation of a tribunal to resolve any conflicts arising from the sharing of water. Thus far, such a tribunal has been formed to settle disputes on five occasions. These are the Godavari Water Disputes Tribunal (April 1969); the Krishna Water Disputes Tribunal (April 1969); the Narmada Water Disputes Tribunal (October 1969); the Ravi and Beas Water Disputes Tribunal (April 1986); and the Cauvery Water Disputes Tribunal (1991). These conflicts have been significant in the political agenda of regional parties in the contending states.[1]

Pakistan

Pakistan was mainly constituted from a hinterland that had provided agricultural raw materials for mills in India (jute for Calcutta in the case of East Bengal; cotton for Bombay in the case of West Pakistan). It had comparatively low levels of industrialisation and as such there was not an indigenous bourgeoisie that could assist the state with development in the way that it could in India. Much of the entrepreneurial and professional classes emigrated to India at partition (Ali 2004). The major political force in Pakistan was the (West Pakistani) agrarian elite. This class had actively cooperated with the British in the colonial period, with the Punjab's canal economy strengthening their position. As such, while there were subsequently attempts to create an industrial class, this was not at the expense of the rural elites. Émigré Gujarati trading classes were relied on by the new state to create a commercial and industrial base. By 1968, just 22 families controlled the vast majority of Pakistan's economy. Investment patterns and industrial licensing reflected this bias, with investment in many sectors in Karachi exceeding that for the whole of East Pakistan (Nations 1971)!

The military-bureaucratic oligopoly that has, in various guises, controlled the state in Pakistan since partition, has functioned to the advantage of the Punjabi landlord class. Wealth accumulation for the industrial classes has been built on patronage from the Pakistani civil service. However, political power remains with the military and bureaucracy, who were recruited from the traditional landed gentry and aristocracy (Nations 1971). In the post-East Pakistan phase, the Pakistani state has continued to intervene to assist the rural elite. Measures under Zulfikar Ali Bhutto included the formation of public sector trading companies to protect export crops and the nationalisation of agribusiness sectors, which was decisive in the 1977 election (Ali 2004). There also continues to be strong antagonism by the provinces of Baluchistan, NWFP and Sindh over what is seen as a development process centred on the interests of Punjab.

Provincial rivalry over the division of the water in the Indus basin was an issue of considerable debate as early as 1920, with Sindh objecting to projects involving the Sutlej river valley and Sukkur barrage, which were proposed by Punjab. The then Central Government of India attempted to resolve these disputes, either through commissions or negotiation between the provinces. The earliest attempt, the Anderson Commission (1935), achieved little in mollifying opposition and it was the Rau Commission (1942) that provided the framework for allocating water between what were to become the provinces of Pakistan.

In this respect, the 1960 Indus Water Treaty was significant for inter-provincial rivalry within Pakistan, particularly between Punjab and Sindh. The Jhelum and Chenab have both drained into the Indus by the time they reach Sindh, meaning that Punjab maintained a greater degree of control over volume of water available to its lower riparian counterpart. Since all the provinces of Western Pakistan were amalgamated following the military take-over in 1958, these rivalries were largely ignored in negotiations, much to the chagrin of the Sindhis, who felt that their interests had been passed over in favour of those of Punjab and have been ever since (Gazdar 2005). Although further challenges to the validity of this earlier framework were evident from the Water Allocation and Rates Commission (1968 – otherwise known as the Akhter Hussain Commission) and the Fazle Akbar Committee (1970), neither had any influence in changing the status quo (Mansoor 2002).

The Water Apportionment Accords were negotiated between the four provinces of Pakistan in 1991, with a regulatory authority to supervise the implementation of its provisions, called the Indus River System Authority (IRSA), established in 1993 (Mansoor 2002). The purpose of these accords was to establish recognition of existing canals and apportion future supplies. This was done by dividing water on the basis of the previous seven years supply, which many have suggested unduly favoured Punjab (Mansoor 2002). The accords worked reasonably well until the first shortages occurred in 1994, at which point a new Water Sharing Agreement was negotiated (Shahzad 2002). This agreement shared water between the provinces according to the aggregate use of the previous seven years, a formula that Sindh immediately dismissed as unjust and which has been the basis for agitation and resentment ever since (Mansoor 2002).

Resentment has also arisen within Baluchistan among those who feel that Sindh is not releasing adequate amounts of water. The disputes over water distribution have continued, with tensions particularly during the Rabi season when shortages of water are acute. A large bureaucratic system has developed to mediate decisions about water sharing but has thus far been largely unsuccessful in finding technical solutions to what are perceived within Pakistan to be political issues.[2]

Bangladesh

Bangladesh is a country with more than sufficient water but insufficient capacity to store the highly seasonal variation of rainfall, so that it periodically varies between acute shortages and over abundance, despite efforts to expand irrigation canals and embankments. Perhaps surprisingly, the division of water has not been as internally divisive between provincial entities in Bangladesh as it has been in other countries in the region.

At partition from India in 1947, the economy of Bangladesh, the erstwhile East Pakistan, was reliant upon several industries that were fading in global importance, most notably jute (Khan 1999). The period between the formation of Pakistan and independent Bangladesh in 1971 served to exacerbate these problems, with East Pakistan having poor infrastructure and a lack of skilled manpower and capital (Kochanek 1996: 708). Initially, the Pakistani government favoured the domestic capitalist classes of West Pakistan. Indeed, it was not until the late 1960s that East Pakistan began to receive substantial assistance towards industrialisation, a problem exacerbated by the fact that there was almost no East Pakistani capitalist class (Khan 1999: 16).

With Independence in 1971, the Awami League (AL) government, led by Sheik Mujib Rahman, attempted to pursue a program of nationalisation and state-directed economic growth. Again, this was done with little attention to the rural areas, which were dominated by a (jotedar) land-holding class. After Mujib's assassination in 1975, General Ziaur Rahman (hereafter Zia) undertook a rapid reversal of Mujib's state-led policies. Since the majority of beneficiaries of this system were large, family run business houses, the distorted liberalisation of this era set in place a patrimonial system that in subsequent periods has seen greater direct and indirect influence by these dominant classes on the workings of politics. Thus accumulation has been to the almost complete detriment of the vast majority of the country's population, who remain among the poorest in the world. From 1978 onwards, the newly formed Bangladesh Nationalist Party (BNP) under Zia dominated weak and fragmented opposition. In return for their support, the dominant classes were shielded from scrutiny over the increasingly large revenues being gained from legal and illegal use of public resources (Quadir 2000: 201).

The system of kleptocracy accelerated during the almost decade long military rule of General Hussain M. Ershad (hereafter Ershad) from 1982 onwards. Although elections were held in 1986 and 1988, it is widely believed that Ershad bribed opposition parties to stand in order to lend him legitimacy (Kochanek 1993: 226–7). With little popular support, Ershad nevertheless managed to sustain his rule by appeasing the multilateral donor community and enriching business elites. During the governments of Khaleda Zia's BNP (1991–96), the Awami League (1996–2001) and again the BNP, the process of liberalisation gained further momentum.

In all three of these countries, then, the class interests of the polity have been a vital determinant of the kinds of development strategy followed, with a preference for the interest of the dominant classes only tempered when absolutely necessary. The class structure has also impacted upon the structure of water resource policy. In some cases, this has been through an unwillingness to monitor the wasteful and inefficient use of water by industry. In other cases, it has been by supporting large landholders. In each case, it has meant that there remains a large section of the population – in both the rural and urban areas – who do not have adequate access to water for livelihoods or food security.

Dams in South Asia

A significant insight into the contours of the political economy of development in India and Pakistan is afforded by an examination of dams. Indeed, aside from the bilateral sharing of surface water, the other major, mostly intra-national, water controversy prevalent in South Asia has been the location and construction of dams. India, with approximately 4,300 dams in 1994, can claim to be one of the world's major builders of dams (Bosshard 2004). Indeed, dams were one of the centrepieces of the Nehruvian strategy of planned industrialisation, along with the other 'temples' of modernisation, such as steel refineries and factories.

Critics of the reliance upon large-scale dams suggest that several factors render this strategy unsustainable and inequitable. The International Rivers Network (IRN), for example, highlights four areas of objection. First, large dams are usually associated with large-scale displacement. The IRN suggests that large dams in India have displaced at least 42 million people, a disproportionately high number of them tribal people. Second, they note the environmental damage associated with clearing of forests and the impacts accompanying road-building, so that the building of the dam has a pronounced local effect. Third, they highlight possible dangers arising from dams being built in areas of high seismic activity. Fourth, critics question the long-term effectiveness of these dams on the basis that siltation will considerably reduce their expected capacity over time (Bosshard 2004). The Tehri Dam, in Uttaranchal in the Indian Himalayas, is the most emblematic of these campaigns.

The Tarbela Dam in Pakistan has also been criticised for the above failings. This is one of the world's most significant dams, providing 9 per cent of the Indus system's total irrigation water and 28 per cent of Pakistan's electric power. From the outset, the dam has been beset with problems, which led to a significant overrun of costs. At least 96,000 people were displaced, of whom 20,000 have still not been resettled. Of those who were compensated, estimates suggest that the long delays meant that the compensation had devalued by half. The ecological impacts include loss of fish diversity, salination, enormous loss of forest cover, increased intrusion of seawater up the Indus, depletion of mangrove forests and severe flooding. The Tarbela has also exacerbated provincial rivalries, since most of the benefits of the project accrue to Punjab, while most of the damage is borne by Sindh (World Commission on Dams 2000).

This inter-provincial tension is evident in many dam projects in South Asia, precisely because the states that receive the greatest benefit from the dams are not always the same as those that have to compensate the losers. The Narmada Valley Development Project, which has now been in process for three decades, involves the construction of 30 large, 135 medium and 3,000 small dams on the Narmada River and its tributaries (Bavadam 2003). This scheme involves the governments of Gujarat, Madhya Pradesh and Maharashtra. Although most of the costs, including rehabilitation and construction, will be borne by Madhya Pradesh, the state will benefit the least from the dam complex when it is finally finished. This has led to political disputes between the three states. Similarly, in Pakistan, the majority of the provinces have opposed the construction of the Kalabagh Dam on the Indus. The political representatives of the provinces of Sindh, the NWFP and Baluchistan all argue that the construction of this dam serves only the interests of Punjab (World Commission on Dams 2000).

Water, agriculture and rural development

The increasing disputes over the allocation of water in the region impact significantly on food security. Agriculture remains the most significant factor in food security in rural areas throughout South Asia, the development of which is intimately linked to the control of irrigation. While much of the agricultural growth in the 1950s and early 1960s came from an increase in net sown area, the improvements thereafter have come to principally form changes in productivity as yields have increased for several major crops. A changed agricultural strategy, based on higher usage of water and other inputs to increase productivity, began to become generalised in most South Asian countries in the mid-1960s. To supplement this, the dominant approach to rural development in the post-independence period in South Asia has rested on supplying subsidised inputs to farmers, which it was hoped would rapidly increase agricultural production and thus reduce rural poverty. The spread of Green Revolution technology throughout South Asia was assisted by the supply of inputs through extension activities and complimentary infrastructure, as successive governments provided the means to build deep tubewells and extend canals through poverty alleviation plans (Osmani 1999).

In the Indus Basin, where many of the pilot programs were pioneered, agricultural productivity initially increased rapidly as a consequence of the widespread adoption of Green Revolution technology. Shallow and deep tubewells and low-lift irrigation pumps began to be sunk in this part of India in the 1950s and were adopted in (West) Pakistan in the 1960s and 1970s. The growth in groundwater complemented the already extensive canal system, which was also increased. In the current era, almost 90 per cent of Pakistan's most important primary products, including rice, wheat and cotton, come from the Sindh and Punjab provinces. Similarly, while India's agricultural base has become somewhat more spatially diversified over time, Punjab and Haryana continue to be the most significant agricultural states.

In contrast, the Ganges region of South Asia experienced a long period of agricultural stagnation from the mid-colonial period. The populous Indian states of the Hindi belt (in central and western India), fed only by the Ganges system, have suffered from shortages of water relative to the amount of cultivable land. This situation has worsened as population has increased. The Bengal Delta, where the rivers of the Ganges Basin drain into the ocean, is far better endowed with water resources than the part of the basin further to the west, although until recently this potential has failed to translate into agricultural growth. Agricultural growth remained stagnant in both East and West Bengal, from around 1860 until the mid-1980s (Rogaly *et al.* 1999).

Studies of agricultural performance in Bengal (Bangladesh and West Bengal) have been preoccupied with the question of why, with such favourable conditions, the region was slow to adopt Green Revolution technology (Rawal 1999; Rawal and Swaminathan 1998; Rogaly *et al.* 1999). James Boyce's landmark study, examining the period up to the mid-1980s, argued that the inadequate control of irrigation water was 'the leading input' contributing to the region's continuing stagnation[3]. He reasoned that institutional factors were also significant. In particular, the hierarchical nature of Bengal's agrarian structure led to an under-utilisation of labour and discouraged cooperation in increasing access to controlled water. Surface water was not adequately controlled and much of the flow remains seasonal, with monsoonal flooding followed by dry season shortages.

The impact of the expansion of groundwater

While the initial stages of the Green Revolution were built around supplementing the already existing canal system, the latter stages are more associated with a notable increase in groundwater extraction throughout previously undeveloped parts of South Asia (particularly in the Ganges basin). This development has been less visible and contentious than the state-supported development of surface water in the post-colonial period, since much of the increase has occurred through privately owned, small-scale tubewells. The development of groundwater resources is often heralded as more accessible than surface water irrigation, since it is less capital intensive and is less restricted by topography than canal development.

India is perhaps the most dramatic example in South Asia of the recent rapid expansion of groundwater. A recent study suggested that 60 per cent of the country's irrigated area now comes from groundwater. In Bangladesh, groundwater accounts for 75 per cent of the total water use and 95 per cent of water for domestic use comes from groundwater. Pakistan has seen significant development of groundwater resources in the past 30 years. Large capacity tubewells were installed by the state and this was a spur to the proliferation of smaller private tubewells (Akhtar Bhatti 2002). In Pakistan, 70 per cent of the groundwater development is also in areas where canals are prevalent, which is evidence of the concentrated nature of agriculture, confined as it mostly is to the Punjab and Sindh provinces. Estimates suggest that between 1972 and 1997 the contribution of groundwater to irrigated agriculture in Pakistan nearly doubled and the number of irrigation tubewells increased by almost 500 per cent from 1970 to 1996 (World Commission on Dams 2000).

The effects of the adoption of the Green Revolution strategy have been mixed. In the short term, there have definitely been productivity improvements and increasing yields. India and Pakistan have achieved self-sufficiency in food grain production, which represents a remarkable feat given the dire predictions of Malthusian doom accompanying the region's rapid population growth. However, this is far from uniform across regions, and the broader, long-term social and environmental effects of the Green Revolution are contentious. There is now considerable evidence that the growth of groundwater expansion is associated with resource over-exploitation, particularly in the heavily populated western and central areas of the Gangetic belt, which are poorly served by canal irrigation (Vaidyanathan 2001). According to World Bank reports, 38 per cent of Pakistan's irrigated land area is waterlogged and soil salinity has caused a 25 per cent reduction in the production of Pakistan's major crops (Bosshard 2004). The lack of coordination among users of groundwater heralds a classic 'tragedy of the commons' scenario. Evidence across South Asia suggests problems with the growing salinisation of aquifers (seawater intrusion) and arsenic and chromium pollution.

The increased use of groundwater has also spurred a growing local market in water-selling. For example, 88 per cent of pump owners in Bangladesh, 60 per cent in Nepal and 48 per cent in West Bengal reported selling water (quoted in Mukherjee 2004). Some have argued that this increased marketisation of water will slow the overexploitation of groundwater. However, early micro-scale case studies refute this optimism, as exploitation continues apace. These studies also suggest that the growth of water markets is reinforcing inequalities in the agrarian structure, with those having ownership of pumps generally drawn from the rural elite. There is evidence that the pattern of ownership has broadened in some places, although not as far as the landless or marginal farmers. While some of these transactions involve money, there are also many examples where they involve interlinkages with credit or labour, thus, further reinforcing class relationships within the agrarian structure (Hanan *et al.* 2004; Ali and Byerlee 2002).

An evolving 'tragedy of the commons', leading to ecological problems and increasing inequality, is not a problem unique to water resources. Other common pool resources, such as forests, have experienced similar problems in much of South Asia. However, in the forestry sector, co-management schemes, involving community groups in the management of resources in collaboration with the state, have enjoyed notable success in slowing resource degradation in many parts of South Asia (Kothari *et al.* 1998). There has been less activity in promoting schemes for the co-management of groundwater, although this is obviously an area that may warrant further effort in the future.

While the social and ecological impacts of the Green Revolution in South Asia are well known outside the region, the political consequences have received less attention. From the 1970s onwards, farmer's movements have become an increasing force in Indian and Pakistani politics. There is considerable debate about the class representation of the New Farmers' Movement in India, although the main interests represented are large and medium farmers (Banaji 1994). Similar movements have developed in Pakistan. In the Pakistani province of Punjab, the main class composition is reported to be large and middle peasants, whereas in Sindh it covers all classes to a much greater degree (Gazdar 2005). The main platform of these movements has been to lobby for subsidised cultivation inputs and assured minimum prices for their produce. This has assisted the over exploitation of resources like water since electricity and diesel technology have remained relatively inexpensive.

Increased demands from groundwater have led to new forms of contestation. For example, localised and pre-existing inequalities within the agrarian structure impact upon the distribution and usage of tubewells. Individual private actors drawing upon common property, in this case aquifers, in an unregulated fashion, are a cause of coordination issues. Farmers' movements have a strong presence in provincial and national-level politics in both Pakistan and India. The demands for cheaper, heavily subsidised cultivation inputs (fertiliser, pesticides and electricity) by these Farmers Movements have contributed to the largely unregulated over-exploitation of groundwater resources.

Conclusion

The chapter has outlined some of the major dimensions of the contestation over water in the South Asian countries of Pakistan, India and Bangladesh. The processes involved in regulating this contestation have at various times strained the relationships between all three countries. There are also significant clashes over water within these countries. These take the form of both inter-state and inter-class contestation, which are exemplified by the emphasis on large dams. Agricultural intensification has significantly increased the use of water. The increased use of groundwater has made the benefits of the Green Revolution far more accessible to a greater number of people than the previous system that was overly reliant upon seasonal flow from canals and rivers. However, there have been significant ecological and social costs associated with this process, which suggests that the current pattern is unsustainable.

While market-based solutions for water-selling may in theory assist in reducing degradation of water resources by assigning private property rights to usage, the over-exploitation of groundwater will not be adequately regulated unless a greater emphasis is placed upon community based resource management solutions. Moreover market-based solutions exclude the asset-poor, not least the many landless and those others who are not cultivators. Whether there is adequate political will to alter the current scenario will be one of the factors defining future contestations over water in the region.

Notes

1 Godavari Water Disputes Tribunal was formed to adjudicate between Maharashtra, Madhya Pradesh, Karnataka, Andhra Pradesh and Orissa; the Krishna Water Disputes Tribunal was between Maharashtra, Karnataka and Andhra Pradesh; the Narmada Water Disputes Tribunal was between Madhya Pradesh, Gujarat, Maharashtra and Rajasthan; the Ravi and Beas Waters Tribunal was between Punjab, Haryana and Rajasthan; and the Cauvery Water Disputes Tribunal was between Karnataka and Tamil Nadu.

2 The bureaucracy charged with dealing with these issues includes the following bodies: the Ministry of Water and Power, Wapda, Indus River System Authority, Technical Committee on Water Resources, National Assembly's Standing Committee, Senate Standing Committee and Federal Flood Committee, Council of Common Interests and the Inter-Provincial Coordination Committee.

3 The experience of South Asian countries largely confirm the hypothesis of Ishikawa (1967) who, in studying agricultural change in various other Asian countries, found that irrigation was the 'leading input' in the first three of his four stages of agriculture contributing to growth. In doing so, he distinguished four different stages of productivity. While irrigation is the leading input in the first three stages of this transition, by the fourth stage fertiliser, better seeds and improved techniques become the 'combined leading input'. Inputs such as labour, fertiliser and seeds are also all important in influencing these changes (Boyce 1987: 33).

Bibliography

Akhtar Bhatti, M. (2002) 'Groundwater Management in South Asia – A Regional Initiative', paper presented at the International Network of Basin Organisations General Assembly, Quebec, Canada, 28–30 May 2002.

Ali, I. (2004) 'Historical Impacts on Political Economy in Pakistan', *Asian Journal of Management Cases* 1(2).

—— (2005) 'Business, Stakeholders and Strategic Responses in Pakistan', *UNEAC Asia Papers* (8).

Ali, M. and Byerlee, D. (2002) 'Productivity Growth and Resource Degradation in Pakistan's Punjab: A Decomposition Analysis', *Economic Development and Cultural Change* 50(4): 839–63.

Anwar, S. (1996) 'Opposition Slams Bangladesh Water Deal with India' *Reuters News*, 14/12/1996.

Banaji, J. (1994) 'The Farmers' Movements – a Critique of Conservative Rural Coalitions', *Journal of Peasant Studies* 21(3/4): 228–45.

Bandyopadhyay, J. (1995) 'Water Management in the Ganges–Brahmaputra Basin: Emerging Challenges for the 21st Century', *Water Resources Development* 11(4): 411–42.

Bardhan, P. (1984) *The Political Economy of Development in India*, Delhi: Oxford University Press.

Bavadam, L. (2003) 'Narmada Valley Project: Rising Concerns', *Frontline* 20(12), www.frontlineonnet.com/fl2012/stories/20030620002404100.htm.

Bosshard, P. (2004) 'World Bank: Lessons not Learnt' www.sanctuaryasia.com/features/detailfeaturescategory.php?id=647&catid=52H (accessed 5 June 2006).

Boyce, J.K. (1987) *Agrarian Impasse in Bengal: Institutional Constraints to Technological Change*, Oxford: Oxford University Press.

Brichieri-Colombi, S. and Bradnock, R.W. (2003) 'Geopolitics, Water and Development in South Asia: Cooperative Development in the Ganges–Brahmaputra Delta', *The Geographical Journal* 169(1): 43–64.

Chakrabarti, A. and Cullenberg, S. (2003) *Transition and Development in India*, New York and London: Routledge.

Corbridge, S. and Harriss, J. (2000) *Reinventing India: Liberalization, Hindu Nationalism and Popular Democracy*, Cambridge: Polity Press.

Gazdar, H. (2005) 'Baglihar and Politics of Water', *Economic and Political Weekly* 40(9): 813–17.

Hanan, G., Jacoby, Rinku Murgai and Saeed Ur Rehman (2004) 'Monopoly Power and Distribution in Fragmented Markets: The Case of Groundwater', *The Review of Economic Studies* 71(248): 783–808.

Haq, K. (2003) *Human Development in South Asia 2002: Agriculture and Rural Development*, Oxford: Oxford University Press.

Hindu Businessline, The (2005a) 'Baglihar project talks fail; Pak threatens to move World Bank', 8/1/2005.

—— (2005b) 'World Bank may help resolve Baglihar row', 9/3/2005.

Hindustan Times (2006a) 'Is Baglihar turning a white elephant?' 5/2/2006.

—— (2006b) 'Kashmir gets special aid for development, power' 28/2/2006.

Hossain, I. (1998) 'Bangladesh–India Relations: The Ganges Water-Sharing Treaty and Beyond', *Asian Affairs* 25(4): 131–50.

Kaviraj, S. (1998) 'A Critique of the Passive Revolution', in P. Chatterjee (ed.) *State and Politics in India*, Delhi: Oxford University Press, pp. 45–87.

Khan, M. (1999) 'The Political Economy of Industrial Policy in Pakistan 1947–1971', Working Paper, Department of Economics, SOAS, University of London.

Kochanek, S. (1993) *Patron–Client Politics and Business in Bangladesh*, Dhaka: Dhaka University Press.

—— (1996) 'The Rise of Interest Politics in Bangladesh', *Asian Survey* 36(7): 704–22.

Kothari, A., Pathak, N., Anuradha, R.V. and Taneja, B. (eds) (1998) *Communities and Conservation: Natural Resource Management in South and Central Asia*, New Delhi: Sage.

Mansoor, H. (2002) 'Water Wars: Sindh's Struggle for Control of the Indus', *Himal*, July.

Mukherjee, A. (2004) 'Groundwater Markets in Ganga–Meghna–Brahmaputra Basin: Theory and Evidence', *Economic and Political Weekly* 30(31): 3514–20.

Nations, R. (1971) 'The Economic Structure of Pakistan: Class and Colony', *New Left Review* (68) July–August: 3–26.

Noorani, A.G. (2002) 'A Treaty to Keep', *Frontline* 19(8): 13–26.

Osmani, S.R. (1999) 'Social Security in South Asia', in E. Ahmad, J. Dreze, J. Hills and A.K. Sen (eds) *Social Security in Developing Countries*, New Delhi: Oxford University Press, Indian Edition, pp. 305–55.

'Pakistan: Focus on the dams dispute in Pakistan', www.irinnews.org/report.asp?ReportID=36592&SelectRegion=Central_Asia&SelectCountry=PAKISTAN (accessed 16 June 2007).

Pakistan Water Gateway, www.waterinfo.net.pk (accessed 26 July 2006).

Quadir, F. (2000) 'The Political Economy of Pro-market Reforms in Bangladesh: Regime Consolidation Through Economic Liberalization?', *Contemporary South Asia* 9(2): 197–212.

Rawal, V. (1999) *Irrigation Development in West Bengal 1977–78 to 1995–96*, unpublished PhD thesis, Indira Gandhi Institute of Development Research, Mumbai.

Rawal, V. and Swaminathan, M. (1998) 'Changing Trajectories: Agricultural Growth in West Bengal, 1950 to 1996', *Economic and Political Weekly* 33(4): 2595–602.

Rogaly, B., Harriss-White, B. and Bose, S. (eds) (1999) *Sonar Bangla? Agricultural Growth and Agrarian Change in West Bengal and Bangladesh*, Dhaka: Dhaka University Press.

Shahzad, I. (2002) 'A Nation Divided Over Water', *Dawn*, 18/3/2002.

Vaidyanathan, A. (2001) *Water Resource Management: Institutions and Irrigation Development in India*, New Delhi: Oxford University Press, Paperback Edition.

'The World Bank and Large Dams: Failure to Learn from History', www.environmentaldefense.org/documents/3011_Gambling_Dams.pdf (accessed 26 July 2007).

World Commission on Dams and Asianics (1999) *Review of the Performance and Development Effectiveness of Tarbela Dam in the Context of the Indus Basin Scoping Report*, Islamabad and South Africa.

World Commission on Dams Case Studies (2000) *Tarbela Dam and Related Aspects of the Indus River Basin Pakistan Final Draft Report*, World Commission on Dams, www.dams.org/kbase/studies/pk (accessed 24 May 2008).

—— (2000) *Pakistan: The Tarbela Dam and Indus River Basin Final Paper – Executive Summary, November 2000*, www.dams.org/kbase/studies/pk/pk_exec.htm (accessed 1 May 2008).

Wright, D. (2002) 'The BJP and Bangladesh', *South Asia* XXV: 381–93.

7 Intellectual critiques, people's resistance and inter-riparian contestations

Constraints to the power of the state regarding flood control and water management in the Ganges–Brahmaputra–Meghna Delta of Bangladesh

Shapan Adnan

This chapter attempts to identify the nature of constraints faced by a state which undertakes water management programmes on river systems that are also shared with other sovereign states.[1] Such constraints can arise from cross-border contentions as well as internal contestations by concerned social groups. The roles of such internal and external constraints are explored below in the specific context of water management and flood control programmes in the Ganges–Brahmaputra–Meghna (GBM) Delta lying within the boundaries of Bangladesh. The analysis focuses on the roles of (i) intellectual critiques of flood control from academics and professional groups; (ii) resistance to harmful project structures by adversely affected people at the grassroots and wider society; and (iii) interventions in shared rivers by upper riparian states.

The context

Geopolitical and hydrological considerations

During the British colonial period, the territory comprising present-day Bangladesh had constituted the eastern part of the erstwhile province of Bengal. At the end of colonial rule in 1947, it became a province of the newly-formed federal state of Pakistan – initially known as East Bengal and, subsequently, East Pakistan. In 1971, domestic conflicts between a Bengali nationalist movement and the Pakistani state led to a war between India and Pakistan, as a result of which the province of East Pakistan broke apart from the rest of the country and became transformed into the independent state of Bangladesh. Territorially, Bangladesh (East Pakistan) was surrounded by post-British India on virtually all sides, except for Myanmar in the extreme southeast and the Bay of Bengal in the south. As a result of the geo-political reconfigurations in 1947 and 1971, new international borders were imposed across the GBM river basins, creating lines of potential tension between the co-riparian countries of the region. The combined catchment area of these rivers is spread out over five countries: India, China, Nepal, Bhutan and Bangladesh (Bricheri-Colombi and Bradnock 2003: 44–5, Figure 1). Consequently, Bangladesh was in the position of having to share these river basins with different sets of co-riparian countries, as follows:

i the Ganges Basin with India and Nepal;
ii the Brahmaputra Basin with India, China and Bhutan;
iii the Meghna-Barak Basin with India.

Combined catchment area of the Ganges–Brahmaputra–Meghna river systems

The Ganges, Brahmaputra and Meghna Rivers enter Bangladesh across its border with India, and merge within its territory before flowing southwards into the Bay of Bengal. Their combined basins cover approximately 80 per cent of Bangladesh's surface area of 144,000 km^2 (Broadus 1993: 265, 274). In contrast, only 8 per cent of the total drainage area of these river systems actually lies *within* the territory of Bangladesh, i.e. more than 90 per cent of the area is

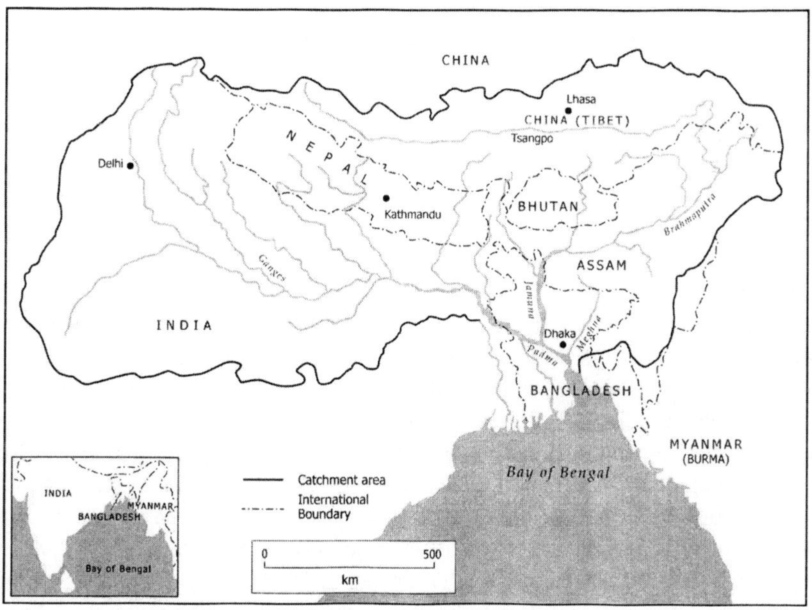

Figure 7.1 Catchment of the Ganges–Brahmaputra–Meghna Rivers.

subject to the sovereign control of other co-riparian states. These strategic geo-political parameters serve to delimit the options and constraints faced by Bangladesh in its attempts to manage the part of the GBM river system lying within its territorial borders. Specifically, upstream interventions on river flows can undermine the hydrological conditions required for the viable operation of flood control, drainage and irrigation works, as well as the technical options of agricultural production in downstream tracts.

Floods and flood control

While physical and technical considerations have tended to dominate the debate on flood control in Bangladesh, the discourses on both sides are informed by social and cultural understandings about ways of utilizing and managing water flows and river systems. At work are contrary visions of the delta as 'wetland' and 'dryland', associated with corresponding technologies and farming systems, espoused by distinct social groups and disciplinary experts.

For the floodplain peasantry of Bangladesh, involved in wet-rice cultivation, normal flooding is an indispensable element in the annual agricultural cycle. It serves to regenerate soil fertility, recharge surface and groundwater reserves, flush out agrochemicals and other pollutants, and facilitate movements of fish for feeding and breeding (Hughes *et al.* 1994: 10–11). From its vantage point, the coming of the monsoon rains, leading to normal flooding, is welcome news and celebrated as such (Boyce 1990). However, *excessive or abnormal* flooding, which is of greater depth and duration, occurs much less frequently. Such severe flooding damages homesteads, standing crops and livestock, while also bringing destitution, starvation and disease in its wake. Floodplain dwellers, therefore, typically want protection against *abnormal* floods, while regarding normal ones as essential and largely beneficial.

Significantly, agronomists and other agricultural scientists have largely endorsed this indigenous view of floodplain management, because it is conducive to ecological sustainability and allows for diversified agricultural production systems, subsuming crop production, livestock and fisheries. This kind of farming system, based on normal flooding, has been regarded as the 'wetland' scenario (BARC, 1989).

As opposed to this, there is the viewpoint which maintains that it is essential to prevent the excessive damages caused by flooding through construction works for flood control and drainage (FCD). In this 'dryland' scenario, floods would be kept out of agricultural fields during the monsoon in order to increase agricultural production. Such structures could optionally include facilities for irrigation (FCD/I) from surface water sources during the dry winter. However, given the overwhelming concern to control floods to the virtual exclusion of other considerations, loss of the beneficial aspects of normal flooding because of flood control structures is largely ignored or underplayed. Such a flawed understanding of the *nature* of the 'flood problem' also leads inexorably to the misconception that structural flood control must represent its 'solution'.

The 'dryland' view has predominated among officials, technocrats and policy-makers of the government and donor agencies, largely influenced by the advice of their consultants and experts. Not surprisingly, this vision has provided the impetus for numerous 'development' interventions in Bangladesh aimed at structural flood control. However, this official view is at variance with the social and cultural perceptions of the floodplain dwellers, and largely ignores the views of concerned professional experts on agricultural and environmental issues (BARC 1989; Adnan 1991). The dryland scenario may be regarded as the product of a technocratic culture in which scientific principles and skills are marshalled to address a narrowly defined 'problem', without adequate concern for the wider picture, particularly the social, economic and environmental impacts of structural works on floodplain dwellers.

Two of the largest programmes of flood control undertaken in the GBM Delta of Bangladesh were the Master Plan of 1964 (in the then East Pakistan) and the Flood Action Plan (FAP) of 1989. Both of these were mammoth undertakings consisting of a large number of individual FCD/I and other projects. As with most water sector programmes in Bangladesh, both these plans were substantially funded by bilateral and/or multilateral donor agencies. The various individual components of these plans were formulated and implemented by multinational corporations, usually working as project contractors and consultants, in collaboration with concerned government agencies, local companies and professional experts. It was this multi-layered development apparatus, consisting of an ensemble of government and donor agencies, business houses and individual experts, which played the most influential role in the formulation and implementation of the dryland strategy embodied in these flood control plans (Adnan 1991; Adnan *et al.* 1992; Hughes *et al.* 1994).

Intellectual contestations

The first major landmark in the intellectual history of these contestations is a study of the causes of catastrophic flooding in North Bengal during 1922 and the possible means of dealing with such occurrences by Prasanta Mahalanobis, a professor of Presidency College, Calcutta. In the results, published in 1927, he noted that decay of important river channels had resulted in deterioration of the drainage system such that flood-water could not easily get out from the low-lying depressions (*beel*) of the region. Significantly, he predicted that while riverbank embankments might prevent overflow for a while, siltation would tend 'to raise the bed of the rivers still further, and thus make the situation much worse in the long run' (Mahalanobis 1927: 6–7). However, Mahalanobis' seminal work and conclusions about the futility of trying to control floods with embankments were generally ignored or forgotten by policy-makers in subsequent decades.

The Master Plan

In 1964, a massive flood control programme was launched under the 'Master Plan' in response to devastating floods during 1954–56 in the then East Pakistan (Adnan *et al.* 1992: 36–9). This huge enterprise consisted of 58 separate FCD/I projects with an estimated cost of US$2.1 billion (in 1964 prices), partly funded by donor agencies such as the World Bank and USAID (EPWAPDA 1964a: 4; Adnan *et al.* 1992: 36).

Significantly, however, the flood control works of the Master Plan were constructed *despite* cautionary advice from concerned experts, including hydraulic engineers. In 1963, General Hardin, a former chairman of the Mississippi River Commission, suggested that the possible impacts of seismic disturbances should be taken into account when designing large structures for flood control in East Pakistan. He also underscored the need for a better understanding of changes in the river system and formation of the active delta (Hardin 1963: 4, cited in Rahman 1989: 46–7). During 1964–65, Professor J. Th. Thijsse of the Netherlands noted that big and unstable rivers such as the Ganges and the Brahmaputra, with massive discharges, could not be regulated (Thijsse 1964: 6–17, 1965: 5–6). He advised the government against construction of embankments alongside these rivers before adequate knowledge had been gathered. Echoing Mahalanobis, he noted that sedimentation in river channels between embankments would lead to the raising of riverbeds and flood levels. He was also apprehensive about the potentially catastrophic consequences of embankment failure, given the deceptive sense of security felt by those living inside the 'protected' areas.

It is important to note that *prevention or reduction of flood damage alone was not sufficient* to justify the massive investment required for the capital-intensive engineering works of FCD/I projects. The economic value of postulated increases in agricultural output also had to be included among the benefits in order to make them viable. The *economic* justification of the projects of the Master Plan was thus based on the claim that agricultural production would rise because of increased cropping intensity, made possible by flood protection during the monsoons (as well as by irrigation during the winter in those projects with such a component) (EPWAPDA 1964b: CIV-1; Adnan *et al.* 1992: 36).

In practice, the agricultural performance of the Master Plan and comparable projects proved to be mixed, and did not necessarily validate such claims of increased output and returns. Subsequent evaluation of a representative sample of 17 completed FCD/I projects found that, while some had attained economic rates of return of more than 30 per cent, about half had rates of return below the required level of 12 per cent (World Bank and GoB 1992: 20; Adnan and Sufiyan 1993: 46). Such variable economic performance served to fuel controversy about the purported agricultural claims used to justify flood control projects.

The Flood Action Plan

Nearly a quarter of a century after the Master Plan, the Flood Action Plan (FAP) was launched in 1989, in response to the catastrophic floods in Bangladesh during 1987 and 1988. A large consortium of multilateral and bilateral donors, led and coordinated by the World Bank, provided funds for the various components of FAP (World Bank 1989b: 23, Annex A; World Bank 1989c; Adnan 1991: 8–10).[2] Even though the cost of the initial phase of 'studies' amounted to a modest US$136 million (FPCO 1992a; Adnan *et al.* 1992: 8–9), estimates of

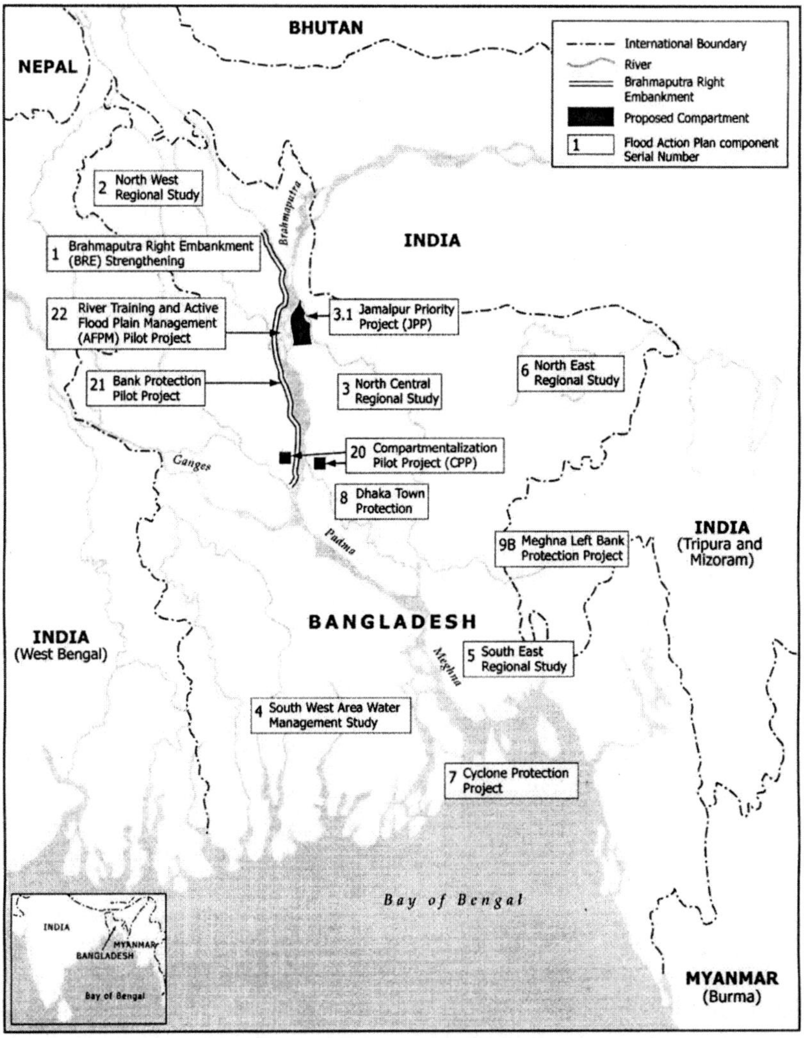

Figure 7.2 The Bangladesh Flood Action Plan of 1989.

longer-term construction and implementation costs ranged up to several billion US dollars (CCEC 1994: 15).

At its origin, the Flood Action Plan had 26 distinct elements, consisting of 11 main components and 15 'supporting studies'. Unlike the Master Plan, the FAP incorporated *non-structural* components which reflected limited attempts at finding ways of 'living with' floods for the floodplain peasantry. However, the contents of the plan left no doubt that its central concern was to *control trans-boundary river floods through structural works*: 'Safe conveyance of the large cross border flows to the Bay of Bengal by channelling it through the major rivers with the help of embankments on both sides' (World Bank 1989c: 3; Adnan 1991: 11–13).

Sites of major components of the Bangladesh FAP of 1989

In terms of technical innovation, the FAP put forward the idea of 'controlled flooding and drainage' (CFD) based on structures termed 'compartments' (Adnan *et al.* 1992: 75; Hughes *et al.* 1994: 42). Despite this refinement, however, the strategy was essentially a sophisticated variant of structural flood control. The central core of the plan aimed at constructing an extensive honey-comb of interlinked compartments across the GBM Delta. In order to work, however, this approach depended crucially upon 'beneficiary participation' in the form of *cooperation of the local people*, who were required to share the responsibility of compartment management by regulating inflows and outflows of water. It is striking that, despite the need for 'beneficiary participation', the entire process of plan formulation took place *without* any consultation with the floodplain dwellers – the supposed beneficiaries – or the broad spectrum of professional and public opinion within Bangladesh (Adnan 1991: 94). Implementation of the plan was initiated by donor agencies working closely with the then government of Bangladesh – a thinly disguised military regime headed by President (General) Ershad, which lacked legitimacy and popular support.

As with the Master Plan, the economic justification for the massive investments required by the FAP was based upon claims of inducing agricultural growth, over and above the benefits of flood control. However, since expansion of rice production during the dry winter had been already attained through groundwater irrigation, a new rationale for investing in flood control works was called for. This was formulated in terms of a particularly cumbersome demographic-cum-agronomic argument. It was claimed that since irrigation-based dry winter cropping would soon reach a technical limit, there was no other way of meeting the increasing demand for grain of a growing population than expanding rice output during the monsoons (*aman* paddy) through flood control works. However, this purported rationale was shown to be largely untenable on both logical and empirical grounds (Hughes *et al.* 1994: 56, Box 11). It was pointed out that Bangladesh could make use of international trade to import rice rather than necessarily having to produce it, that meeting the varied nutritional needs of the growing population required more than increasing rice output, and that flood control was not the only means of increasing rice production during the monsoons, nor was it necessarily the most cost-effective (e.g. long-stemmed, deep-water, high-yielding rice varieties could grow and 'float' with rising flood waters) (Catling 1992). Furthermore, the FAP approach simply ignored the fact that conversion of wetlands into 'drylands' through flood control structures for expansion of rice monoculture during the monsoons would lead to the loss of indigenous varieties of both rice and non-rice crops, as well as damage to open-water capture fisheries, the primary source of animal protein and vitamins for the rural poor (Adnan and Sufiyan 1993).

Both the flood control strategy and economic justification of FAP were strongly contested by academics and researchers from home and abroad. A discussion forum of agricultural scientists, economists, and other social scientists, organized by the Bangladesh Agricultural Research Council (BARC), strongly contested the FAP strategy of transforming Bangladesh's floodplains from 'wetlands' to 'drylands' by excluding surface water during the monsoon period (BARC 1989: 2–3; RAS 1995a: 6–9). Claims about increased rice production during the *monsoon* season due to flood control were regarded as exaggerated, thereby challenging the very basis of the economic justification of FAP. The discussion also sounded a cautionary note against manipulation of the environment of the delta without adequate understanding of the potential impacts on floodplain ecology, inclusive of fishery and forestry. This critique was subsequently circulated in the form of a policy brief entitled *Floodplain Agriculture.* In the signed foreword to this publication, Dr M.M. Rahman, BARC's Executive Vice-Chairman, echoed the earlier views of Mahalanobis, Hardin and Thijsse by recommending that there should be no rush into massive investment in embankment-centred flood control without more considered assessment of alternative ways of coping with floods (BARC 1989: 1; RAS 1995a: 6–7).

The Ershad regime's response to this intellectual critique from BARC – a public sector research organization largely funded by government grants and foreign aid – was swift and ruthless. The Executive Vice-Chairman was summarily retired on a flimsy technical excuse (Adnan 1991: 94–6; RAS 1995a: 2–5). The expatriate and Bangladeshi professionals closely involved with drafting the policy brief were marginalized in various ways by concerned government and donor agencies, as well as the networks of multinational and local corporations with huge stakes in the contracts being handed out for FAP implementation (Hughes *et al.* 1994: 47–50).[3] The suppression of the BARC critique was symptomatic of the generally authoritarian response towards criticisms of the FAP by the military regime controlling state power (Boyce 1990: 419–28; Adnan 1991).

However, after the fall of the autocratic Ershad regime in December 1990 following widespread popular protests, a 'National Task Force on the Flood Action Plan' was set up, consisting of Bangladeshi academics, engineers, geographers, economists and other professionals (Adnan 1991: 96, 124–5). The report of the Task Force was severely critical of the flood control strategy of the FAP, as well as the harsh suppression of dissenting views by the preceding regime (Task Force 1991: 370–1). Furthermore, within the first few years of launching the FAP, a sizeable number of critical reviews of the plan entered the international development discourse (Boyce 1990; Dalal-Clayton 1990; Counsellor and Reinhardt 1992; Custers 1992; Kvaloy 1994; Hughes *et al.* 1994). Ironically, as the reports of the FAP projects began to become available during the early 1990s, their research findings acknowledged that the people of the country generally perceived floods as *beneficial*, and did *not necessarily* want protection against flooding unless it was very severe (World Bank and GoB 1992: 15–21; FAP 14, 1992: i). Reviews by the FAP studies concluded that critical problems encountered by earlier FCD projects were in part due to the 'failure to involve local people in planning, design and operation' (FAP 13, 1992: S-13–14; World Bank and GoB 1992: 21).

Resistance by affected people and wider contestations

Flood control structures built by the Master Plan and other programmes did not always provide protection from floods and, in some cases, made the situation worse through drainage congestion or structural collapse (World Bank 1989a: 13; Adnan 1991: 71–81; Hughes *et al.* 1994: 22). Such constructions generally had adverse impacts on open-water capture fisheries and river transport, affecting occupational groups such as professional fishermen and boatmen, as well as ordinary peasant households catching fish or plying boats for everyday needs (FAP 12, 1992; Adnan *et al.* 1992: 47–51; Adnan and Sufiyan, 1993: 38–41; Hughes *et al.* 1994: 90–1). Indeed, these were symptomatic of *second-generation problems created* by FCD projects, which made the supposed 'beneficiaries' worse off compared to their pre-project situation.

Faced with such adverse impacts of a project, the affected groups gave vent to their resentment and anger against the state and the project management in various ways. Even if they were powerless to do anything else, people could still *refuse to cooperate*, for instance by not surrendering land to the state for construction of embankments (Adnan *et al.* 1992: 45–6). Furthermore, when the actual or apprehended damage from river floods or FCD structures became sufficiently great, the floodplain peasantry had a tradition of taking matters into its own hands. Ahmed Kamal (2006: 207–9) documents an attempt by the peasantry in southern Bangladesh during 1948 to implement its own solution to flooding by cutting canals to shorten meandering river courses, despite opposition from the state and its security forces.

The classic instance of such people's intervention took the form of breaching flood control embankments at critical points in the expectation of relieving waterlogging caused by drainage congestion. These acts, termed 'public cuts' in official parlance, were viewed as illegal by the state and could lead to prosecution of those responsible in the courts of law (World Bank 1989b: 8; World Bank and GoB 1992). Despite the formal illegality of the act, however, embankments were deliberately breached by local people who believed, rightly or wrongly, that this would help to drain out accumulated water from their affected areas (FAP 13, 1992; Adnan 1991: 98–101). The nature and complexities of such contestations between the state and the floodplain peasantry may be illustrated by relevant instances of actual or threatened public cuts.

Public cuts in Chalan Beel Polder-D

Polder-D is one of several polders constructed in the low-lying Chalan Beel area in northern Bangladesh (a polder consists of an area protected from flooding by a peripheral 'ring embankment' which completely surrounds it). During the severe floods of 1987, the homesteads and standing crops of the villages *outside* the polder were damaged by prolonged inundation by floodwater, while the area *inside* the polder remained protected. After their petitions and procedural protests to the concerned authorities failed to produce any effective remedy, the affected villagers mobilized themselves and made several breaches in the peripheral embankment of the polder (BWDB 1987: 48–9; Adnan *et al.* 1992: 47–8). While these initial public cuts relieved drainage congestion outside the polder, they also led to inundation of the area *inside* the polder. Consequently, the people there had no option but to breach the embankment at other points to flush the flood waters outside, producing a 'chain reaction' of public cuts.

This was not an exceptional instance, and dozens of public cuts were made in the FCD structures of various northern districts of Bangladesh during the catastrophic floods of 1987, as well as in other parts of the country in later years (BWDB 1987: 48–66; Adnan *et al.* 1992: 47–8). Since these were illegal acts, groups making public cuts generally tended to do so at times and places where they would not be easily observed or opposed (e.g. under the cover of darkness, in remote sections of embankments).

Mass mobilization in Beel Dakatia

However, there were also circumstances which led to public cuts being made *openly*, in clear defiance of state authority. One of the most remarkable instances of such mass action took place in Beel Dakatia, covering the area of Polder 25 in southwestern Bangladesh (Adnan 1991: 72). This had been built under the Coastal Embankment Project (CEP) of the Master Plan, which had aimed at reducing salinity inside the polder by controlling tidal inflows from surrounding rivers (EPWAPDA 1968: 33–5; Adnan *et al.* 1992: 49–50). These objectives had appeared to be successful in the short run but, from 1982, the polder began to display technical problems leading to drainage congestion. By 1990, nearly 40,000 acres of land, including homesteads, had become perennially waterlogged and crops could be no longer grown in the submerged fields. Without agricultural production and employment, the local peasantry faced chronic hunger and destitution. Their appeals, petitions and other forms of procedural protest did not lead to any effective remedial measures being taken by the concerned authorities. In mid-1990, the 'Beel Dakatia Action Committee' was formed as a public platform to protest against the state's inaction and take initiatives to solve the problem on their own. This committee represented a broad-based coalition of affected people and local social groups, members of local government councils (Union and Upazilla Parishads), local branches of national political parties and peasant associations, as well as various other sympathetic groups and organizations.

The Action Committee put forward a 'people's solution' to the problem which proposed to breach the peripheral embankments at certain points so as to re-connect the waterlogged area inside the polder with the tidal rivers outside. It was predicted that this would lead to resumption of siltation through tidal activity, thereby raising the ground level inside the polder and enabling gravity flow to drain out the waterlogged area. When the committee called for a mass mobilization (*mahashamabesh*) of the local population in support of this programme on 17 August 1990, the administration attempted to stop it by bringing in armed police and imposing a curfew prohibiting public assembly during the preceding 24 hours (Adnan *et al.* 1992: 51). Nonetheless, thousands of men and women came out in procession, defying the curfew despite the presence of armed police. Faced with this massive show of popular resistance, the administration decided to hold fire and back down. A month later, on 18 September 1990, the embankments of the polder were publicly breached by masses of local people, while the agencies of the state stood by without attempting to intervene.

The resumption of tidal activity did lead to siltation and the formation of a small delta in the erstwhile waterlogged area adjoining one of the cuts (FAP 4, 1992: 2–29; Haskoning *et al.* 1992: 8, Appendix B; Adnan *et al.* 1992: 52). Predictably, however, this successful challenge to the 'modern knowledge and technology' of the state and the donor-funded development apparatus, based on the traditional knowledge system and active resistance of the floodplain peasantry, was not allowed to exist for very long. A new project was initiated soon after by the government and donor agencies to 'fix' the problems of Beel Dakatia, as part of which the public cuts made by popular resistance were plugged. This was reflective of a process of *continuing contestation* between floodplain dwellers and the state, donor agencies and the development apparatus.

The mass mobilization in Beel Dakatia represents one of the rare instances of *open confrontation* between the floodplain peasantry and the state. However, even though hundreds of other public cuts – such as those in the Chalan Beel polders – took place *covertly*, these also embodied people's contestation of the state's authority and monopoly power over management of the delta. Indeed, public cuts were the most powerful expression of the fact that floodplain dwellers not only had their own social and cultural understandings of how water should be used and managed, but also possessed the capability to act against harmful flood control structures to protect their own interests – if necessary, in open defiance of state power.

Contestations regarding the Jamalpur Priority Project (JPP)

The JPP (or FAP 3.1) of the FAP, funded by France and the European Commission, aimed at constructing embankments on the left bank of the Brahmaputra–

Jamuna. However, since there was already an embankment on the right bank, construction of a new one on the opposite bank was likely to raise flood levels in the river channels lying in between. There were nearly half a million people living on islands and sandbars on this stretch of the Brahmaputra–Jamuna, the braided channels of which were several kilometres wide. Their homesteads and agricultural lands were likely to be partially submerged by the expected rise in flood level resulting from construction of the new embankment (Adnan *et al.* 1992: 83–5). This prospective scenario aroused public concern in the donor countries belonging to the European Union when a television documentary was screened, highlighting the threat to local inhabitants from the JPP's embankment construction. Furthermore, representations on behalf of the local people regarding this potential threat were made at the International Water Tribunal in Amsterdam during 1991–92 (Counsellor 1991; Hughes *et al.* 1994: 51–3, fn. 39). In parallel to the above, activists among the local people made them aware of the threat of a rise in the flood level in the Brahmaputra–Jamuna that would result from construction of the embankment by the JPP. Members of parliament in the affected area were lobbied and leaders of local self-government institutions mobilized. As a result, by late 1992, some sections of the local inhabitants began to oppose the JPP and threatened to cut open the embankment, if it were to be built (Adnan *et al.* 1992: 84–5).

As noted above, there was little that the government and donor agencies could have done to protect the embankment of the JPP, had it been constructed, against public cuts made by aggrieved people. Without the agreement and cooperation of the local inhabitants, the viability of the project remained uncertain. Partly as a result of such considerations, construction works of the JPP were never begun, despite it being the 'priority' project of the FAP earmarked for speedy implementation. This outcome is indicative of the way in which counter pressure exerted by the threat of people's resistance could undermine unilateral plans to impose flood control projects, thereby also helping to bring about shifts in government and donor policies from afar.

Contestations about the Compartmentalization Pilot Project (CPP)

The CPP (or FAP 20) funded by the Netherlands and Germany, was intended to test the structural and institutional viability of the concept of compartmentalization. This involved not only the construction of an experimental (pilot) compartment in Tangail, but also setting up the social-institutional arrangements necessary for obtaining the *collaboration of the local people* in its operation and maintenance, i.e. 'beneficiary participation'. Furthermore, since compartmentalization was also intended to be the principal means of expanding rice production during the monsoons through the technology of 'controlled flooding and drainage', the project was absolutely crucial for *validating the postulated economic justification* of the FAP.

However, during the public consultation process at the outset, the people of Tangail almost unanimously expressed preference for measures to *improve drainage* to facilitate growing crops during the dry winter, rather than flood control for rice production during the monsoons, as specified in the project objectives (FAP 20, 1992: 35, 89–91). Paradoxically, after finding out people's preferences, the public consultation process was abruptly stopped by the intervention of central FAP management, its international panel of experts, as well as representatives of one of the donor agencies (Adnan *et al.* 1992: 158–69). The latter insisted that, even though the local people preferred simple drainage options, the project must continue with the predefined objective of constructing the physical structures of the compartment (FPCO 1992b: 2; Adnan *et al.* 1992: 74–81, 160). This turn of events in the CPP was, however, hardly surprising, given that the strategy of the FAP as a whole depended crucially upon building and operating this prototype so as to 'prove' that it was technically and institutionally viable. Also at stake were potential investments worth billions of dollars in large-scale replication of compartments.

However, the situation began to change after an independent research report on people's participation in the FAP investigated and exposed the way in which people's preferences and 'beneficiary involvement' in the CPP had been arbitrarily sidelined by the interference of government and donor officials and the experts advising them (Adnan *et al.* 1992: 74–81). Once brought out into the public domain, the matter was taken up in reports of other researchers, publicized by activists in NGOs and advocacy networks, and transmitted through the local and international media. Furthermore, public demonstrations against the CPP by people living in Tangail town and surrounding villages began to take place soon after construction work on the compartment was begun in 1992–93, and continued despite threats and intimidation by interest groups having a stake in the project (Hughes *et al.* 1994: 51, fn.; Kvaløy 1994).

Contestations in the national and international arena

During the early 1990s, opposition to the FAP expanded from localized protests in project impact areas to coordinated campaigns by broad-based coalitions of affected people, NGOs and other support organizations from home and abroad. At the national level, this was manifested in growing numbers of professional groups and associations declaring their opposition to the FAP's flood control strategy (Hughes *et al.* 1994: 50). In parallel, the press, radio and television in various countries of Europe and North America broadcast programmes on issues raised by flooding and flood control in Bangladesh, which served to influence public opinion and policy-making in the FAP donor countries.

These processes at the local, national and international levels paved the ground for a landmark conference on the FAP at the premises of the European Parliament in Strasbourg over 27–28 May 1993, held under the auspices of the Green Party and organized by a coalition of political organizations and NGOs in Europe. Face-to-face debates took place between (i) FAP critics and activists from Bangladesh and (ii) representatives of donor agencies, inclusive of the World Bank, the European Commission and several European governments

(CCEC 1994: 9–19). One of the significant political fallouts of the conference was the adoption of a resolution on the FAP by the European Parliament on 24 June 1993 which was critical of its flood control strategy and likely adverse impacts on the people and environment of the floodplains (CCEC 1994: 18, 137–8; Hughes *et al.* 1994: 50, 93–4). It explicitly urged that 'no major physical works in the area of water management be implemented in rural areas in the short run, including the area of the JPP (FAP 3.1)'. It also called upon the European Commission and member states of the European Union to reconsider their involvement in the various FAP projects. At the end of the conference, the International Flood Action Plan Campaign Coalition was formed, consisting of a large number of NGOs and research institutions as well as people's and political organizations, based in Europe and North America (CCEC 1994: 139–40; Hughes *et al.* 1994: 50).

Policy reversals

In early 1999, a new National Water Policy (NWP) was announced by the government of Bangladesh (MOWR 1999). Within this policy framework, a long-term National Water Management Plan (NWMP) (WARPO 1998: 4) was formulated in 1998, followed by a detailed draft of its development strategy in mid-2000 (WARPO 2000a, 2000b) and an official summary in mid-2001 (WARPO 2001). Prepared by consultants appointed by the government and donor agencies, these documents provided *official acknowledgement of the failure of the flood control strategy*, as embodied in the projects of the Master Plan and the FAP.

To illustrate, the performance of FCD projects was found to have been quite negative on multiple counts, displaying a host of technical, environmental and social complexities, as well as unsatisfactory economic performance and significant adverse social effects (WARPO 2000b: 235–40). Evaluation of the CPP in Tangail concluded that compartmentalization is 'not an attractive option' because of the high costs as well as the operational and institutional difficulties encountered. This meant that the foremost technological and institutional innovation proposed by the FAP had not proved to be viable. The NWP declared that the scope of flood control works in the future would be drastically reduced and that no new FCD projects would be undertaken in rural-agricultural areas (except in the coastal belt) (MOWR 1999: 4; WARPO 2000a: 36, 2000b: 209). In sharp contrast to the erstwhile preoccupation with expansion of *rice monoculture* for attaining domestic self-sufficiency in food grain, the NWP explicitly supported the strengthening of 'crop diversification programmes for efficient water utilization' (MOWR 1999: 8). This policy shift also signified that the purported economic rationale of the flood control strategy, based on claims about attaining *food-grain self-sufficiency*, had been undermined by the disappointing agricultural performance of FCD projects.

Upstream interventions on cross-border river flows

Constraints to Bangladesh's water management and flood control programmes also arose from inter-riparian contestations regarding the sharing and management of common rivers. Around 56 rivers, large and small, flow into Bangladesh from India, when account is taken of the tributaries of the three major rivers as well as other minor rivers (Adel 2001: 357, Fig. 1). The upper tracts of some of these also pass through Nepal, Bhutan and/or China. Structures for upstream interventions on water flows have already been constructed, or are being currently designed, on many of these international rivers, including the Ganges, the Brahmaputra, the Teesta and the Barak (Islam 1992: 211–12). It is estimated that India makes upstream diversion of water on nearly 30 of its common rivers with Bangladesh (Adel 2001: 366, Fig. 10). Nepal and China also have existing or planned structures for intervening in the flows of some of these common rivers. Since Bangladesh is the lowest riparian in all cases, such interventions are beyond its control, putting it in a weak bargaining position in relation to these upper riparian states.

The construction of hydroelectricity dams and FCD and irrigation works on upper tracts of the Ganges, Brahmaputra, Meghna and their tributaries, in sites located in India, Nepal, Bhutan or China, can seriously affect the flow of common rivers entering Bangladesh, potentially undermining the hydrological conditions required for water management and flood control projects. This is illustrated by the decline in volume of water flow at the Hardinge Bridge (Islam 1992: 214, Table 1) and the general worsening of dry season water shortage and saline intrusion in the southwestern parts of Bangladesh after India began to divert water at the Farakka Barrage on the Ganges from 1975 (Bradnock and Saunders 2000: 75; Chapman 1995: 175–6). Another case in point is the massive Tipaimukh Dam for generating hydroelectricity, located in the upstream tract of the Meghna–Barak in northeastern India (Thakuria 2003). It is apprehended by Bangladesh that operation of the project by Indian power-generating agencies would result in the worsening of water *shortage* in its groundwater-short eastern regions during the dry season, as well as *increased* downstream flooding during the monsoons (Talukdar 2004).

Actual or prospective scenarios such as the above are the result of the exclusively *self-oriented* water utilization plans pursued by each of the co-riparian countries, with little concern for the potential impacts on the others (Crow and Singh 2000: 1922–3). Nor is there any serious effort at integrated basin-wide water management, involving some or all of the concerned co-riparian countries for their mutual benefit. One of the factors exacerbating this impasse has been India's long-standing insistence on conducting *only bilateral* negotiations with each of the other co-riparian states, while excluding multilateral ones (Crow and Singh 2000: 1910). Consequently, inter-riparian relations in the region have been tense and sour, largely characterized by the features of an adversarial two-party zero-sum game.

However, it is evident that water management and flood control programmes by Bangladesh within its own territorial limits stand a much better chance of success if these are not undertaken 'single-handedly', as had been the case with the Master Plan and the FAP. Rather, effective agreement on transboundary flows of common rivers with the upper riparian countries, particularly India, provide a less uncertain basis for undertaking such programmes. Since 1995, plans and policies of the Bangladesh government have acknowledged the need for the country to enter into collaborative arrangements with upper riparian states to 'share the water resources of the international rivers to mitigate floods and augment flows of water during the dry season' (MOWR 1999: 2–3; FPCO 1995: 5–6, 10–12; Adnan and Sufiyan 1995: 56–7). It was also noted that the inflows of 'all transboundary rivers need to be secured by treaties' between the concerned co-riparian states (WARPO 2000a: 53).

It was at this conjuncture that India began to show a greater readiness to negotiate agreements with its co-riparians and to shift marginally from its long-standing insistence on bilateralism. Thus, during 1996, India signed four international treaties with three of its neighbours (Nepal, Bhutan and Bangladesh), and in 1997 it took part in a meeting with the same three countries to consider 'forming a sub-regional group within the SAARC framework that would include the shared rivers of the four countries' (Crow and Singh 2000: 1917–20). One of these agreements was the 1996 Ganges Water Treaty between Bangladesh and India which, in a formal sense, demonstrated the benefits of negotiated water-sharing between co-riparian states (Bradnock and Saunders 2000: 76; Kamal 1997).

However, in terms of actual results, Bangladesh fared worse in terms of its share of Ganges flow in the 1996 treaty compared to the previous one signed in 1977 (Tanzeema and Faisal 2001). Furthermore, up to 2007, no comparable agreements were reached on sharing the waters of any of the other common rivers from which India was making upstream diversions, so that Bangladesh continued to face uncertainty about the timing and volume of such cross-border river flows reaching its territory. While, in theory, collaborative sharing of water flows with co-riparian states, particularly India, is the best option for Bangladesh, in practice geopolitical constraints arising from multiple sovereignties on common rivers have made it extremely hard to realize (MOWR 1999: 3). Realistically, as the lowest riparian in the GBM delta, 'Bangladesh has to live with the second best option of trying to manage her water resources as best as she can till (international) basin planning becomes a reality' (Huda 2005: 128).

Concluding remarks

This brief review of the contestations regarding water management and flood control in the GBM Delta of Bangladesh indicates the ways in which the powers of a state can be constrained by both internal and external factors. State-sponsored programmes were called into question not only by intellectual critiques but also by resistance of the floodplain peasantry, while upper riparian interventions in some instances undermined the hydrological and technical conditions necessary for such country-specific programmes to operate in a viable manner. Significantly, some of these constraining factors interacted in practice, making their combined resistance to state power that much more effective.

Even though academics and professionals did provide incisive critiques of the technical aspects of the Master Plan and the FAP, these views were either ignored or marginalized by the government, donors and corporate agencies concerned. Intellectual critiques became effective only when these were disseminated to the general public in simplified forms and began to inform the activities of affected social groups, people's organizations, NGOs, advocacy networks, and other concerned social and political actors. Most crucial was the emergence of organized resistance among the floodplain peasantry in the project impact areas, which could then be picked up and transmitted more widely by advocacy campaigns and the media in Bangladesh and the donor countries. However, the government's typical response to instances of intellectual dissent and grassroots movements by affected people was to crush such resistance through the exercise of state power – if necessary, through the deployment of security forces. Even international donor agencies, the prime movers of projects and the paymasters of multinational and local consultants and contractors, were not particularly averse to showing their disapproval of critical dissent by pulling on the purse strings.

Underlying these multi-layered contentions were the opposed cultural views about the use and management of water espoused by (i) the floodplain peasantry and (ii) the planners and policy-makers. People's cultural understanding about floods and water use were pitted against a technocratic culture of flood control and river management, which exuded confidence in the powers of modern technology, but had little understanding of the traditional knowledge system and resilience of the floodplain peasantry. It was this cultural divide that was embodied in the contestation between 'wetland' and 'dryland' visions of managing the delta and dealing with floods.

Although the drastic policy changes regarding flood control were eventually made by the government and donor agencies, the forces initiating and driving them can be traced back to contestations at the grassroots between the state and people adversely affected by flood control structures. Pre-eminent among the forms of resistance of the floodplain dwellers were the public cuts of embankments, which the state and the development apparatus were powerless to prevent or stop. Indeed, it was the spectre of public cuts that served to bring about the eventual realization among government and donor agencies – perhaps not without elements of enlightened self-interest – that the long-term sustainability of project structures could not be ensured unless people in the impact areas also felt that these were beneficial to themselves (Adnan *et al.* 1992: 57, S-2–S-4).

Another set of independent factors which contributed to shifts in Bangladesh's country-oriented water management and flood control policies arose from the constraints resulting from interventions in international rivers by upper riparian states. Given the virtual absence of collaborative planning among co-riparian states, upstream diversion of water through barrages and hydroelectricity projects not only undermined the viability of water management in

Bangladesh, but also provided upstream states with political leverage and bargaining chips against the lowest riparian. Furthermore, contestations about cross-border river flows did not take place in isolation but rather as one element among many in the total matrix of operating hydrological, economic and political contentions between the co-riparian states. It was the overall resultant of these forces which determined the eventual outcomes.

Notes

1 The discussion draws upon my earlier work (Adnan 1991, 2006a, 2006b; Adnan *et al.* 1992). Many of the ideas put forward here were developed through years of fruitful interaction with Bruce Currey, Aminur Rahman, Eirik G. Jansen and Khushi Kabir. The present version owes much to the interest of Heather Goodall and to help with access to relevant literature from Ahmed Kamal and Shithi Kamal.

2 Among the multilateral agencies were the World Bank (IDA), UNDP, Asian Development Bank and the European Commission, while the bilateral donors included France, Japan, the Netherlands, Germany, Denmark, Canada, the UK, the USA, Sweden, Finland and Switzerland.

3 Dr Bruce Currey, who had played a key role in organizing the forum and bringing out and circulating *Floodplain Agriculture*, was pressurized to leave his position at BARC by the international foundation funding him.

Bibliography

Adel, M.M. (2001) 'Effect on Water Resources from Upstream Water Diversion in the Ganges Basin', *Journal of Environmental Quality* 30, March–April: 356–68.

Adnan, S. (1991) *Floods, People and the Environment: Institutional Aspects of Flood Protection Programmes in Bangladesh, 1990*, Dhaka: Research and Advisory Services (RAS).

—— (2006a) 'Le retrait de la politique de lutte contre les inundations dans le delta du Ganges–Brahmpoutre au Bangladesh', *Herodote: Revue de geographie et de geopolitique* (121): 95–118. Special issue *The Geopolitics of Land and Water Management in the Deltas of the Asian Monsoon Belt.*

—— (2006b) 'Explaining the Retreat from Flood Control in the Ganges–Brahmaputra–Meghna Delta of Bangladesh', paper presented at the Department of History, Kolkata (Calcutta) University, 6–8 March.

Adnan, S. and Sufiyan, A.M. (1993) *State of the FAP: Contradictions between Policy Objectives and Plan Implementation*, Dhaka: RAS.

—— (1995) 'A Trojan Horse? Review of the Latest FAP "Strategy" Report, March 1995', *Monitor* 1(1), April, Dhaka.

Adnan, S., Barrett, A., Alam, S.M.N. and Brustinow, A. (1992) *People's Participation, NGOs and the Flood Action Plan: An Independent Review*, Dhaka: RAS.

Bangladesh Agricultural Research Council (BARC) (1989) *Floodplain Agriculture*, Dhaka: BARC.

Bangladesh Water Development Board (BWDB) (1987) *Flood in Bangladesh 1987: Investigation, Review and Recommendation for Flood Control*, Dhaka: Ministry of Irrigation, Water Development and Flood Control.

Boyce, J.K. (1990) 'Birth of a Megaproject: Political Economy of Flood Control in Bangladesh', *Environmental Management* 14(4): 419–28.

Bradnock, R.W. and Saunders, P.L. (2000) 'Sea-level Rise, Subsidence and Submergence: The Political Ecology of Environmental Change in the Bengal Delta', in P. Stott and S. Sullivan (eds) *Political Ecology: Science, Myth and Power*, London and New York: Arnold and Oxford University Press.

Bricheri-Colombi, S. and Bradnock, R.W. (2003) 'Geopolitics, Water and Development in South Asia: Cooperative Development in the Ganges–Brahmaputra Delta', *The Geographical Journal* 169(1), March: 43–64.

Broadus, J.M. (1993) 'Possible Impacts of, and Adjustments to, Sea Level Rise: The Cases of Bangladesh and Egypt', in R.A. Warrick, E.M. Barrow and T.M.L. Wigley (eds) *Climate and Sea Level Change: Observations, Projections and Implications*, Cambridge: Cambridge University Press.

Catling, D. (1992) *Rice in Deep Water*, London: McMillan, International Rice Research Institute.

Chapman, G.P. (1995) 'Environmental Myth as International Politics: The Problems of the Bengal Delta', in G.P. Chapman and M. Thompson (eds) *Water and the Quest for Sustainable Development in the Ganges Valley*, Calcutta: Mansell Publishing.

Coordinating Committee European Conference (CCEC) (1994) *The Proceedings of the European Conference on the Flood Action Plan in Bangladesh: European Parliament – Strasbourg, May 27–28, 1993*, Amsterdam: CCEC on the Flood Action Plan in Bangladesh, BPSC.

Counsellor, R.W. (1991) *Case Submission to the International Water Tribunal Concerning Bangladesh Flood Action Plan and Flood Protection 1 Project*, Dhaka, (mimeo).

Counsellor, R.W. and Reinhardt, D. (1992) 'Flood Action Plan in Bangladesh', paper presented at the Third Workshop of the European Network of Bangladesh Studies, Copenhagen, 28–30 August.

Crow, B. and Singh, N. (2000) 'Impediments and Innovation in International Rivers: The Waters of South Asia', *World Development* 28(11): 1907–25.

Custers, P. (1992) 'Banking on a Flood-free Future? Flood Mismanagement in Bangladesh', *The Ecologist* 22(5), September/October.

Dalal-Clayton, D.B. (1990) *Environmental Aspects of the Bangladesh Flood Action Plan*, Issues Series No. 1, *Sustainable Agriculture Programme*, London, International Institute for Environment and Development (IIED).

EPWAPDA = East Pakistan Water and Power Development Authority

East Pakistan Water and Development Authority (EPWAPDA) (1964a) *Master Plan, Main Report: Vol. I*, International Engineering Company Inc. (IECO), Dhaka: EPWAPDA, December 1964.

—— (1964b) *Master Plan, Supplement C: Economics*, International Engineering Company Inc. (IECO), Dhaka: EPWAPDA, December 1964.

—— (1968) *Coastal Embankment Project, Engineering and Economic Evaluation: Volumes 1 and 2*, Leedshill-De Leuw Engineers, December.

FAP 4 (1992) *Inception Report*, Southwest Area Water Resources Management Project, Halcrow *et al.*, Government of Bangladesh, January.

FAP 12 (1992) *Final Report, Vol. 1: Main Report*, Hunting Technical *et al.*, Government of Bangladesh, February.

FAP 13 (1992) *Final Report, Vol. 1: Main Report*, Hunting Technical *et al.*, Government of Bangladesh, March.

FAP 14 (1992) *Draft Final Report: Preliminary Review Draft*, ISPAN, Government of Bangladesh, July.

FAP 20 (1992) *Tangail Compartmentalization Pilot Project, Interim Report, Annex 1.1: Household Survey, Appendix 2: Questionnaires – English*, Euroconsult *et al.*, Government of Bangladesh, September.

Flood Plan Coordination Organization (FPCO) (1992a) *Bangladesh Flood Action Plan Review Report*, Dhaka: Ministry of Irrigation, Water Resources and Flood Control, September, (mimeo).

—— (1992b) *Compartmentalization Pilot Project, FAP-20: Minutes of the Meeting on Concepts of Compartmentalization*, Memo No. 1504/FPCO/A-020/90, dated 15 July.

—— (1995) *Bangladesh Water and Flood Management Strategy*, Dhaka: Ministry of Irrigation, Water Resources and Flood Control, March.

Government of Bangladesh (GoB) and Netherlands Technical Assistance Programme (NTAP) (1989) *Report of the Project Identification Mission*, Compartmentalization Pilot Project, Dhaka, December 1989.

Haskoning *et al.* (1992) *Second Coastal Embankment Rehabilitation Project, Inception Report Draft*, Government of Bangladesh and Asian Development Bank, June.

Huda, A.T.M. Shamsul (2005) 'Integrated Water Resources Management in Bangladesh: An Assessment', in A.K. Biswas, O. Varis and C. Tortajada (eds), *Integrated Water Resources Management in South and Southeast Asia*, New Delhi: Oxford University Press.

Hughes, R., Adnan, S. and Dalal-Clayton, B. (1994) *Floodplains or Flood Plans? A Review of Approaches to Water Management in Bangladesh*, London: International Institute for Environment and Development (IIED) and Dhaka: RAS.

Islam, N. (1992) 'Indo-Bangladesh Common Rivers: The Impact on Bangladesh', *Contemporary South Asia* 1(2): 203–25.

Jansen, E. (1992) 'Interest Groups and Development Assistance: The Case of Bangladesh', *Forum for Development Studies*, No. 2, NUPI, Oslo.

Kamal, A. (2006) 'Living with Water: Bangladesh since Ancient Times', in T. Tevdt and E. Jakobsson (eds) *A History of Water. Volume 1: Water Control and River Biographies*, London: I.B. Tauris.

Kamal, S. (1997) 'The Politics of Water Sharing: A New Shift in Indo-Bangladesh Relations', dissertation submitted to Swarthmore College (mimeo).

Kvaløy, F. (1994) *The Role of NGOs and People's Participation in Relation to Bangladesh Flood Action Plan: Special Focus on the Compartmentalisation Pilot Project in Tangail*, Ministry of Foreign Affairs, Oslo.

Mahalanobis, P.C. (1927) *Report on Rainfall and Floods in North Bengal 1870–1922*, Calcutta: Ministry of Water Resources.

Ministry of Water Resources (MOWR) (1999) *The National Water Policy*, Government of Bangladesh, Dhaka. (Reproduced as Appendix 1 of WARPO, 2000b, *National Water Management Plan Project: Draft Development Strategy, Vol. 2: Main Report*, Dhaka: Water Resources Planning Organization (WARPO), MOWR, Government of Bangladesh, August.)

Rahman, M.A. (1989) 'In Search of Flood Mitigation in Bangladesh', in M. Ahmed (ed.) *Flood in Bangladesh*, Dhaka: Community Development Library (CDL).

Research and Advisory Services (RAS) (1995a) '"Floodplain Agriculture": Six Years Later ... The first critique of FAP in Bangladesh', *Monitor* 1(2) August, RAS.

—— (1995b) 'A 'Second Opinion' on FAP: The UNDP Independent Review Mission Report', *Monitor* 1(2) August, RAS.

Talukdar, S. (2004) 'Dhaka to Oppose Tipaimukh Dam Project', *Sify News*, Internet edition, 29 November 2004.

Tanzeema, S. and Faisal, I.M. (2001) 'Sharing the Ganges: A Critical Analysis of the Water Sharing Treaties', *Water Policy* 3: 13–28.

Task Force (1991) *Report of the Task Forces on Bangladesh Development Strategies of the 1990s, Vol. 3: The Flood Action Plan*, Dhaka: Dhaka University Press.

Thakuria, N. (2003) 'Tribesmen Protest against Tipaimukh Project', *Holiday*, Dhaka, Internet edition, 24 October.

Thijsse, J.T. (1964) 'Report on Hydrology of East Pakistan', May–October (mimeo).

—— (1965) 'Additional Report on Hydrology of East Pakistan', March–April (mimeo).

Water Resources Planning Organization (WARPO).

—— (1998) *National Water Management Plan Project: Inception Report, Vol. 1: Main Report*, Dhaka: WARPO, MOWR, Government of Bangladesh, prepared by Halcrow and Mott MacDonald, December.

—— (2000a) *National Water Management Plan Project: Draft Development Strategy, Vol. 1: Summary of Options*, Dhaka: WARPO, MOWR, Government of Bangladesh, prepared by Halcrow and Mott MacDonald, August.

—— (2000b) *National Water Management Plan Project: Draft Development Strategy, Vol. 2: Main Report*, Dhaka: WARPO, MOWR, Government of Bangladesh, prepared by Halcrow and Mott MacDonald, August.

—— (2001) *National Water Management Plan Development Strategy*, Dhaka: WARPO, MOWR, Government of Bangladesh, June.

World Bank (1989a) 'Bangladesh: Five Year Action Plan for Flood Control', draft for discussion, 31 August.

—— (1989b) 'Bangladesh: Action Plan for Flood Control', draft, 7 November.

—— (1989c) *Bangladesh: Action Plan for Flood Control*, Asia Region Country Department, 1 December.

World Bank and Government of Bangladesh (GoB) (1992) *Proceedings of the Second Flood Action Plan Conference*, Dhaka, 1–5 March.

8 Issues of scale in governing water as a common good

The Mekong River Basin

Philip Hirsch

Introduction

Two hundred and sixty-one of the world's river basins are shared by more than one country. Some 45 per cent of the world's land territory lies within international river basins, and 40 per cent of the world's population shares water across borders by living in such basins. Sixty per cent of the world's freshwater surface flow is within basins that are used in common between two or more countries (Wolf *et al.* 2003). Transboundary water management is thus one of the key areas in which there is a need to find common approaches to dealing with what may be considered the transnational commons. Unlike the global commons of the oceans, the atmosphere, Antarctica or biodiversity, transboundary rivers involve management by a set number of geographically contiguous states, and this means that management occurs within a much wider set of neighbourly political relations. Further, the often unequal levels of power, commonalities and differences of culture, shared histories, economic interaction, demographic movements and so on that shape such relations have superimposed on them the geographies of upstream and downstream position, geographically differentiated vulnerabilities to water use and development elsewhere in the basin, and other specific conditions that make shared management anything but a level playing field.

Like the global commons, however, managing water across and within borders as a common good raises some key issues of scale. In particular, questions arise when the establishment of transnational institutions to manage the resource in common – in this case water within its river basin ecosystem context – brings with it an associated developmentally oriented set of arrangements that serve to intensify pressure on the resource in question. This in turn has implications for more local commons management of the same resource, and it sets in train scaled relations of power over and beyond the transnational relations that the institutional arrangements are primarily designed to deal with (Hirsch and Jensen 2006).

In their critique of the Brundtland Commission's 'Our Common Future', *The Ecologist* turned the issue into a question of 'Whose Common Future?' (*The Ecologist* 1993). The main area of concern here is the construction of a global commons that arrogates wisdom and management of these commons to global institutions such as the World Bank. In so doing, biodiversity and other resources deemed to have world heritage value are deemed too important for local management. The same global commons discourse neglects cultural means of managing resources in favour of neo-liberal property rights regimes and market mechanisms to deal with perceived local 'tragedies of the commons' (Hardin 1968), creating a vision of sustainable development predicated on enclosure. This has been given a further boost in recent work by neoliberal economists and conservative think tanks such as the Centre for Independent Studies, who see customary tenures and practices as absolute obstacles to development (Hughes 2004; Hughes and Warin 2005). In turn, such thinking has been critiqued in a number of publications by the radical environmental and social justice think-tank, Cornerhouse (e.g. Lohmann 2002), by the Australia Institute (Fingleton 2005), and in a more wide-ranging critique of enclosure and market-based solutions as the dominant and universalistic basis for mainstream environmental governance (Zerner 2002).

In this chapter, I examine parallel issues in what might be termed a 'bioregional transboundary commons', in the sense that the Mekong River Basin is a transnational area defined by a natural boundary within which the commonality of the shared resource is based on the interconnected nature of the river system. I start with an overall account and history of the framework for managing the Mekong as a shared resource, and then consider how development options associated with this framework place actual or potential additional pressure on the resource. This in turn poses questions for shared use of the more localized commons, for their tenure and their management. These themes are illustrated through case studies in water governance, water infrastructure and commodification of water.

Transnational commons in water and their management: the Mekong

Transboundary management of rivers whose waters and catchments are shared by several countries is clearly an important concern. This concern was expressed dramatically in 1995, when the then World Bank Vice-President stated famously that, 'if the wars of this century were fought over oil, the wars of the next century will be fought over water' (Shiva 2002: ix). Since that time, there has been much critique of such an analysis, in part because it is seen to be alarmist, in part because shared rivers have in fact often served as a basis for cooperation rather than conflict (Wolf 1998), and in part because the primary dimensions and scale of conflict over water are constructed more locally and socially than globally and geopolitically (Boesen and Ravnborg 2004). However, in transboundary river basins, the local and the social are also affected in various ways by the internationally shared nature of water and related resources. It is this fact and the conundrums posed by it that I wish to illustrate in this chapter.

The Mekong River and the territory in its basin are shared by six countries: China, Burma, Thailand, Laos, Cambodia and Vietnam. Seven hundred and ninety-five thousand square kilometres in area, the Mekong is the world's twelfth longest river (4,800 km), eighth largest in terms of average freshwater discharge (475 billion m^3), second most biodiverse (up to 1,700 endogenous fish species, compared for example with 27 endogenous species in the Murray-Darling), and it maintains the world's largest freshwater fishery (two to three million tons annually, 80–90 per cent of which comes from artisanal capture fisheries, providing between 40 and 80 per cent of animal protein in the diets of the rural poor dependent on this resource).

The Mekong has been managed as a transboundary basin for longer than most international river systems, despite the region having been ravaged by geopolitical conflict from the 1950s to 1980s. The Mekong Committee was established by the four lower Mekong countries in 1957, under the auspices of the United Nations, but at a time when the region covered was largely under the hegemony of the United States and was in the front line of the Cold War and then caught up in the Second Indochina War. China and Burma were not included in this framework for cooperation. The US Army Corps of Engineers and Bureau of Reclamation were central in the formation and formulation of the Mekong Committee, and an engineering-led development agenda dominated the business of the committee. Large-scale plans were drawn up for cooperation to build a cascade of dams along the length of the Lower Mekong from northern Laos to the head of the Delta in Cambodia.

The development vision of the 1950s and 1960s was not realized because of the escalating conflict. The organization went into abeyance after Cambodia withdrew in 1975 under Pol Pot, and it was reconstituted as the Interim Mekong Committee in 1978 with only three members. The organization was reinvented in its current form as the Mekong River Commission (MRC) under the Agreement for the Cooperation for Sustainable Development of the Mekong River Basin in 1995. The Mekong cooperation framework has only been partial, as the two upstream countries – China and Burma – have never joined, although they hold observer status. It has also continued to be associated with planning and promotion of large-scale water resource infrastructure, notably large dams but also irrigation and flood control. Since the early 1990s, dams have been very much back on the agenda, even though the MRC itself has moved away from hydropower planning and development as a driving activity. MRC has also taken on an environmental portfolio and a robust fisheries programme.

The transboundary nature of the Mekong River tends to supersede many other ways in which, and levels at which, water and resources or livelihoods dependent on it are held and managed in common (e.g. Ahmed and Hirsch 2000). Water as common property is manifested in traditional irrigation structures (e.g. *muang-faai* in Thailand and Laos), in community-based artisanal fisheries and in the commons of seasonally flooded lands and forests that have great livelihood significance for riparian communities. There are thus multiple local commons associated with water that are, at best, secondary considerations in transboundary river basin management. Relegation of local commons issues outside the purview of transboundary river basin management has created an unfortunate disconnect that underlies a number of barriers to a fully integrated approach to river basin management in the Mekong.

Development and the water commons: issues of scale

Intergovernmental management of the Mekong as a transboundary commons has been inseparable from the agenda of development. In a region in which three of the economies (Vietnam, Laos and Cambodia) are still among the poorest in the world when measured on a per capita income basis, it is not surprising that development dominates all else. Further, development in the Mekong cooperation context has been closely tied with dominant geopolitical agendas. An early illustration of this can be seen on the cover of *National Geographic* in December 1968, where the Mekong was featured as a 'river of terror [communism] and hope [dams]'. Dams were seen as the hope to pull the region out of poverty through industrialization facilitated by hydropower generation and food production facilitated by irrigation development. These would tug remote rural areas out of the grip of subversive ideology preying on poverty and hopelessness. While this belongs to a past ideological era in terms both of geopolitical and environmental understandings, developmentalism lives on. For example, the Asian Development Bank's (ADB) infrastructure-oriented Greater Mekong Subregion development program is replete with discourse on reaping 'peace dividends' through its investment strategy and the prosperity and cooperation that will flow from a fully integrated regional economy (e.g. Pante 1996).

With the development era that has come with the end of geopolitical conflict, the pressing question that arises is what alternative conflicts are generated, and what other common property arrangements are impacted upon, by the mainstream growth and integration agenda associated with transboundary cooperation and MRC- or ADB-style management. In the remainder of this chapter, I suggest and illustrate three key areas of tension associated with water as a shared resource, which are all closely related to mainstream development: water governance, water infrastructure and water as commodity.

Water governance

Water governance has become an important part of water reforms and of development assistance in the water sector (Lebel *et al.* 2007). In many respects, this is a widely welcomed move away from old-style 'hardware' financing dominated by engineering projects, towards the 'software' of seeking to maximize the triple bottom line through equitable, efficient and sustainable approaches to water management. High on the agenda of water governance in its river basin context is the establishment of river basin organizations. Ironically, however, river basin organizations can both enhance and undermine governance for the common good, depending on how they deal with commonality of interest in freshwater at various scales. Bureaucratization of process is one threat to managing the local commons in water. Such organizations may end up being formalized 'solutions looking for a problem' (Molle 2007). Issues of representation present another rarely resolved question in governing river basins through centralized organizations. In the Mekong, these issues can be illustrated through governance at the level of the MRC, and through the river basin committees being established in Thailand and mooted elsewhere.

As an intergovernmental organization, the MRC is in principle owned and governed by its member countries (the four lower Mekong nations of Lao PDR, Thailand, Cambodia and Vietnam). In fact, as an organization whose budget is almost entirely dependent on foreign grant aid, the MRC remains aid donor-driven. The nature of governmental control through the Ministerial Council and Joint Committee is such that two major barriers exist to representation of the local commons in water and fish. First, it is Water Resources departments and related ministries who represent 'national interests' on the Joint Committee and MRC Council, lending a strong bias towards construction and 'developing' the river. This simply reinforces the legacy of the Mekong cooperation framework in the old impoundment-oriented Mekong Committee. Cambodia is represented by the Minister for Water Resources and Meteorology; Lao PDR is represented by the Minister of the Water Resources and Environment Agency; Thailand is represented by the Ministry of Natural Resources and Environment, on the basis that it houses the Department of Water Resources; and Vietnam is represented by the Ministry of Agriculture and Rural Development, home to the Department of Irrigation. Second, the diplomacy and international relations bound up in the organization lead to a culture of non-interference, non-confrontation and deference of weaker to stronger countries. At one level this is simply in keeping with the so-called 'ASEAN Way', but it lacks the incremental moves that ASEAN has made towards a more rules-based regime on the basis of trust (Hirsch and Jensen 2006). The implications for local interests of this culture of non-interference and deference at higher levels is illustrated by the difficulty of indigenous community voices and civil society interests being heard in a case where lives and livelihoods have been badly damaged by Vietnam's Yali Falls Dam and its downstream impacts in Cambodia, which have destroyed fisheries, livestock and riverside gardens. MRC did establish a government-to-government forum to address this case, but it has not had the capacity or provided the access for local communities to put their grievances in the trans-border arena in which this governance problem is set (Hirsch and Wyatt 2004).

At the national level, establishment of River Basin Committees (RBCs) raises similar concerns. In Thailand, RBCs have been established for each of the country's 25 river basins. At one level, RBCs are the product of a progressive move to establish a basis for administration within bioregional rather than provincial administrative boundaries, based on integrated water resources management principles. However, there is little or no articulation of the Thai RBCs with more local structures, such as traditional irrigation systems. Half the representation on RBCs is by ex-officio government staff. The other half comes from non-governmental representatives such as chambers of commerce and an ad hoc mixture of respected persons and organizations, but without systematic village-based representation. As a result, RBCs tend to be seen as an instrument of the Department of Water Resources and as a means to secure funds to build weirs, small reservoirs and other water infrastructure rather than to establish or enhance the management of water as a local commons. To date they have had a very limited water allocation function, despite the increasing awareness of water as a scarce resource in Thailand.

Water infrastructure

The greatest physical threat to common property values of water at a livelihood level is the further construction of large-scale infrastructure. Since its establishment in 1995, MRC has certainly moved away from a dam-first mentality towards river basin development and management, and indeed the largest donor funding has gone into the fisheries and environment programs. More recently, there has been a return to an investment-led notion of sustainable river basin development, under the influence of a Chief Executive Officer of the Secretariat who saw the role of the Commission as an 'investment facilitator' – albeit 'with due regard for the environment' (MRC 2004: 29). While some have seen the large scale infrastructure approach as a thing of the past, and the World Commission on Dams seemed to signal a closure of the build first, ask questions later approach to impoundment and diversion of rivers, there is something of a resurgence in dams and diversions in the Mekong. Two current projects illustrate this quite dramatically.

At the end of March 2005, the Board of Directors of the World Bank voted in favour of Bank support for the Nam Theun 2 Dam in Laos, in the form of loans and sovereign risk guarantees. This marks the culmination of a heated debate that has raged over more than a decade (Hirsch 1991, 2002), and it also marks a return by the Bank to what it now terms 'high risk, high return' projects. That the risks and returns fall on different sets of shoulders is, in principle, supposed to be taken care of by better planning, resettlement and compensation programs. Nevertheless, the fact remains that this project, which will be the largest transboundary energy project in Asia (almost all the electricity generated is for sale to Thailand) and requires an investment roughly equivalent to the annual GDP of the country in which it is being built, involves a loss of public resources that are used and managed in common by affected communities, and it also imposes changes in ways in which these resources will be managed. These include not only the sections of the Nam Theun River, forests and farmlands of 6,000 people from ethnic minority groups that will go under the 450 km^2 reservoir, but also the downstream fisheries on the Xe Bang Fai River, accessed by up to 100,000 people, and riverbank gardens along the same river. The proposed compensation for loss of these common resources is an unspecified 'replacement' of lost fisheries through aquaculture ponds. Another loss of local commons will be in the use of upstream forest lands in the headwaters area by remote indigenous minorities whose livelihood activities will be circumscribed in the name of protecting both biodiversity (a global common) and the investment in the reservoir in the form of 'ecosystem services'. Michael Goldman has written of the 'eco-governmentality' that such abrogation of rights to manage entails in the context of Nam Theun 2 and more generally under projects where the World Bank conflates environmental and economic objectives (Goldman 2004).

A second major infrastructure project that has been slated recently is the Thai Water Grid (the common term for a project whose official name translates as the 'Sustainably Integrated Water Management Project'). Requiring an investment of some 200 billion baht (about AU$7 billion), the project is designed to address Thailand's water crisis by linking river basins that have surplus water with those that have insufficient water – a scheme reminiscent in some ways of Australia's Snowy Mountains Project or of the idea of taking water from the Kimberley to Perth, and mirrored in India's river-linking program and China's South–North diversions linking the Yangtze waters with the moribund Yellow River. The Water Grid would also access water from Cambodia, Laos and Burma. In the case of Laos, this involves piping water from the Nam Ngum and Xe Bang Hieng tributaries under the Mekong to water the dry northeastern region. The reason for not taking water straight out of the Mekong itself is bound up in the water-sharing rules under the 1995 Agreement, which would make such a move a multilateral rather than bilateral matter among Mekong countries. In fact, the existing but toned down Khong–Chi–Mun diversion scheme is based on a somewhat similar principle, and some of the most controversial projects in Thailand have been part of this, including Pak Mun and Rasi Salai Dams. Indicative of the implications of such 'water sharing' for the local commons are the destruction of artisanal fisheries in the case of Pak Mun and of the seasonally flooded gallery forests (*paa thaam*) in the case of Rasi Salai, which used to provide an important dry season food source for affected communities but have not been taken into account in project planning by the very fact of their being common property and, therefore, without official individual land title.

Water as a commodity

There is a fundamental tension between water as a common resource and water as a commodity. This has been debated since the signing of the 1992 Dublin Principles that established an international understanding of the economic nature of water. Water has been established as a commodity, albeit in a highly contested manner, as part of the mainstream development thrust in the Mekong region. Two dimensions of water as a commodity stand out in particular.

First, the pressure by some external development agencies to price water as part of neoliberal reforms packages has led further to discussion of water as a tradeable – and by implication alienable – commodity. The Asian Development Bank attempted to set conditions as part of its 1999 Agricultural Sector Program Loan (ASPL) in Thailand that would require water pricing. Immediately this provoked a backlash by NGOs and farmer groups already facing financial hardship in the wake of the 1997 financial crisis (which, ironically, the ASPL was designed to alleviate). In fact, the notion of water as a free good is something of

Water as a commodity is another way regional states have resisted new development norms a myth – villagers have long paid for water by mobilizing labour, materials and 'social capital' in local irrigation systems and have paid for the use of water through rice or cash payments to locally elected irrigation managers in *muang-faai* systems. Elsewhere, locally managed pump irrigation attracts a fee that farmers have willingly paid and managed in common. Thus, the issue of pricing per se is subsidiary to the imposition of new centrally imposed charges, and in particular to the question of alienable water rights.

A second dimension of water as a commodity is the valorizing of rivers inherent in large dam projects, particularly as the private sector now makes the running on projects such as Nam Theun 2 as described above. Ironically, part of the discourse of the Nam Theun 2 'consultation teams' involved in the public relations work to bring affected communities on-side was to talk of 'rivers of gold and silver' (*Dateline* 1996) that would bring untold wealth to the country and its citizens alike once projects like Nam Theun 2 get off the ground. Here, the national 'common good' evoked through the 'national interest' takes precedence over and usurps the local commons.

Conclusion

Transboundary rivers such as the Mekong are, and need to be, managed in common. However, without scale sensitivity to what commonality of interest and the commons themselves mean and imply, there is a tendency for the transnational (i.e. broad-scale) commons to dominate and become tied closely to a mainstream developmentalism. In this chapter, I have sought to demonstrate some of the dilemmas this creates for the local commons associated with water in its river basin context.

There is nothing to suggest that concern for transboundary commons is incompatible with an understanding of, and respect for, the commons at other scales. Rather, the status quo, particularly as manifested in the governance structures associated with large-scale and bureaucratically and developmentally inclined river basin institutions, mitigates against simultaneous multi-scale understandings of water as a shared and jointly managed resource. Progressive moves toward a scaled approach to governance that incorporates civil society and community interests can only serve to enhance equitability and sustainability in managing these commons. – is this happening now.
* are these norms setting in?
need to see if norms are bypassing
Regional committee barriers.

Bibliography

Ahmed, M. and Hirsch, P. (eds) (2000) *Common Property in the Mekong: Issues of Sustainability and Subsistence*, Penang: International Centre for Living Aquatic Resources Management and Australian Mekong Resource Centre.

Boesen, J. and Ravnborg, H.M. (2004) *From Water Wars to Water Riots: Lessons from Transboundary Water Management*, Copenhagen: Danish Institute for International Studies.

Dateline (1996) 'Dam Destiny', Sydney: SBS Television, 7 August.

Fingleton, J. (ed.) (2005) 'Privatising Land in the Pacific: A Defence of Customary Tenures', discussion paper. Canberra: Australia Institute.

Goldman, M. (2004), 'Eco-governmentality and Other Transnational Practices of a "Green" World Bank', in R. Peet and M.J. Watts (eds) *Liberation Ecologies: Environment, Development, Social Movements*, London: Routledge.

Hardin, G. (1968) 'The Tragedy of the Commons', *Science* 162: 1243–1248.

Hirsch, P. (1991) *Environmental and Social Implications of Nam Theun Dam, Laos*, Working Paper No. 5, Economic and Regional Restructuring Research Unit, Departments of Economics and Geography, University of Sydney.

—— (2002) 'Global Norms, Local Compliance and the Human Rights-Environment Nexus: A Case Study of the Nam Theun II Dam in Laos', in L. Zarsky (ed.) *Human Rights and the Environment: Conflicts and Norms in a Globalizing World*, London: Earthscan.

Hirsch, P. and Jensen, K.M. (2006) *Transboundary Water Governance in the Mekong River Basin*, Sydney: Australian Mekong Resource Centre in collaboration with Danish International Development Assistance.

Hirsch, P. and Wyatt, A. (2004) 'Negotiating Local Livelihoods: Scales of Conflict in the Se San River Basin', *Asia Pacific Viewpoint* 45(1): 51–68.

Hughes, H. (2004). 'The Pacific is Viable!', *Issue Analysis*, 53, Sydney: Centre for Independent Studies.

Hughes, H. and Warin, J. (2005) 'A New Deal for Aborigines and Torres Strait Islanders in Remote Communities', *Issue Analysis*, 54 Sydney: Centre for Independent Studies.

Lebel, L., Dore, J., Daniel, R. and Saing Koma, Y. (eds) (2007) *Democratizing Water Governance in the Mekong Region*, Chiang Mai: Unit for Social and Environmental Research.

Lohmann, L. (2002) Polanyi along the Mekong: New Tensions and Resolutions over Land, Sturminster Newton, Cornerhouse. URL www.thecornerhouse.org.uk.

Mekong River Commission (MRC) (2004) *Annual Report*, Vientiane: Mekong River Commission.

Molle, F. (2007) 'Irrigation and Water Policies: Trends and Challenges', in Louis Lebel, John Dore, Rajesh Daniel and Yang Saing Koma (eds) *Democratizing Water Governance in the Mekong Region*, Chiang Mai: Unit for Social and Environmental Research.

Pante, F. (1996) 'Investing in Regional Development: Asian Development Bank', in B. Stensholt (ed.) *Developing the Mekong Subregion*, Clayton: Monash Asia Institute.

Shiva, V. (2002) *Water Wars: Privatization, Pollution and Profit*, London, Pluto Press.

The Ecologist (1993) 'Whose Common Future? Reclaiming the Commons', London: Earthscan.

Wolf, A. (1998) 'Conflict and Cooperation along International Waterways', *Water Policy* 1(2): 251–265.

Wolf, A., Stahl, K. and Macomber, M.F. (2003) 'Conflict and Cooperation within International River Basins: The Importance of Institutional Capacity', *Water Resources Update*, Vol. 125, Oregon State University, Universities Council on Water Resources. URL www.transboundarywaters.orst.edu/publications/Wolf_2003.pdf (accessed 27 March 2008).

Zerner, C. (ed.) (2002) *People, Plants, and Justice: The Politics of Nature Conservation*, New York: Blackwell.

9 Managing the Yellow River

Questions of borders, boundaries and access

Michael Webber, Jon Barnett, Brian Finlayson and Mark Wang

Introduction

The Yellow River Basin is the site of myriad water resource problems. Some of these have geomorphic causes, such as seasonally variable flow, very high sediment load and a capacity to flood with devastating effect. However, the problems of managing the Yellow River now also reflect the ways in which people use water. Reductions in the quantity and quality of water in relation to human demands limit the attainment of things that people value, like good health, economic growth and employment. Nowadays, the Yellow River Basin is a region of water scarcity, pollution (Lohmar *et al.* 2003; SEPA 2002) and risk of flood (Li and Finlayson 1993; Mei and Dregne 2001).

In this chapter, we deploy an analysis of the problems of the Yellow River to question the significance of borders, boundaries and access in understanding the management of water. Events and conditions in particular localities have local causes, and in this sense the bounding of regions is significant. Yet those events and conditions also have causes that are extra-local, deriving from conditions in neighbouring and distant regions, or operate at a larger scale, reflecting national or global conditions. Borders, like the regions they bound, are hierarchical, scaled and porous. However, analyses of the causes and consequences of events are also bounded by the habits of scientific and social thought, producing boundaries that circumscribe the terms of debates over prescriptions for policy. In the case of the Yellow River a localised understanding of its problems as regional rather than national, and as technical rather than social, is inhibiting appropriate policy responses.

The chapter has two principal sections. In the first, we trace the emergence of the problems of the Yellow River through an historical analysis of the effects on its condition of the economic transition that has been underway in China since 1978. With this groundwork, we turn in the second section to identify some of the key issues involved in managing the Yellow River, illustrating the interaction of local and larger scale issues. We conclude by reflecting on the manner in which the management of the river reveals national priorities and goals – that is, on the manner in which debate over the management of the river has been circumscribed.

The Yellow River

The transition was the result of a set of incremental policy experiments. Its effects on water resources were unintentional and unanticipated. Evidence of these problems has emerged since the early 1990s, yet understanding their extent, causes and solutions is far from complete. That understanding traditionally identifies the problems of the Yellow River as constrained spatially (to the basin) and causally (to certain technical problems of industrial and agricultural demand and use). However, the way in which the economic transition has driven water resource problems in the Yellow River Basin suggests that technical solutions implemented within the basin may not be sufficient – that social solutions and integrated water resource management at the national level may also be needed. An appropriate scale of analysis identifies those borders that must be respected and those that inhibit understanding.

China's economic transition

The economic reforms in China since 1978 have entailed a shift away from central economic planning towards more market-oriented forms of economy that include state, collective and private forms of business. This transition has been endogenously driven, and has occurred through gradual, regular and incremental adjustments in institutions. China's transition has involved moves to 'open up' the economy to international markets. The changes have seen increased foreign direct investment (Wang *et al.* 2002a) and the marketisation of production and distribution systems. In almost all sectors of production, including agriculture, state-directed production has now been replaced by market-directed production (Webber *et al.* 2002a). Centralised political control and market-oriented firms, and state owned enterprises and capitalist foreign-funded firms, now coexist as competing economic systems. State-owned and private enterprises compete to attract resources (including labour and land), and to sell their products or services; individuals now compete and choose among different forms of activity; and central and regional governments can choose among different systems depending on their capacity to dispense revenues or power, to ameliorate social conflict, or to deliver on the promise of economic growth (Webber *et al.* 2002a). The effect has been a new division of activities between the various ways of organising social, political and economic life within China (Webber *et al.* 2002b), including countless changes in water use.

The Household Responsibility System (HRS)

The HRS created the opportunity for farmers to expand their incomes by intensifying agricultural production (Blaikie 1985; Muldavin 1998, 2002). This included greater consumption of irrigation water, particularly in north China, leading to increased withdrawals of both surface and groundwater. Fertiliser use increased by 260 per cent between 1980 and 2002 (FAOSTAT 2004), causing increased water pollution in parts of the Yellow River Basin. There was also a three-fold increase in the area of land under permanent crops between 1978 and 2002 (FAOSTAT 2004).

High population densities and the more or less equal allocations of land under the HRS together mean that land holdings are small and fragmented (Hu 1997), precluding the possibility of saving water by investing in large-scale irrigation. The low rate of returns from farming relative to other sectors has also constrained investments in sustainable water use. Still, between 1980 and 1997 agriculture's share of all Chinese water use decreased from 88 per cent to 72 per cent (Mei 1999). Though agriculture remains the largest user of water in China, the water scarcity problem may be largely a product of the growth of industrial and urban uses which are consuming an increasing share of available water resources, and demanding yet more.

Urbanisation and increasing affluence

In 1978, at the start of transition, China's urban population was officially 80 million (Wang *et al.* 2002b). This had increased to 490 million by 2002 (UNDP 2004) – a rate of increase far in excess of national population growth. Urban growth has contributed to water scarcity problems in China because, as more people live within cities and become more affluent, they each consume and demand more water. Urban use has been the fastest growing sector of water use in China, with municipal uses of water increasing by over 10 per cent per annum throughout the 1990s (Economy 2004). For example, Beijing's growing demand for water has translated directly into reduced allocations of water to agriculture and to rapid decreases in aquifers around the city (Jun 2004).

Relative to other regions in China, water is scarce in the Yellow River Basin (Cai and Rosengrant 2004). Urban uses of water in the basin increased by 245 per cent between 1980 and 1993 (Heilig 1999; YRCC 2005). Urban demands are likely to be increasingly influential as urban centres are the basis of political power in China, as in almost every country. Nevertheless, the welfare of urban residents is rarely as sensitive to changes in water supply as the welfare of resource-dependent rural people.

As incomes continue to rise there has been a decline in the proportion of cereals being consumed, and an increase in consumption and production of more expensive, higher quality food products, especially animal products. Between 1979 and 2002, meat production and the supply of calories from animal products more than quadrupled; the production of fruits increased more than eight-fold; production of vegetables increased more than seven-fold (FAOSTAT 2004). Increasing production of meat has entailed increased production of feed grains, so that between 1991 and 1996, the production of coarse feed grain increased more than any other cereal.

These changes in demand and supply are important for water use since fruits, vegetables, nuts, dairy products and meat are *less* water efficient (they use more water per calorie delivered) than wheat or corn. Nevertheless, fruit, vegetables and animal products are economically more efficient than grains, in the sense that they yield more dollars' worth of output per cubic metre of water applied. In other words, the development of a market economy is leading farmers to become more economically efficient, but less water efficient. Corn is more efficient than wheat, with corn's water efficiency at 1.96 kg/m^{-3}. While the conversion of farmland to horticulture (and fish ponds) has been greatest in the populous southern areas, increased production of non-grain foods has also occurred in the Yellow River Basin. For example, in Henan and Shandong food production now includes an increasing proportion of non-grain crops as farmers seek higher returns per unit of water used. There has also been an increase in corn production for feed grain.

Industrialisation

Transition led to large-scale industrialisation in some regions of China. Of the 980,235 hectares of cultivated land converted for industrial and urban uses between 1988 and 1995, 34 per cent was converted in the coastal and southern provinces (Heilig 1999). In these regions both the area under cultivation and agricultural output have declined and industrial water use has trebled (Heilig 1999). Nationwide, industrial uses of water doubled between 1980 and 1997 (UNDP 2002), and again since (Economy 2004). These industrial uses have contributed to increased demand (and therefore increased scarcity) for water and to water pollution. In particular, more than 500,000 TVEs seem to be exempt in both policy and practice from environmental regulation and their emissions are not monitored, even though they are thought to be responsible for approximately half of all pollution in China (Economy 2004; Vermeer 1998).

In the regions where industrialisation has been most rapid there have been the largest declines in allocation of labour, land and finance for agricultural purposes. This shift of capital away from agriculture occurred rapidly in the southern and coastal regions that have the most abundant water resources and are climatically the most suitable for agriculture. This has in turn caused a relocation of agricultural production in China.

The changing geography of agriculture

The areas where industrialisation has been relatively less rapid have taken up the resulting gap in agricultural supply, particularly of less profitable crops such as wheat. However, these areas are generally dry, and three of the five provinces with largest net gains in the area of cultivated land between 1988 and 1995 were in the Yellow River Basin (Gansu, Ningxia and Qinghai). These areas cannot meet the gap in supply created by reduced production in the South without using irrigation and fertilisers, leading to overdrawing of groundwater and excessive water pollution. As a proportion of all water use, irrigation use is high in the Yellow River Basin (Heilig 1999). According to Cai and Rosengrant (2004), the area of irrigated land in the basin increased more than nine times between 1950 and 2000. Agriculture accounts for perhaps 80–90 per cent of all water withdrawals in the basin (Cai and Rosengrant 2004; Heilig 1999; YRCC 2005).

Agriculture has intensified significantly on the North China Plain for four reasons: first, it is one of the few areas of China in which flat land is abundant; second, restrictions on migration coupled with a relatively low level of industrialisation mean that people in the North China Plain have had few better income earning opportunities than agriculture; third, increasing incomes and urbanisation in the south coupled with population growth have increased demand for all kinds of food; and fourth, much of this increased demand is not being met by production in the wetter southeast of the country. So, the North China Plain now produces 60 per cent of China's wheat and 40 per cent of its corn, even though the region has only 22 per cent of China's cultivated land and just 4 per cent of its water resources.

Intensification of agricultural production on the North China Plain has been achieved principally through increasing irrigation and fertiliser use. Shandong and Henan are the highest users of fertilisers in China, and use is also high in Shaanxi (UNDP 2002). Agriculture in the North China Plain is now nearly totally dependent on irrigation, and the volume of water used for irrigation on the plain is three or four times annual rainfall. Much of the water used for irrigation, therefore, comes from groundwater, extraction of which exceeds groundwater recharge rates (Liu and Xia 2004). There is a lot of evidence to suggest that irrigation on much of the North China Plain is unsustainable.

So: development and water in the Yellow River

The changing geography of agriculture in China, which is driven by the way the 1978 reforms triggered rapid industrialisation in the south and on the coast, means that agriculture has intensified in the Yellow River Basin. Most people in the basin depend on agriculture for their livelihoods, with generally fewer alternative opportunities for income generation than among urban and southern people (Wu and Pretty 2004; Yang *et al.* 2003). This is reflected, in part, in data about development in the basin: of the nine provinces in the Yellow River Basin, seven are in the lower half of China's 31 provinces when they are ranked according to the human development index (HDI) (UNDP 2002). Levels of human development in these provinces are well below the Chinese average. (The HDI is comprised of composite measures representing life expectancy, education and income.) Household incomes, particularly in rural areas, are low. This means that access to water is critical to the livelihoods of most of the ~130 million rural people who depend on water from the Yellow River Basin.

So, while industrial water use and pollution in the Yellow River Basin are both growing, and while urban demands are rising, it is farmers who are the group most sensitive to water problems. The implications of changes in farmer's entitlements to useable water (a function of quantity, cost and water quality) may be profound, not just for individual rural households, but also for North China, and perhaps even China as a whole. Indeed, it may be prudent for policy-makers to consider these farmers as the most important stakeholders in water reforms in the basin. Solutions require an understanding of the vulnerability of rural livelihoods to changes in entitlements to water.

Questions of borders, boundaries and access

The historical sketch provided above identifies the ways in which the current problems of the Yellow River have emerged or intensified during the broad changes in social organisation that comprise the transition in China. In other words, the interaction of regional conditions, developments in other provinces and supra-regional policies defines the nature of and the solutions to the problems of managing the water supply of the Yellow River. We now identify some of the key issues involved in managing the Yellow River, illustrating the interaction of local and larger scale issues.

Scale, boundaries and governance regimes

Many bodies are responsible for various aspects of water regulation and management in the Yellow River Basin. The Ministry of Water Resources (MWR) is a principal responsible State body, though it delegates some responsibility to the Yellow River Conservancy Commission, irrigation districts and the Provincial Water Resource Bureaus and Offices (Lohmar *et al.* 2003). At the sub-provincial level there are prefecture, county and township water management stations, and at the village level there are water management committees. Other State agencies are also involved in water resource management. Whereas water supply is the principal concern of the Ministry of Water Resources and its subordinate agencies, water pollution is largely the concern of the State Environmental Protection Administration (SEPA). Other national level agencies involved are the Ministry of Geology and Mining, the Ministry of Agriculture, the State Forest Administration, the State Development Planning Commission, the State Economic and Trade Commission, the Ministry of Construction and the State Price Bureau (Lohmar *et al.* 2003; UNDP 2002). Effective water management is, therefore, contingent on a high degree of cooperation among agencies and between agencies at different administrative levels. However, this cooperation rarely occurs. The dichotomy of power and authority in Chinese is referred to as *tiaotiao-kuaikuai fenge* or the conflict between the vertical *tiao* lines of authority and horizontal *kuai* lines of authority and the division between these within the bureaucracy.

An improved governance regime is critical to managing the Yellow River Basin's problems (Economy 2004; UNDP 2002; Vermeer 1998; Wang and Ongley 2004; World Bank 2002). If governance means the mechanisms through which people and groups express their concerns, negotiate their differences, exercise their obligations and ensure fulfilment of their rights, then governance in this sense necessarily includes *people* and their regular practices, rules, laws, behavioural norms, conventions and organisations (*institutions*), as well as *governments*. However, improved governance in this sense may be difficult to achieve: for example, it is difficult to couple local people and their resource management institutions to larger scale institutions without losing the advantages of local 'fit' (Folke *et al.* 1998).

Given the existing complexity of actors in water resource management in the Yellow River Basin, it may be desirable to move towards a system of nested, cross scale institutions in which responsibility for making, implementing, monitoring and adapting policies rests with the most appropriate level. Folke *et al.* (1998a) call such a system a 'nested system of governance'; Ostrom (2001) refers to a similar idea as a 'polycentric' governance system. Key issues in refining the current system into this more nested and polycentric ideal include: balancing the degree of autonomy of institutions with a need for overall coordination; spreading power throughout various institutions in the system; clarifying roles and responsibilities of institutions; identifying aggregate outcomes that are not allowed; making explicit who is allowed to use resources, where and when; determining who is allowed to make decisions and how decisions are to be made; and establishing clear channels of communication throughout the governance system (Folke *et al.* 1998b; Gunderson *et al.* 1995; Handmer and Dovers 1996; Ostrom 2001). Such a system of governance – that collects and distributes information, negotiates the definition of problems, agrees policy goals and sets measurable policy targets, monitors policy implementation and outcomes, and adapts policies as required – is far more important than actual policies (Dovers 1995).

Choice of policy instruments

Once established, the governance system decides on policy goals and targets, and then selects instruments for implementing policy. Too frequently the choice of policy instruments is framed as a debate between regulation and market-based mechanisms (Dovers and Gullett 1999; Fiorino 1995), and this is true of discussions about solutions to water problems in the Yellow River Basin. Yet there are many more policy instruments than these. Dovers (1995) lists 13 instruments for implementing policy, including: education and training; consultation, mediation and negotiation; agreements and conventions; regulation by the State; self-regulation by users; community involvement in management; removal or adjustment of distorting policies; and market mechanisms. Even market mechanisms include a variety of instruments, including taxes, user charges, subsidies, penalties, tradeable permits, and performance or assurance bonds (Dinar *et al.* 1997). This variety of policy instruments suggests that there are many choices for achieving policy goals and that there is likely to be an effective instrument for each particular water use and user. Regardless of the instrument chosen, all policy instruments are best seen as information that requests, orders, encourages, warns and creates incentives for desirable forms of action (Dovers and Gullett 1999).

Commonly, the selection of policy instruments depends on the biases of agencies and advocates and on traditional ways of doings things (Dovers and

Gullett 1999). Yet there are more rational criteria for selecting the best policy instrument, including: equity – since the distributional outcomes of one instrument choice can undermine larger policy goals; political feasibility – since some instruments may not be accepted by groups and/or users with power; institutional feasibility – since some institutions may not be capable of implementing some instruments (for reasons ranging from legal mandate through to staff skills); the ability to monitor progress of the instrument's effectiveness (or not); the degree to which an instrument can be enforced; and the degree to which the operation of an instrument and the reasons for its use can be communicated to those with which it engages (Dovers 1995). Policy instruments are not always transferable between cultures: Cassar (2004), for example, identifies the ineffectiveness of regulation in the management of Ramsar-listed wetland sites in China because of people's unwillingness to deliberately participate in the legal system.

Access: the price of agricultural water in the Yellow River Basin

Some studies suggest that unsustainable water use in the basin is largely due to the low cost of irrigation, and propose that commodity pricing would encourage more efficient water use in rural areas. The principal effect of this policy will be to increase the cost of inputs into farming. Farmers' responses to changes in the price of irrigation water depend on its price (Yang *et al.* 2003), but in general price increases induce rather small reduction in the use of water for irrigation in China (Cai and Rosengrant 2004). In other words, farmers lose income when the price of water is increased.

Those whose livelihoods most depend upon water (farmers) are typically poor and their incomes may not support a sudden shift to market-valuation. The net effect of increased production costs is to transfer income out of agriculture, so that small farmers become uncompetitive and production becomes dominated by fewer but larger farms, with a net loss of employment in agriculture, increased number of landless labourers and rural–urban migration. So, the social impacts of water pricing are significant, and the identification of winners and losers from such a policy – including the implications for China as a whole – is important. If pricing is to be a regulatory tool, it is important to determine a price of rural water that avoids adverse social consequences but achieves gains in efficiency.

Thus, the implications of changes in farmer's entitlements to useable water may be profound, not just for individual rural households, but also for North China, and perhaps even China as a whole. It is in this sense that such plans as the South–North water transfer reflect the centrality of water availability and farmers' entitlements to the political economy of China.

Regional borders: south–north water transfers

The South–North Water Transfer Scheme involves constructing a network of canals to divert water from the Yangtze (south) to the Yellow River Basin (north). It began in December 2002 and the full project is expected to take 50 years to complete at a cost of US$58 billion. Should the economic costs of the project ever be fully incorporated into the price of water, North China's farmers may be no longer competitive. Barnett *et al.* (2005) calculate that the price of this water would exceed the value of the incremental output of crops such as wheat. The south–north transfer cannot resolve farmers' entitlement failures, unless the water is not going to be priced to cover costs.

The place of the south–north transfer in China's development policy thus needs to be questioned. If at least some of the water is to be used for agriculture, then it will have to be subsidised; so commitment to the scheme signals that the state intends to subsidise farmers, keeping them in rural areas and producing food – for reasons of national food security or to prevent mass migration of pauperised farmers to the cities, perhaps. If most of the water is sold to urban-industrial consumers, then the scheme will increase their total entitlement and perhaps improve the cleanliness of supply; farmers will retain access to Yellow River water. There may be other benefits too – for example, lower flood risk on the Yangtze River and hydropower development. In other words, the State's endorsement of this project implies a commitment to keep China the way it is: China can more or less feed itself; most peasants remain on the land; urbanisation and industrialisation can proceed at its current pace.

Conclusions

There do not seem to be any simple solutions to water problems in the Yellow River Basin. If nothing else, our analysis suggests that at least some solutions to water problems in the Yellow River lie outside the basin and beyond the realm of science or technology. There is a lot of interest in increasing the cost of water, particularly to farmers, as a way of encouraging more efficient use of water in the Yellow River Basin. However, bearing in mind the relative poverty of most farmers in the basin, and that water costs are already high in many places (Yang *et al.* 2003), higher water prices will merely raise poverty by increasing farmers' production costs (Lohmar *et al.* 2003; Yang *et al.* 2003). If it is to be implemented, water pricing will require careful central government control in establishing, maintaining, and monitoring water markets and their potential social repercussions. National solutions require local understanding.

Some important factors in the livelihoods of farmers and their use of water are also determined by the central government. Increasing the profitability of farming is as important as increasing water price. Because farming is not the most profitable activity for people in rural areas, they do not invest in it. If more income could be earned then households might invest to sustain their businesses. Perhaps the central government should increase the length of land leases – and provide firm guarantees of tenure – to encourage capital investment and to consolidate land holdings to create continuous blocks. Perhaps cooperative farming based on pooled land would share the costs of irrigation while achieving some economies through scaling up of irrigation projects. Clear property rights over small irrigation systems would encourage towns and villages to maintain and improve them (Lohmar *et al.* 2003). Increasing farm profits could also be achieved through more direct measures such as a non-production based transfer to farmers in water scarce regions, low rates of taxation to increase profitability, subsidies on certain forms of production to encourage farming in the most ecologically suitable places, and subsidies on water conservation technologies.

National-level water planning may also help to locate some of the most water intense forms of agricultural and industrial production in the places where water is most abundant (the south and east). During the transition, power was decentralised to provincial and lower level governments, whose increasingly autonomous development plans in effect set these jurisdictions in competition with each other for the available water resources. An effective water governance system requires national coordination to clarify the jurisdictions, roles and authorities of various central government agencies, river valley commissions, provincial governments, municipalities, counties, irrigation districts and water management committees. The problems of the Yellow River are national and resolution of them requires national initiatives.

Bibliography

Barnett, J., Webber, M., Wang, M.Y., Finlayson, B. and Dickinson, D. (2005) 'Ten Key Questions About the Human Dimensions of Water in the Yellow River Basin', *Proceedings of the 2nd International Yellow River Forum on Keeping Healthy Life of the River*, Zhengzhou, China (18–21 October): 127–135.

Bellier, M. and Zhou, Y. (2003) *Private Participation in Infrastructure in China. Issues and Recommendations for the Road, Water and Power Sectors*, Washington: The World Bank.

Bezlova, A. (2004) 'Water Woes Threaten to Dry Out North', Inter Press Service English News Wire, 10 June 2004.

Blaikie, P. (1985) *The Political Economy of Soil Erosion in Developing Countries*, London: Longman.

Cai, X. and Rosengrant, M. (2004) 'Optional Water Development Strategies for the Yellow River Basin: Balancing Agricultural and Ecological Water Demands', *Water Resources Research* 40(8)W08S04, doi:10.1029/2003WR0024.

Carter, C.A., Zhong, F.N. and Cai, F. (1996) *China's Ongoing Agricultural Reform*, San Francisco: 1990 Institute.

Cassar, A. (2004) 'The Application of International Water Agreements: The Case of the China–Australia Migratory Bird Agreement', unpublished PhD Thesis, University of Melbourne.

Chen, C., Findlay, C., Watson, A. and Zhang, X. (1994) 'Rural Enterprise Growth in a Partially Reformed Chinese Economy', in C. Findlay, A. Watson and X. Wu (eds) *Rural Enterprises in China*, New York: St Martin's Press.

Dinar, A., Rosegrant, M.W. and Meinzen-Dick, R. (1997) 'Water Allocation Mechanisms – Principles and Examples', World Bank Working Paper #1779.

Dovers, S. (1995) 'Information, Sustainability and Policy', *Australian Journal of Environmental Management* 2(3): 142–156.

Dovers, S. and Gullett, W. (1999) 'Policy Choice for Sustainability: Marketization, Law and Institutions', in K. Bosselmann and B. Richardson (eds) *Environmental Justice and Market Mechanisms*, London: Kluwer Law International.

Economy, E. (2004) *The River Runs Black: The Environmental Challenge to China's Future*, Ithaca: Cornell University Press.

FAOSTAT (2004) *Agricultural Data*, Food and Agriculture Organization of the United Nations: Statistical Data. Available Online at http://Faostat.Fao.Org. (last accessed 16 August 2004.)

Findlay, C., Watson, A. and Wu, X. (eds) (1994) *Rural Enterprises in China*, New York: St Martin's Press.

Fiorino, D. (1995) *Making Environmental Policy*, Berkeley and Los Angeles: University of California Press.

Folke, C., Berkes, F. and Colding, J. (1998b) 'Ecological Practices and Social Mechanisms for Building Resilience and Sustainability', in F. Berkes and C. Folke (eds) *Linking Social and Ecological Systems: Management Practices and Social Mechanisms for Building Resilience*, Cambridge: Cambridge University Press.

Folke, C., Pritchard, L., Berkes, F., Colding, J. and Svedin, U. (1998a) *The Problem of Fit Between Ecosystems and Institutions*, IHDP Working Paper No. 2, International Human Dimensions Programme on Global Environmental Change: Bonn.

Foster, S., Garduno, H., Evans, R., Olson, D. and Tian, Y. (2004) 'Quaternary Aquifer of the North China Plain – Assessing and Achieving Groundwater Resource Sustainability', *Hydrogeology Journal* 12: 81–93.

Gunderson, L., Holling, C. and Light, S. (eds) (1995) *Barriers and Bridges to the Renewal of Ecosystems and Institutions*, New York: Columbia University Press.

Handmer, J. and Dovers, S. (1996) 'A Typology of Resilience: Rethinking Institutions for Sustainable Development', *Industrial and Environmental Crisis Quarterly* 9(4): 482–511.

Heilig, G. (1999) *Can China Feed Itself?* Laxenburg, Austria: IIASA CD-Rom.

Hu, W. (1997) 'Household Land Tenure Reform in China: Its Impact on Farming Land Use and Agroenvironment', *Land Use Policy* 14: 175–186.

Jun, M. (2004) *China's Water Crisis*, Norwalk: Eastbridge Books.

Kang, S.Z., Zhang, L., Liang, Y.L. and Cai, H.J. (2002) 'Effects of Limited Irrigation on Yield and Water Use Efficiency of Winter Wheat on the Loess Plateau of China', in T.R. McVicar, R. Li, J. Walker, R.W. Fitzpatrick and C.M. Liu (eds) *Regional Water and Soil Assessment for Managing Sustainable Agriculture in China and Australia*, ACIAR Monograph No. 84. 105–116.

Krusekopf, C. (2002) 'Diversity in Land-Tenure Arrangements under the Household Responsibility System in China', *China Economic Review* 13: 297–312.

Li, S. and Finlayson, B. (1993) 'Flood Management on the Lower Yellow River: Hydrological and Geomorphological Perspectives', *Sedimentary Geology* 85: 285–288.

Liu, C. and Xia, J. (2004) 'Water Problems and Hydrological Research in the Yellow River and the Huai and Hai River Basins of China', *Hydrological Processes* 18: 2197–2210.

Lohmar, B., Wang, J., Rozelle, S., Huang, J. and Dawe, D. (2003) *China's Agricultural Water Policy Reforms*, Washington: United States Department of Agriculture.

Mei, C. and Dregne, H. (2001) 'Review Article: Silt and the Future Development of China's Yellow River', *The Geographical Journal* 167: 7–22.

Mei, X. (1999) 'Water Shortage and Food Production in China: Issues, Potential and Solutions' paper presented at the US–China Water Resources Management Workshop, Tuscon, Arizona, 18–22 April.

Muldavin, J. (1998) 'Agrarian Change in Contemporary Rural China', in I. Szelenyi (ed.) *Privatizing the Land. Rural Political Economy in Post-Communist Societies*, London: Routledge.

—— (2002) 'The Paradoxes of Environmental Policy and Resource Management in Reform-Era China', *Economic Geography* 76: 244–271.

Nyberg, A. and Rozelle, S. (1999) *Accelerating China's Rural Transformation*, Washington: The World Bank.

Oi, J. (1999) *Rural China Takes Off*, Berkeley: University of California Press.

Ostrom, E. (2001) 'Vulnerability and Polycentric Governance Systems', *IHDP Update* 3: 1–4.

Panagariya, A. (1993) 'Unraveling the Mysteries of China's Foreign Trade Regime', *World Economy* 16(1): 51–68.

Pereira, L., Cai, L. and Hann, M. (2003) 'Farm Water and Soil Management for Improved Water Use in the North China Plain', *Irrigation and Drainage* 52: 299–317.

Pomfret, R. (1996) *Asian Economies in Transition: Reforming Centrally Planned Economies*, Cheltenham: Edward Elgar.

Shu, G., Zhou, Y., Zhang, M., Smallwood, K. (2001) 'A Sustainable Agro-ecological Solution to Water Shortage in the North China Plain (Huabei Plain)', *Journal of Environmental Planning and Management* 44: 344–355.

State Environmental Protection Administration (SEPA) (2002) *Report on the State of the Environment in China 2002*, Beijing: Environmental Information Center (SEPA).

Tian, W. and Chudleigh, J. (1999) 'China's Feed Grain Market: Development and Prospects', *Agribusiness* 15: 393–409.

United Nations Development Program (UNDP) (2002) *China – Human Development Report 2002: Making Green Development a Choice*, New York: Oxford University Press.

—— (2004) *Human Development Report 2004*, Oxford: Oxford University Press.

Varis, O. and Vakkilainen, P. (2001) 'China's 8 Challenges to Water Resource Management in the First Quarter of the 21st Century', *Geomorphology* 41: 93–104.

Vermeer, E. (1998) 'Industrial Pollution in China and Remedial Policies', *The China Quarterly* 156 (Special Issue): 952–985.

Wang, M., Webber, M. and Zhu, Y. (2002a) 'Managed Openness: Opening China's Door', in M. Webber, M. Wang and Y. Zhu (eds) *China's Transition to a Global Economy*, New York: Palgrave Macmillan.

—— (2002b) 'China's Puzzle Game: Four Spatial Shifts of Development', in M. Webber, M. Wang and Y. Zhu (eds) *China's Transition to a Global Economy*, New York: Palgrave Macmillan.

Wang, X. and Ongley, E. (2004) 'Transjurisdictional Water Pollution Disputes and Measures of Resolution: Examples from the Yellow River Basin, China', *Water International* 29: 282–289.

Wang, Y. (2003) 'Water Dispute in the Yellow River Basin: Challenges to a Centralized System', *China Environment Series* 6: 94–98.

Watson, A., Findlay, C. and Chen, C. (1996) 'The Growth of Rural Industry: The Impact of Fiscal Contracting', in R. Garnaut, S. Guo and G. Ma (eds) *The Third Revolution in the Chinese Countryside*, Cambridge: Cambridge University Press.

Webber, M., Wang, M. and Zhu, Y. (2002a) 'Making Markets', in M. Webber, M. Wang and Y. Zhu (eds) *China's Transition to a Global Economy*, New York: Palgrave Macmillan.

—— (2002b) 'Knocking on WTO's Door', in M. Webber, M. Wang and Y. Zhu (eds) *China's Transition to a Global Economy*, New York: Palgrave Macmillan.

World Bank (2002) *China. Country Water Resources Assistance Strategy*, Washington: The World Bank East Asia and Pacific Region.

World Trade Organisation (WTO) (2003) *International Trade Statistics 2003*, Geneva: WTO.

Wu, B. and Pretty, J. (2004) 'Social Connectedness in Marginal Rural China: The Case of Farmer Innovation Circles in Zhidan, North Shaanxi', *Agriculture and Human Values* 21: 81–92.

Xu, C. (1995) *A Different Transition Path*, New York: Garland.

Yang, H. and Zehnder, A. (2001) 'China's Regional Water Scarcity and Implications for Grain Supply and Trade', *Environment and Planning A* 33: 79–95.

Yang, H., Zhang, X. and Zehnder, A. (2003) 'Water Scarcity, Pricing Mechanisms and Institutional Reform in Northern China Irrigated Agriculture', *Agricultural Water Management* 61: 143–161.

Yellow River Conservancy Commission (YRCC) (2005) 'Development and Utilization of Water Resources'. Available online at www.yellowriver.gov.cn/eng/ (accessed May 2007).

Zhen, L. and Routray, J. (2002) 'Groundwater Resource Use Practices and Implications for Sustainable Agricultural Development in the North China Plain: A Case Study in Ningjin County of Shandong Province, PR China', *Water Resources Development* 18: 581–593.

10 Watered down?

Legal constructs, tradable entitlements and the regulation of water

Janice Gray

Introduction

Water is a great unifier. It binds society on many different levels including the spiritual and the pragmatic. Creation stories commonly feature water.[1] In some, including Darwinian theory, the human form emerges from water while in others, such as Noah in the Bible or Nun in Egyptian mythology, water tests and challenges the inhabitants of earth. In many cultures, water is simply there: a gift to planet Earth. But water is also a divider, a boundary maker and a site of contestation. Its very existence is essential to human life. While water was both plentiful and present it was convenient to conceive of water as a commons, that is, something available to all; something in which people could freely share, but as water has become scarcer (or at least less available where it is needed) positions have changed and there is now a growing push for at least aspects of this multi-use resource to be seen as a commodity, regulated in part, by the market rather than the state.[2] The rationale for commodification is that the resource will be treated more efficiently and carefully; a rationale which has, in turn, raised issues of distributive justice.

One of the challenges, therefore, has been to develop legal constructs and frameworks able to protect the resource in the long term but simultaneously provide for its present use (Godden 2003). In this regard the idea of a partial water market has gained favour and hence the development of suitable frameworks and mechanisms for water trading in the wider context of environmental protection and sustainability have become important. In order to examine that challenge more carefully, this chapter explores the shifting positions on how, historically, water has been legally classified and, in so doing, considers the relationship between classification and management of the resource. For example, it considers the different types of rights (such as a commons, common property, public property, common law riparian rights and statutory rights) which have been relied upon to manage access, use, control, quality and quantity of water.

Historical approaches to water rights

Often prior legal understandings and rules are helpful in formulating, refashioning or even inventing new legal constructs to deal with a modern problem. Here historical water concepts are enlisted to understand the idea of water trading and the preservation and protection of the resource itself for present and inter-generational users. Adopting these insights, this chapter explores a number of concerns related to water trading such as the nature of the right to be traded, market unpredictability, stranded assets, social equity and costly infrastructure. They provide a start to thinking about water trading and an agenda for future research on modern water regulation.

Roman Law – water as *res communes*

Although the law of England (and later Australia) has never been directly derivative of Roman Law, a brief consideration of Roman classifications is informative, particularly given that the common property doctrine has resonances in Roman Law. In Roman law, as in common law, not all rights were conceived of as private. *Res nullius* belonged to nobody, *res publicae* belonged to the state and *res communes* belonged to everyone. Justinian classified the air, running water, the sea and the sea-shores as *res communes*. Rights over these objects were collectively referred to as *ius naturale*.[3] One of the key grounds on which a resource could be classified as *res communes* was that the substance in question was both plentiful and pure (Fisher 2000: 65). As running water was seemingly in abundance it made sense to characterise it in a way that allowed it to belong to everyone. However, the right of 'use' (as opposed to the right to 'own') water was restricted to those who had access to water, such as those owning land which adjoined or abutted the water source. Consequently, those who could not gain access without committing trespass, did not have a water right, unless the water was regarded as being in the 'public domain' (Getches 1997). Water was, therefore, largely unregulated under the Roman system of law and the resource itself was categorised along the lines of common property.

Water as a commons

The concept of 'a common' is well entrenched in English land law and is based on ancient rights etched in tradition and custom which predate formalised law. In practice, a land common has meant that a community of users has had the right to exercise 'rights of common' including the right to pasture cattle (common pasture), the right to fish (common piscary), the right to take sods of turf (common tubury) and estover (the right to take sufficient wood for household or agricultural purposes). Hence a common has been understood as a piece of land over which neighbours could exercise a number of rights.[4] These 'sharing' rights were heavily relied on prior to the enclosure Acts.[5]

The term 'a commons' is both a modification and extension of the land common concept. The former has come to apply to *any* set of resources that a community recognises as being available to be shared by members of that community, such as air or certain digital information technology, for example (Fitzgerald 2004: 137–40; Lessig 2001, 2002; Starr 2000; Hess 2000; Bollier

2002: Ch 7). Consequently, the nature of a commons will vary between societies but often includes both cultural and natural resources. Further, the meaning of the term may vary from discipline to discipline. For example, an economic understanding may relate to the use and management of a resource that is held by a community of users rather than to the rights which support that use and management of the resource, the latter being more likely to be seen as a legal understanding (Fisher 2004; Tarlock 1988).

Legally, the concept of a commons demonstrates some synonymy with the doctrine of 'common property'.[6] Under the common property paradigm all people are able to have a share in the available water without regulation, with some people taking more than others. While water was abundant, at least superficially, heavy consumption mattered little. The overwhelming concern was to preserve the quality of the water, not the quantity. Hence, classification as a commons or common property had some appeal in those conditions.

Problems with the *res communes*/common property approach

The egalitarian idea of sharing an essential resource(s) as a commons, common property or *res communes* has both a moral and commonsense attraction.[7] Yet people are often rapacious, short sighted and self motivated. Individuals may put their needs above those of the society more generally and the preservation of the resource might not be given priority. It might be ill-treated or ultimately destroyed. Such concerns lay behind Garret Hardin's cry for control and regulation of resources that are shared as a commons. A central point of Hardin's thesis was that '[f]reedom in a commons brings ruin to all'. Put another way, Hardin's thesis is that resources on which we all depend as a community need to be regulated because we cannot rely on Adam Smith's belief that individuals will be 'led by an invisible hand to promote the public interest' (Smith 1776, 1937: 423). Hardin saw a range of resources such as water, air, national parks and farming land being degraded by the unregulated use of society. Hence he suggested that:

> [we] have several options. We might sell them [commons] off as private property. We might keep them as public property, but allocate the right to enter them. The allocation might be on the basis of wealth, by the use of an auction system. It might be on the basis of merit, as defined by some agreed upon standards. It might be by lottery. Or it might be on first-come, first-served basis, administered to long queues. These, I think, are all objectionable. But we must choose – or acquiesce in the destruction of the commons…
>
> (Hardin 1968: 1243–8)

While Hardin acknowledged that he did not particularly like any of the options above, he felt compelled to make a choice in favour of one of them because to sit back and do nothing would have, in his opinion, meant the destruction of the particular commons and made it of 'no value to anyone'. Further, he was not of the view that an action taken to regulate the commons needed to be a perfect solution, pointing out that in other domains of our lives we regularly accept imperfect solutions. In that regard, he suggested that anyone is capable of owning property through inheritance but if we sought a perfect solution to the issue of property ownership we would be compelled to place property only in the hands of those who were 'biologically more fit to be the custodians of property'. He concluded this argument by stating that accepting '[i]njustice is preferable to total ruin' (Hardin 1968: 1243–8).

Where the balance between rights and obligations among users of a commons is maintained, it may perhaps be possible to conclude that the unregulated management of the resource will bring no harm. However, pollution and overconsumption both indicate that at some point the mutuality of rights and obligations has broken down, or at least been impaired, in relation to water. Where that is the case, alternatives require consideration and in that regard it would seem a variety of options is available, ranging from the Hobbesian Leviathan model – which gives power to a central authority in order to monitor the conduct of users and sanction the non compliant users – on the one hand, to the Smithsonian free market model on the other.[8]

Interestingly, in relation to water, the courts and legislators could be said to have responded to Hardin's call for regulation and management of shared resources long before he made it in the 1960s. Several legislative regimes had already been introduced across Australia, including the *Water Rights Act* 1896 (NSW), the *Water Act* 1912 (NSW), *Rights in Water and Irrigation Act* 1914 (WA), *Water Act* 1957 (TAS). Arguably the responses were woefully inadequate and insufficiently rigorous. They do, nevertheless, demonstrate a trend away from the total freedom of the commons that so concerned Hardin. They also reflect attempts to affix the State with the overall responsibility for the welfare of the resource, with micro-management falling initially to government agencies and their servants. The following briefly tracks some of the various attempts to manage and regulate water in the English and Scottish jurisdictions before moving onto the Australian context. Due to limitations of space, the Australian example will be confined to New South Wales.

Early moves towards rights classification and regulatory frameworks

According to Fisher, prior to the feudal system, Anglo-Saxon law 'disclosed similar approaches'[9] to those of Roman law i.e. in England water was largely unregulated and regarded as common property (Holdsworth 1936 vol. 11: 72–6 as cited in Fisher 2004: 203–4; Tan 2005: where Tan refers to water as 'publici juris'). After the Norman Conquest, Anglo Saxon law ultimately gave way to the common law which fashioned a new set of rules for water (Plucknett 1956; Dorsett 2002). In this context 'common law' simply means the law that was applicable to the whole of the country in common and which was administered by the King's ordinary courts rather than the ancient customary laws which varied from one part of the country to the next and which were administered locally, unhindered by any central control.[10]

Under the English common law system, 'rights of common' developed.[11] According to Holdsworth (1936 vol. 11: 72–6 as cited in Fisher 2004: 204) while rights of common included *profits a prendre*[12] (as common piscary and estover are described), significantly rights of common did *not* extend to the taking of water (Fisher 2004: 204). Instead *access* to water from rivers and streams came to be regulated by the law relating to land use and the associated doctrine of riparian rights.[13] Further, things common to all, such as the 'air and sea' were not, by their nature, subject to ownership but running water was not mentioned along with the air and sea.[14]

As the law relating to water developed further it emerged that different legal rules applied according to whether the water was, for example: (a) in flow in a river;[15] (b) falling on high land and naturally draining to lower land;[16] (c) falling on high land and artificially draining to lower land;[17] (d) collecting on the surface of the earth in indefinite channels;[18] (e) underground;[19] (g) captured in a dam; (h) being pumped out of a river or; (i) being carried away in a vessel. It also became obvious that the English common law was concerned about rights of access to water rather than property rights in water.

Water in flow

Although England and Scotland merged in 1707 their legal systems remained separate. Throughout the nineteenth century both English and Scottish courts worked at refining water law.[20] In Scotland, where a civil law system based on Roman law developed, the case of *Linlithgow Magistrates* v. *Elphinstone* demonstrated an early attempt at the classification of water in a river.[21] The following extract from *Linlithgow* notably echoes some of the Roman law concepts discussed above. Lord Kames stated:

> At advising this cause much darkness was occasioned by a notion which some of the judges unwarily adopted, as if a river could be appropriated like a field or a horse. A river, which is in perpetual motion, is not naturally susceptible of appropriation; and were it susceptible, it would be greatly against the public interest that it should be suffered to be brought under private property. In general by the laws of all polished nations, appropriation is authorised with respect to every subject that is best enjoyed separately; but barred with respect to every subject that is best enjoyed in common ... Water drawn from a river into vessels or into ponds becomes private property; but to admit of such property with respect to the river itself, considered as a complex body, would be inconsistent with the public interest, by putting in the power of one man to lay waste to a whole country...
>
> A river may be considered as *the common property of the whole nation* [author's emphasis]; but the law declares against separated property of the whole or part ... A river is a subject composed of a trunk and branches. No

> individual can appropriate a river, or any branch of it; but every individual of the nation, those especially who have land adjoining, are entitled to use the water for their private purposes. . . .[22]

Under this conception of common property everyone, including both riparian owners *and* others, could use river water in flow. As Lord Kames expressed it, these rights resembled a blend of Justinian's *res communes* (common) and his *res publicae* (belonging to the public, state or nation).[23]

Meanwhile, the common law of England (at least according to *Embrey* v. *Owen*) declared that water *in flow* was not the subject of property.[24] The idea that something lay outside the property classification was not unfamiliar to English law. At common law, for example, there was no property in a wild animal.[25] It was only when the captor of the animal was able to demonstrate 'possession' of it that he or she could protect his or her right in the animal against the rest of the world. Put another way, it was only then that the captor had a proprietary right and the wide sphere of enforceability associated with private property rights became available to him or her.[26] Cases such as these often turned on the question of what acts demonstrated 'possession'. In more recent times other things (such as a spectacle[27] and a cell line[28]) have been found not to be the subject of property.

In keeping with these cases, it would seem that the reason water in flow was held not to be the subject of private property was that possession, observed through an ability to *control* the object in question, could not be demonstrated.[29] While moving water is transitory and unstable, the requisite ability to control it cannot be readily legally demonstrated. Further, it is likely that social policy and cultural reasons also contributed to water in flow being outside the proprietary classification in a raft of nineteenth century English cases that developed the law on water. Such cases may well have been responses to the view that water was, after all, necessary for the maintenance of life. It was simply there, as a gift from 'God', to be shared by all creatures rather than appropriated privately.[30] It followed from this that there was no property interest, at common law, in the water of a free flowing river. One simply had the right to use it, treating one's 'neighbours' fairly by sharing the resource with them.[31]

Access to water in flow

As noted, the situation was different when the subject of discussion was *access* to water rather than water in flow itself, according to Baron Parke in *Embrey* v. *Owen*.[32] While free flowing water itself was not the subject of private property, access to water was regarded as possible by virtue of riparian ownership. This echoes, at least to some extent, the position in Roman Law. The water to which riparian landholders had access, although described as a *publici juris* (a public right), was a term which, in Baron Parke's lexicon, appeared to represent something of a hybridisation. It involved Justinian's concepts of *res communes* (belonging to everyone) and *res publicae* (belonging to the state).[33]

> The right to have the stream to flow in its natural state without diminution and alteration is an incident to the property in the land through which it passes: but flowing water is *publici juris*, not in the sense of a *bonum vacans*,[34] to which the first occupant may acquire an exclusive right, but that it is public and common in this sense only, that all may reasonably use it who have *a right of access* to it, *that none have any property in the water itself*, except in the particular portion which he may take into his possession, and that during the time of his possession only. But *each proprietor of the adjacent land has the right to the usufruct of the stream* which flows through it.
>
> This right to the benefit and advantage of the water flowing past his land, is not an absolute and exclusive right to the flow of the water in its natural state; if it were, the argument of the learned counsel, that every abstraction of it would give a cause of action, would be irrefragable; but *it is a right only to the flow of the water, and the enjoyment of it, subject to the similar rights of all the proprietors of the banks on each side to the reasonable enjoyment of the same gift of Providence.*
>
> It is only therefore for an unreasonable and unauthorised use of this common benefit that the action will lie;[35]
>
> [Emphasis added]

Like Baron Parke, Starkie on Evidence[36] also referred to flowing water as *publici juris* but he also understood only riparian owners to have the right to the usufruct of it.[37]

> The water in a running stream is *publici juris*, which each successive proprietor has a *right to use in passing, but which is the property of no-one*; but if one of such owners appropriates the water by applying it to a particular purpose, he has a right to do so, provided he does not thereby prejudice any other owner in his previous use and appropriation of the water to other purposes.[38]
>
> [Emphasis added]

Hence the riparian rights doctrine regulated the number of users by tying water access rights to ownership of land adjoining rivers. It imposed further restrictions on use by denying the right to degrade the water quality or quantity of another potential user.[39] Riparian rights represented a limited form of control over access to and the treatment of water but on Hardin's analysis they would have been insufficiently stringent.

Perspectives on the English cases

The nineteenth-century English cases[40] conceived of river water as a gift to the world; a gift from providence to man which had to be shared with neighbours whose use of it could not be seriously impaired. Yet what resonates throughout these judgements is that at the centre of their narratives is 'Man' and 'his' needs and not the preservation of water and the riverine environment.[41] This point of distinction places these judgements in stark contrast to those more recent native title judgements (particularly the fishing cases) which include reflections on Indigenous water management in comparable historical eras.[42] In the native title cases there is a tendency to emphasise notions of stewardship, protection, care and maintenance of water. While Indigenous consumption features in these narratives it is not at the forefront, whereas the picture is largely the reverse in the English cases dealing with water use in the context of water grist mills, irrigation, farming and water diversions. Kent's Commentaries reflect the prominence given by the common law to people rather than the environment, noting that '[s]treams of water are intended for the use and comfort of man' and that

> all the law requires of the party by or over whose land a stream passes, is that he should use the water in a reasonable manner, and so as not to destroy, or render useless, or materially diminish or affect the application of the water by the proprietors above or below on the stream.[43]

People and their needs are at the centre of this understanding of water management.

The Australian position

Prior to 'settlement' Indigenous communities' relationship to water was underpinned by custodial obligations which were later recognised (through native title) as a type of communal property (Bartlett 1997; Behrendt and Thompson 2003; McEvoy 2007). The relationship, however, went largely unrecognised after 'settlement'[44] when Australia inherited as much common law from England as was applicable to the colonists' own 'situation and the conditions of the infant colony' with the result that Indigenous rights were progressively extinguished (Blackstone 1803: 107; Castles 1982: 9–13; Bartlett 2001). Given that English common law evolved in a culturally and geographically different place, several oceans away, arguably little of it was applicable to the Australian conditions. Nevertheless, Justice Windeyer observed, in 1962, that 'it is beyond doubt that these rules [English common law] are a part, and an important part of the common law that Australia inherited'[45] even though the application of the common law rules (with respect to riparian rights) was a 'source of insuperable difficulty'.[46]

New South Wales statutory frameworks for the public management of water

The inherited riparian rights doctrine afforded water rights to a subset of the community – those who occupied land adjoining or abutting rivers. The broad restrictions contained in the common law riparian rights doctrine were developed further by various pieces of state-based legislation. In New South Wales comprehensive water legislation developed in the form of the *Water Rights Act* 1896 (NSW), the *Water Act* 1912 (NSW) and the *Water Management Act* 2000 (NSW).[47] As noted above, all these Acts reflect, in varying degrees and by differing methods, controls on the free use of water.[48]

Water Rights Act *1896 (NSW)*

Significantly, this Act vested rights to the use and flow of water in the Crown[49] but arguably statutory vesting simply expresses the state's ability to regulate and protect the exploitation of a resource rather than the creation of property in the Crown.[50] The Act also sought to manage water by specifying intended outcomes such as conservation, supply, more equal distribution, beneficial use, protection from pollution and the prevention of unauthorised use.[51] The Act attempted to do what Hardin later called for, that is, 'manage' water and place controls on its use so that the resource is not harmed. Yet the methods of achieving the outcomes were quite different from later Acts. For example, whereas the 1896 Act sought to vest rights in the Crown and thereby make the Crown the 'manager' of water, along with the assistance of various administrative regimes, the *Water Management Act* 2000 (NSW) (discussed later) hands over at least some of the management of water to the market.

Water Act *1912 (NSW)*

The *Water Act* 1912 (NSW) retained many of the principles in the 1896 Act but the 1912 Act later became subject to the *Water Administration Act* 1986 (NSW) which vested rights to water in rivers and lakes, water occurring naturally on the surface or ground, water conserved by any works and sub-surface water, in the Water Administration Ministerial Corporation rather than, as had been the case, in the Crown.[52] The Water Administration Ministerial Corporation was also given rights to take measures for specified purposes that went beyond those in the 1896 Act and included flood control and mitigation, as well as environmental protection. By the interaction of s 7 of the *Water Act* 1912 (NSW) and Schedule 2 of the *Water Administration Act* 1986 (NSW) a riparian owner was permitted (without the requirement of a licence) to take and use water in the river (or lake) for stock, to irrigate dwelling house gardens and to irrigate small areas of non commercial land associated with dwelling houses.[53]

The public management of water was, therefore, linked to the shift of rights in or associated with water, from the Crown, to a Corporation responsible for bringing about designated outcomes. This occurred along with the creation of statutory rights vested in riparian owners (Fisher 2000: 94). Although the twentieth century marked an era of prolific statutory growth in regard to water (a growth that often related to the provision of infrastructure and irrigation schemes), the public management regime still made entitlements to water derivative of rights in land (Tan 2002: 15; Godden 2003: fns 72–8).[54] Nevertheless in

1986, the 1912 Act introduced the trading of basic entitlements.[55] That change marked a shift towards the commodification of water entitlements but the shift was not accompanied by the same vocal public discussion as that which accompanied the *Water Management Act* 2000 (NSW). Expansion and modification of the 1912 Act trading regime was taken up in the *Water Management Act* 2000 NSW.[56]

Water Management Act *2000 (NSW)*

The genesis of the *Water Management Act* 2000 (NSW) (WMA) largely lay in the Council of Australian Governments (COAG) meeting in 1994, where an agenda for micro-economic reform of the water industry in NSW was agreed. Two key aspects of the agreed reform were (a) ecological sustainability and (b) the introduction of mechanisms which permitted a more efficient allocation of water. The following principles underpinned the reform package: (1) pricing should be consumption and full-cost recovery based and cross subsidies should be removed; (2) the best scientific information available should be used to review water allocations; (3) environmental allocation should be restored in over-allocated water systems; (4) water allocations should be separated from land title[57] and water allocations should be tradable; and (5) public consultation should take place concerning irrigation management, environmental issues and water trading (Godden 2003: fns 72–8). Dependence on these principles marked an enormous shift from the ethos of previous legislation which had been based on a consumption rather than sustainability principle and had relied on water rights being derivative of those in land. Further, the earlier legislation, which had left much water management to public utilities (whose officers assumed significant responsibility for administrative decision making), gave way under these principles to a system of tighter legislative controls. Another difference between the earlier legislation and the emerging COAG principles was that the former demonstrated little sensitivity to Indigenous water use whereas the latter embraced an integrative management approach which took heed of the Indigenous experience.[58]

The National Competition Council payments (designed to encourage and reward the removal of barriers to competition) which were, in turn, tied to the satisfaction of Competition Policy, provided an impetus for the COAG water reform objectives to be operationalised in legislation (Shadwick 2002). Although the 2000 Act provides that rights to the use and flow of all water in rivers, lakes aquifers and groundwater are 'State's water rights' and vest in the Crown pursuant to s 392, the Act cuts back the role of government (at least, at an operational level). It seeks to manage water, at least partially, by relying on market forces, through the trading of Water Access Licences (WALs). Water management is, therefore, partially dependent upon market turns. The legislation is premised on the view that the trading of WALs will, among other things, promote the efficient and equitable sharing of water from water sources and at the same time give benefits to the environment, urban communities, fisheries, culture, heritage and Aboriginal people.[59] Accordingly, the legislation is designed so that economic goals may be tempered by environmental sustainability objectives and vice versa, giving rise to a situation of 'co-regulation' whereby the efficiency of the resource is largely left to the market within broad goals set by government (Godden 2003; Connor and Dovers 2004).

A detailed discussion of the mechanics of the trading provisions is beyond the scope of this chapter. However, it is worth noting that the whole licence itself and/or its component parts may be traded pursuant to Division 4 of the Act.[60] A WAL has two component parts: (a) the 'share component' which describes the specified share in the available water within a water management area or from a specified source to which the holder is entitled and (b) the 'extraction' component which specifies the conditions under which a holder is entitled to extract water, for example the times, rates or circumstances and locations or areas. Trades may either be permanent or temporary. It is also possible to divide or split a WAL, so that a WAL comprised of a share component of say 120 units becomes divided into two share components of 100 units and 20 units, respectively. Each sub-divided share component may be traded separately. Further, details of WALs are recorded in a register at the relevant government department,[61] in a manner similar to the way in which interests in land are recorded under the Torrens title system of land holding. However, indefeasibility[62] was not initially made a concomitant of registration. The plan is for it to attach only after a series of comprehensive checks have taken place to verify title.

Trading and rights classification

One of the key underlying issues in regard to water trading is the determination of the nature of the right being traded because (a) the right in question must be capable of being traded and (b) the specific procedures relevant to rights of that nature must be followed in order to facilitate a proper transfer (or trade). In regard to (a), the *nemo dat quod non habet* principle (meaning that one cannot give what one does not have) is relevant. Hence, if water itself were simply legally classified as either common or public property, for example, then no individual would be able to trade in water because no individual would have the right to take what belonged to a larger group or body and sell it him or herself. However, as property rights are capable of fragmentation, it is potentially possible to carve out a lesser or particular right from a broader bundle of rights. WALs attempt to do this by allowing individuals to appropriate unto themselves a subset of the rights that exist in or in relation to water itself. It is this subset of rights relating to water access which legislation has made tradable. In turn, a mechanism or procedure must exist which facilitates the transfer of that package of rights as between parties (a trade amounting to a contract of exchange or a transfer, for value). The correct procedure, be it one at common law or under statute, is determined by the nature of the right to be transferred.[63] In this regard there are several possibilities for thinking about the nature of a WAL. Are they property, a contract, a licence or something else entirely different?[64]

The WMA (NSW) 2000 does not specifically label WALs as a form of property although to some extent they exhibit the indicia of common law property.[65] Are they then to be transferred according to the procedures in the statute, on the basis that they are common law property, statutory property or something else? Such concerns raise the fundamental issue of whether anything that is not property is capable of being the subject of trade.[66] Does it matter whether a WAL is classified as common law property, statutory property or something else? The answer to this question is, it may well. For example, if a common law property right is compulsorily acquired (as opposed to being interfered with[67]) by regulatory intervention, according to s 51(xxxi) of the Commonwealth Constitution, compensation is payable in just and fair terms. However, there is a view that compensation is not payable if the lost property is statutory property as opposed to common law property.[68] The reasoning appears to be along the lines that what 'the statute giveth, the statute may taketh away'. Accordingly, compensation will not flow. While WALs presently come under State legislation and the State constitution does not include a right to compensation for loss of property, compensation is only available according to the terms of the statute itself. However, if the States cede the management of water to the Commonwealth[69] and Commonwealth legislation creates WALs, loss of them would potentially be non-compensable.

It does not, however, necessarily follow from the above that WALs should be classified as common law property. It merely demonstrates the importance of legal classification in resource management. In fact, it is suggested that the very special nature of water should be borne in mind when developing suitable legal constructs to help manage it. Water creates boundaries yet knows no boundaries. Rivers, for example, mark out state and territorial limits but the water in them flows irrespective of those boundaries. The water that is accessed today by virtue of an entitlement is not the same water that is accessed tomorrow.[70] The same water molecule may progress from the atmosphere to a stream where it helps support flora and fauna. Later it might support water sports and crop irrigation, while later still it might become groundwater seepage that carries salt onto a neighbour's property or it might become part of a return flow to the streams that drain the earth. Ultimately, it could reach an estuary where as fresh water it will mix with saltwater to have an impact on fish breeding and the commercial and economic wellbeing of coastal towns.[71]

Therefore, it is important to craft legal rights, entitlements or obligations in a way that allows the vast array of water uses to be accommodated. Rights over and in relation to water need to regulate the activities or use to which water is being put at any given time but they also need simultaneously to help ensure the maintenance of the resource for both future uses and future users, a concern that is sometimes expressed in terms of inter-generational equity. How this is to be achieved presents enormous challenges.

One method of management suggested by Epstein is that of co-regulation. He suggested that water should be held as a commons but that 'some limited conversion of water for private use' should be tolerated (Epstein 1994: 28). He continued:

> The underlying instinct shows the importance of making marginal adjustments to fundamental institutions. In principle, the formal problem to be solved (although Justinian and the Romans would scarcely have put it this way) is how to take a body of water, which has value in multiple uses simultaneously, and devise a system of rights that maximises the value for the sum of its common and private uses.
>
> The Romans had an intuitive sense of the relative values at stake because they in fact adopted an intermediate solution that left the commons dominant, but allowed some diversion from it.... It was routinely held that each of the riparians had a 'usufructuary' interest in the water which allowed them to make limited diversions for domestic uses.
>
> (Epstein 1994: 28; Tan 2005: 63)

Epstein's reasoning is attractive but whether it is correct to assume that the commons (or common property) needs to co-exist with private tradable access rights in water, as opposed to co-existing with non-tradable permissions or licences (or some alternative legal entity) made operational through a government controlled regulatory system, is a moot point. Despite some benefits there appear to be several real and potential problems associated with the water market approach and the trading of private access licences. They include: the ineffective operation of the market so as to produce price 'distortions', causing sellers to receive less for water than they would in a truly competitive market; the lack of a synoptic overview of the market itself; 'stranded assets' whereby inefficient producers are forced out of the market leaving efficient producers in the market but stranded without the critical mass needed to sustain the community in which they operate;[72] the reduced number of WALs available for trading because of government 'claw backs' in over-allocated systems (claw backs being introduced to return water to the environment);[73] the fact that externalities such as the cost of storage and evaporation are difficult to factor into pricing; the inconsistency and complexity of the various legal jurisdictions in or between which water is to be traded;[74] the high cost of hydraulic infrastructure, where necessary, to move water between seller and purchaser; the potential for 'water barons' to buy up large numbers of licences; the high concentration of WALs in the hands of irrigation corporations;[75] social equity concerns relating to fairness and distributional impacts being inadequately met;[76] and the need to provide a certain core amount of water at a reasonable price, to individuals as a necessity for existence.[77]

What is emerging more clearly, however, is a growing interest in affixing the State with an overall obligation to steward water on behalf of the whole society.[78] How this can be satisfactorily achieved again raises a number of questions relating to legal classification and mechanisms. Whether it should be by virtue of vesting provisions which may carry with them an implicit duty to protect, care for and guard (similar to those associated with US public trust doctrine[79]) or whether they should arise by virtue of express provisions making water public property (either in terms of proprietorship or sovereignty) is still an open question.[80]

Conclusion

In conclusion, this chapter has offered a description and explanation of the legal classifications and frameworks that have impacted on the development of surface water management in Australia and, more particularly, New South Wales. It has raised a number of issues about trading and the legal constructs which operate to facilitate that process. In so doing it has also explained how legal classifications and frameworks may have a very real impact on legal and commercial outcomes particularly in relation to statutory property and compensation.

The chapter has also pointed to some of the potential weaknesses in using water trading as a tool of water management: weaknesses which have, perhaps, not received sufficient attention in an era where trading has been so readily embraced and posited as a panacea for water management problems. While the focus of debate revolves around the legal mechanisms for trading as well as the economic benefits of trading, the cultural, social and environmental outcomes of the introduction of a market-based approach may not receive due scrutiny. If they do not, the consequences could be far-reaching. Accordingly, one is led to ask, what would be the benefit of a strong market if the community could not use water in a range of socially and culturally valued (but not economically efficient) ways, such as for commemorative fountains, public swimming pools or the greening of public space, for example? Would such deprivation harm the community in non-economic ways? Further, one is led to ask what would be the point of a market if the commodity or resource being traded became so degraded that ultimately it was rendered useless? Presumably this is why the drafters of the NWI emphasised environmental sustainability as key to reform, making it a primary objective in many sections of the NWI instrument.[81] It is important not to lose sight of that environmental priority in any debate focusing on trading regimes and markets.

The issue of co-regulation is related to these concerns about the cultural, social and environmental outcomes of water management being downplayed. This chapter has highlighted how New South Wales has moved towards a system of co-regulation. The control, use and flow of water vests in the State pursuant to s 392 of the WMA and arguably that means that the State has the over-arching duty to guard, steward and protect the water in its care on behalf of the State's people. Meanwhile the trading provisions allow the market, at least in part, to micro-manage water. If, however, there is a total or partial market failure, reliance on the market will not necessarily achieve all the desired outcomes that a diverse community might wish. As a result it may be the case that the role of private property rights (potentially created by statute and/or the common law in the form of tradable licences) will need to be tempered by the intervention of the State, acting benevolently to protect the public property it holds on behalf of its citizens. Co-governance will, therefore, need to involve a genuine respect for the State's role as steward of the commons.[82] If that role of State stewardship comes to the fore it may, in turn, also cause water law to reflect to a greater extent, the ethos of water stewardship observed in the native title fishing cases mentioned previously, bringing the common law approach to water management more into line with Indigenous approaches. That may well be a good thing for a range of reasons, legal, environmental and social.

Notes

1 Water features in the creation stories of the Apache, Navajo, Muslim, Christian, Jewish, Egyptian and Australian Indigenous peoples, to name but a few. It also plays a part in many religious and cultural traditions aside from creation stories.

2 Evidence of the popularity of this approach may be seen in California, Colorado, Chile, Mexico and Indonesia to name but a few places. See Australian Productivity Commission 2003; Bauer 1997, 1998, 2004; Marino and Kemper 1999.

3 *Institutes of Justinian*, Book 11, Title 1, AD 535; see also Moyle 1949: 193–4 and Sandars 1859: 167–70, both as cited in Fisher 2000: 64; Getzler 2004: 65–100.

4 Until late Anglo Saxon times it seems a common was owned communally. Following that period the right to exercise a right of common became restricted to a commoner. The *Commons Registration Act* 1965 (UK) offers an attempt to regularise competing definitions of common land.

5 The Enclosure Acts were passed in order to encourage efficiency in food production which was restricted under the medieval system of communal agriculture. Private Enclosure Acts were passed from the middle of the eighteenth century onwards. The Inclosure Act 1773 (UK); *Inclosure (Consolidation) Act* 1801 and the *Inclosure Act* 1845 facilitated enclosure. See Hill 1969: 269–74 for a discussion of the rural distress created by the Inclosure Acts. A public outcry in response to the diminution of open spaces led to the Inclosure Acts 1852 incorporating a provision that prevented inclosure without the consent of parliament. Later the procedure came to be governed by the *Commons Act* 1876. On the meaning of a land commons see De Vattel, *The Law of Nations* [1760] excerpt in McRae *et al.* 1991: 76–7. It is interesting to note that in modern English law one can observe a slight shift towards the re-instatement of communal access rights such as those seen in the *Countryside and Rights of Way Act* 2000 (UK) which effectively gives ramblers or walkers the right to walk over certain private lands without being liable to be sued in trespass.

6 Property is notoriously difficult to define and its meaning continues to be contentious, generating considerable academic scholarship and judicial consideration. Its indicia commonly include: the right to use and enjoy; the right to exclude all others; and the right to alienate. For an analysis of some of the substantive elements of property see Honore 1961: 107–47; Gray 1991: 252; Cooke 2001–05; Williamson *et al.* 2003: 64 where the authors state that a common is generally taken to mean a right in a resource but that right is taken by a group of individuals.

7 It should be noted that there are differences between these three categories. *Res communes* did not actually accord with a right in property but rather meant that the resource was available for all to use. See Williamson *et al.* 2003 for a discussion of common property and a commons.

8 For a discussion of the regulatory state see Black 2007: 58–73; Gunningham and Grabosky 1998.

9 Fisher 2004 surmises that the form of resource management relating to fodder and fuel also extended to water. That resource management involved an unrestricted use resonating of common property.

10 Megarry and Wade 1984: 7. The authors note that '[W]hen the old local jurisdictions were forgotten, the "common law" came to mean the ordinary judge-made law of the royal courts' where judges laid down new rules.

11 Note that in 1066 when William, the Conqueror, came to Great Britain he claimed almost all the lands for himself and set up a system of feudal tenures which allowed individuals to hold interests in land 'of' the Crown. Indeed the process of subinfeudation, by which more rungs were added to the tenurial pyramid, may be seen as an acknowledgement of private and individual tenures (cf. common property) albeit tenures which involved substantial obligations in return.

12 A *profit a prendre* is a proprietary right and it allows one or more parties to take resources from the land or water of another. It is distinguished from a licence in that it is a property right while a licence is a personal right, amounting to a permission.

13 To some extent easements were also relevant to water access rights.

14 Fisher 2000: 65. By way of comparison, Tan 2005: 70, fn. 12, noted that rivers in Spanish law (influenced by Moorish and Roman law) have been considered public property since the thirteenth century, while since 1669 French law has treated navigable and floatable rivers as available for public use but not susceptible to private ownership. Iranian law treats all waters in their natural state, irrespective of whether they are in public or private use, as in the public domain.

15 *Embrey* v. *Owen* (1851) 6 Exch 353.

16 *Smith* v. *Kenrick* (1849) CB 515; 137 ER 205; *Gartner* v. *Kidman* (1962) 108 CLR 12; *Palmer* v. *Bowman* [2000] 1 WLR 842 (CA).

17 *Whalley* v. *Lancashire and Yorkshire Railway Co* (1884) 13 QBD 131.

18 See *Trinidad Asphalt Company* v. *Ambard* [1899] AC 594 at 601 for a discussion of some of these issues.

19 *Ballard* v. *Tomlinson* (1885) 29 Ch D 115 at 120. Re there being no common law action against a neighbour for extracting groundwater and causing interference see *Chasemore* v. *Richards* (1859) 7 HLC 349.

20 Note that Scottish law has remained independent of English law but Welsh civil matters came under English law in the sixteenth century, criminal law having done so earlier in 1282 with the death of King Llewylyn.

21 *Linlithgow Magistrates* v. *Elphinstone*, 3 Kames 331. The impact of Roman law on Scottish law is commented on by Fisher 2000: 65.

22 *Linlithgow* case quoted in the English case, *Embrey* v. *Owen* (1851) 6 Exch 353 at 361.

23 Australia inherited English common law rather than Roman or Scottish law but the latter two jurisdictions have at times influenced Australian law.

24 *Embrey* v. *Owen* 6 Exch 353 at 369. Note that this discussion relates only to water in flow.

25 *Pierson* v. *Post* (1805) 3 Caines 175 (Supreme Court of New York). There was no property in an oyster either. *R* v. *Toohey; Ex parte Meneling Station P/L* (1982) 158 CLR 327 found that a grazing licence was outside the property paradigm.

26 The benefit of a proprietary classification lies in the extensiveness of the sphere of enforceability. A property right is enforceable against all the world but a right in contract, for example, is *prima facie* enforceable only against the parties to the contract.

27 *Victoria Park Racing and Recreation Grounds Co Ltd* v. *Taylor* (1937) 58 CLR 479.

28 *Moore* v. *Regents of the University of California* (1990) 793 P 2d 479. (American case.)

29 The legal concept of possession has been expressed as the ability to demonstrate sufficient physical control to ground an action in trespass.

30 This approach is reflected in the words, '[Rights to air and light, like water] also are bestowed by Providence for the common benefit of man' see *Embrey* v. *Owen* 6 Exch 353 at 372.

31 Protection of neighbours' rights is evident in the words '[t]he owner must so use and apply the water as to work no material injury or annoyance to his neighbour below him.' See Kent's Commentaries in *Embrey* v. *Owen* 6 Exch 353 at 370.

32 *Embrey* v. *Owen* 6 Exch 353.

33 Baron Parke traced the history of several water law cases before reaching his conclusion. See *Wright* v. *Howard* (1 Sim. & S. 190); *Mason* v. *Hill* (3B. & Ad 304; 5 id 1); *Wood* v. *Waud* (3 Exch. 748).
34 *Bons vacans* (or *bona vacantia*) means ownerless property. Ownerless property traditionally escheated to the Crown.
35 *Embrey* v. *Owen* 6 Exch 353 at 369.
36 Starkie on Evidence, tit. Watercourse (vol. 3, p1249, 3rd edit) quoted in *Embrey* v. *Owen* 6 Exch 353 at 359. This position is in contradistinction to that of Lord Kames in *The Magistrates of Linlithgow* v. *Elphinstone* 3 Kames' Decisions 331 noted above.
37 This means to enjoy all the advantages of something which belongs to another.
38 Quoted in *Embrey* v. *Owen* 6 Exch 353 at 359.
39 *Embrey* v. *Owen* (1851) 6 Exch 353 at 370–371 per Baron Parke stated that the riparian owner 'should use the water in a reasonable manner, and so as not to destroy, or render useless, or materially diminish or affect the application of the water proprietors above or below on the stream. He must not shut the gates of his dam and detain the water unreasonably, or let it off in unusual quantities, to the annoyance of his neighbours'. For a more comprehensive discussion of the common law position in relation to surface water in flow see Fisher 2000: 64.
40 See *Embrey* v. *Owen* (1851) 6 Exch 353 along with *Wright* v. *Howard* (1 Sim. & S. 190); *Mason* v. *Hill* (3 B. & Ad. 304; 5 ld 1) and; *Wood* v. *Waud* (3 Exch 748). Also see the American case of *Blanchard* v. *Baker* (8 Greenl. American Rep.)
41 A similar anthropocentric approach seems to pervade understandings of the enclosure of land commons.
42 *Yanner* v. *Eaton* (1999) 201 CLR 351; *Mason* v. *Tritton* (1994) 34 NSWLR 572, for example.
43 *Embrey* v. *Owen* 6 Exch 362 at 370–371.
44 The term 'settlement' is a contestable one given that Australia was not *terra nullius*. The term invasion is less often used but arguably more accurate, Gray 2007: 128.
45 *Gartner* v. *Kidman* (1962) 108 CLR 12 at 23. In 1992 Australian law generally and more specifically water law also had to take account of the then newly recognised form of title known as native title; see *Mabo* v. *Queensland (no 2)* (1992) 175 CLR 1.
46 *Hanson* v. *Grassy Gully Mining Co* (1900) 21 NSWLR 271 at 275. Note that an alternative approach to riparian rights exists in parts of the USA where a system of 'appropriative rights' emerged and was given legislative recognition in the 1860s and 1870s. The doctrine of appropriation gives the best rights to the person who first used the water. Beginning with miners' use of water, the doctrine was later extended to farmers and other users, who put the water to beneficial use. In terms of the beneficial use aspect there is a conceptual similarity between these rights in water and the adverse possession doctrine in relation to land; see also Getches 1997; Australian Productivity Commission 2003: 42.
47 As noted above, in the interests of space this chapter uses New South Wales as a case study. It does not consider legal developments in other Australian jurisdictions although reforms in other states also took place in response to the 1994 COAG Framework (see '*Water Management Act* 2000' section in this chapter).
48 It is unfortunate that there has been no uniformity of water legislation given that water knows not when it crosses a state boundary. Constitutionally rivers are the responsibility of the states but it is possible for the Federal government to legislate in regard to water under the following sections in the Commonwealth Constitution: s 51 (v) defence; s 128 interstate trade; s 92 commerce; s 96 financial assistance; s 51 (xxix) external affairs.
49 *Water Rights Act* 1896 (NSW) s 1(1).
50 See *Yanner* v. *Eaton* (1993) 73 ALJ 1518; Tan 2005: 65.
51 *Water Rights Act* 1896 (NSW) s 1(1). Whether this section meant that 'the rights of

riparian owners were divested and vested in the Crown' or whether only those riparian rights described in part one were transferred to the Crown is a moot point and has drawn discussion in cases such as *Hanson* v. *Grassy Gully Gold Mining Co* (1900) 21 NSWR 271.

52 See *Water Administration Act* 1986 (NSW) ss 12(1), 3.

53 *Water Act* 1912 (NSW) s 7(1)(a).

54 *Water Act* 1912 (NSW) ss 12, 13A, 16, 18, 20B, 20C and 20F.

55 *Water Act* 1912 (NSW) Div 4C and s 20AG.

56 The WAL trading provisions were amended by the *Water Management Amendment Act* 2004 No 39, the amending Act being repealed by Sch 3 of the *Statute Law (Miscellaneous Provisions) Act (No 2)* 2004 No 91, with effect from 10.12.2004.

57 This later found voice in WMA (NSW) 2000 s 393.

58 How well this has been achieved remains the subject of academic discussion, see Jackson 2005 and 2006.

59 *Water Management Act* 2000 NSW s 3.

60 *Water Management Act* 2000 NSW ss 71 L-ZA, 72, 72A, 73 and 74; Gray 2006: 84–9.

61 Water Access Licences are recorded in a register at the Lands Department, Land and Property Information section.

62 Indefeasibility 'makes the interest one that is unable to be defeated by claims of prior defectiveness', see Gray *et al.* 2007: 290.

63 Hence there are different systems of transfer depending on (a) whether the thing to be transferred is classified as real property, a chose in action (e.g. shares), or a chose in possession (e.g. a chair), or statutory property, for example and; (b) any relevant legislative overlay. A failure to adhere to the procedures for transfer could result in the property remaining in the hands of the vendor which, in turn, could result in unexpected outcomes particularly in relation to taxation liability, succession and commerce.

64 Godden 2003 suggests that since the mid nineteenth century, legal constructs such as contract and statute have also helped facilitate trade.

65 WALS can be used and enjoyed, alienated (or transferred) and their holders have the right to exclude others from interfering with them; see *National Provincial Bank* v. *Ainsworth* [1965] AC 1175 at 1247–8; *Milirrpum* v. *Nabalco Pty Ltd and Commonwealth* (1971) 17 FLR 141. Connor and Dovers 2002: 123 point out that the characterisation of a natural resource as a commons regulated by private property rights carries with it assumptions about human behaviour as well as relying on costs being fully internalised; Gardner 2003: 4.

66 Godden suggests that it is possible for contract and statute to replace property rights in the facilitation of trade. It is, however, arguable that the benefits of a contract are property and it is that property which is transferred according to statutory procedures. Gray 1991: 252 comes at the issue from a different angle suggesting that, historically, rights which could not be transferred were not property. Clearly this is no longer the case because a non-assignable lease is now treated as property.

67 For commentary on the distinction see Gray 2007.

68 *Health Insurance* v. *Peverill* (1994) 179 CLR 226; *Newcrest Mining (WA) Ltd* v. *Commonwealth* (1997) 190 CLR 513.

69 As at March 2008, all States had agreed with the Commonwealth to an independent Commission taking over the management of the Murray–Darling Basin. The scheme includes licence buy-backs and investment in irrigation infrastructure. See Murray–Darling Basin Memorandum of Understanding, 26 March 2008. Available at www.coag.gov.au/meetings/260308/docs/attachment_a.pdf (accessed 16 May 2008).

70 This may cause WALs to resemble *profits a prendre*. A *profit a prendre* is a proprietary right which permits the taking of chattels from another's land, such as the right to hunt and collect rabbits.

71 For further elaboration on this and the importance of fashioning a suitable right for water see Lee 1993: 153; Hatfield Dodds and Syme 2006a: 44.
72 For an explanation of distortions and stranded assets refer to Hussey 2007.
73 This has been a contentious issue. The issue is presently governed by the WMA Division 9. Limited compensation is available. See also NSW Riverbank project which is a $105 million environmental fund to buy back WALs for stressed rivers.
74 Unfortunately there is not uniform water legislation across the Australian states.
75 In NSW approximately 80 per cent of WALs are in the hands of five licence holders who hold on behalf of shareholders in Irrigation Corporations. As Irrigation Corporations tend to buy licences rather than sell them this leaves 20 per cent of WALs for wider trade. Statistics presented by Doug Miell, CEO, Irrigators' Council of NSW, Seminar, Faculty of Law, University of New South Wales, Sydney, May 2005.
76 Hatfield Dodds and Syme 2006b. Yet, it may not be a common goal to remove all inefficient users from the water market because social and cultural considerations will, in some circumstances, outweigh economic efficiencies.
77 The human right to water is identified in many international agreements and covenants including the 1948 Universal Declaration of Human Rights and the 1966 International Convention on Economic, Social and Cultural Rights, Gray 2008. For an analysis of water trading on rural communities see McKay and Bjornlund 2002: 137. Under the WMA, s 52, water used for domestic consumption and taken from a river, estuary or lake to which the land has frontage or from any aquifer underlying the land is not the subject of a WAL.
78 Tan 2005: 70; Barnes forthcoming 2008.
79 *Illinois Central Railroad* v. *Illinois* (1892) 146 OS 387 (applied to land under navigable waters); *National Audubon Society* v. *Superior Court of Alpine County* (1983) 658 P 2d 709, Cal. For discussion see Tan 2005: 67.
80 Tan 2005: 70 favours express acknowledgement that water is public property.
81 See clauses 23, 48 and 49 and Schedule A of the NWI, for example. Schedule A sets out the timetable for sustainability.
82 Or common property or public property.

Bibliography

Australian Productivity Commission (2003) *Water Rights Arrangements in Australia and Overseas*, Melbourne: Australian Productivity Commission, available at www.pc.gov.au/research/crp/waterrights/index.html (accessed 14 April 2008).

Barnes, R. (forthcoming 2008) *Property Rights and Natural Resources*, Devon: Hart Publishing.

Bartlett, R. (1997) 'Native Title to Water' in R. Bartlett, A. Gardner and S. Maschers (eds) *Water Law in Western Australia*, Perth: Centre for Commercial and Resources Law.

—— (2001) *Native Title*, Sydney: Butterworths.

Bauer, C.J. (1997) 'Bringing Water Markets Down to Earth: The Political Economy of Water Rights in Chile 1976–95', *World Development*, 25(5): 639.

—— (1998) 'Slippery Property Rights: Multiple water users and the neoliberal model in Chile, 1981–1985', *Natural Resources Journal*, 38(102): 109–55.

—— (2004) *Siren Song: Chilean Water Law as a Model for International Reform*, Washington DC: RFF Press.

Behrendt, J. and Thompson, P. (2003) 'The Recognition and Protection of Aboriginal Interests in NSW Rivers', Sydney: Healthy Rivers Commission of New South Wales, Occasional Paper 1008.

Black, J. (2007) 'Tensions in the Regulatory State' *Public Law*, Spring: 58–73.

Blackstone, W. (1803) *Commentaries on the Law of England*, 14th edn by T. Caddell and W. Davies, London.

Bollier, D. (2002) *Silent Theft: The Plunder of our Common Wealth*, New York: Routledge.

Castles, A. (1982) *An Australian Legal History*, Sydney: Law Book Company.

Connor, R. and Dovers, S. (2002) 'Property Rights Instruments: Transformative Policy Options', *Property Rights and Responsibilities, Current Australian Thinking*, Canberra: Land and Water Australia.

—— (2004) *Institutional Change for Sustainable Development*, Cheltenham: Edward Elgar.

Cooke, E. (ed.) (2001–05) *Modern Studies in Property*, vols 1–3, Oxford: Hart.

Dorsett, S. (2002) '"Since Time Immemorial": A Story of the Common Law Jurisdiction, Native Title and the Case of Tanistry' *MULR* 26: 32–60.

Epstein, R. (1994) 'On the Optimal Mix of Private and Common Property' in F. Miller and E. Paul (eds) *Property Rights*, Cambridge: Cambridge University Press.

Fisher, D.E. (2000) *Water Law*, Sydney: Law Book Company Information Services.

—— (2004) 'Rights of Property in Water: Confusion or Clarity', *Environmental and Planning Law Journal*, 21(3): 200–27.

Fitzgerald, B. (2004) 'Free Culture: Cultivating the Creative Commons', *Media and Arts Law Review*, 9(2): 137–40.

Gardner, A. (2003) 'The Legal Basis for the Emerging Value of Water Licences – Property Rights or Tenuous Permissions' *Australian Property Law Journal*, 10: 1–18.

Getches, D. (1997) *Water in a Nutshell*, 3rd edn, St Paul, Minnesota: West Publishing Co.

—— (ed.) (1998) *Water and the American West*, Boulder, Colorado: Natural Resources Law Center.

Getzler, J. (2004) *A History of Water Rights at Common Law*, Oxford: Oxford University Press.

Godden, L. (2003) 'Perceptions of Water in Australian Law: Re-examining Rights and Responsibilities', in Australian Academy of Technological Science and Technology (ATSE) Symposium, *Water: The Australian Dilemma*, available at www.atse.org.au/index.php?sectionid=629.

Gray, J. (2006) 'Legal Approaches to the Ownership, Management and Regulation of Water from Riparian Rights to Commodification', *Transforming Cultures eJournal*, 1(2): 64–96.

—— (2008) 'Implementing the Human Right to Water in Australia' in J. Gray and J. Nolan (eds) *Human Rights Defender*, 17(1): 2–5.

Gray, J., Egeworth, B., Forster, N. and Grattan, S. (2007) *Property Law in New South Wales*, Sydney: LexisNexis.

Gray, K. (1991) 'Property in Thin Air' *Cambridge Law Journal*, 50: 252–308.

—— (2007) '"Can Environmental Regulation Amount to a Taking of Common Law Property Rights?" Keynote Address, Beyond Environmental Law Conference, Sydney 16 and 17 February', *EPLJ*, 24: 161–82.

Gunningham, N. and Grabosky, P. (1998) *Smart Regulation: Designing Environmental Policy*, Oxford: Oxford University Press.

Hardin, G. (1968) 'The Tragedy of the Commons', *Science*, 162: 1243–8, available at: www.constitution.org/cmt/tragcomm.htm.

Hatfield Dodds, S. and Syme, G. (2006a) 'Improving Australian Water Management', *Water* 89.

—— (2006b) 'Values Attached to Water and their Shaping of Understanding and Communication of Reform Objectives and Implementation', National Water Conference, Canberra, 4 and 5 December.

Hess, C. (2000) 'Is There Anything New Under the Sun? A Discussion and Survey of Studies on New Commons and the Internet', paper presented at 'Constituting the Commons: Crafting Sustainable Commons in the New Millennium', Eighth Conference of the International Association for the Study of Common Property, Bloomington, Indiana, 31 May–4 June, available at http://dlc.dlib.indiana.edu/archive/00000512/ (accessed 4 April 2007).

Hill, C. (1969) *Reformation to Industrial Revolution*, Harmondsworth: Penguin.

Hobbes, T. (1651, 1969) *Leviathan*, Menston: Scolar Press, facsimile reprint of 1st edn, London: Andrew Crooke.

Holdsworth, W.A. (1936) *A History of English Law*, London: Sweet and Maxwell.

Honore, A.M. (1961) 'Ownership', in A.G. Guest (ed.) *Oxford Essays in Jurisprudence*, Oxford: Clarendon Press.

Hussey, K. (2007) 'Human Rights and the Environment: Reconciling Social-equity Issues in Contemporary Water Policy', paper presented at the Beyond Environmental Law Conference, 16–17 February.

Jackson, S. (ed.) (2005) 'Recognising and Protecting Indigenous Values in Water Resource Management', report from Workshop held at CSIRO, Darwin, NT, 5–6 April.

—— (2006) 'Indigenous Perspectives in Water Management, Reforms and Implementation', paper presented at Australian Government Land and Water Australia, National Water Commission Conference, Canberra, 4 and 5 December.

Lee, K. (1993) *Compass and Gyroscope: Integrating Science and Politics for the Environment*, Washington DC: Island Press.

Lessig, L. (2001) *The Future of Ideas: The Fate of the Commons in a Connected World*, New York: Random House.

—— (2002) 'The Architecture of Innovation', *Duke Law Journal*, 51 (6): 1783–803, available at www.law.duke.edu/pd/papers/lessig.pdf.

McEvoy, A. (2007) 'Indigenous Law and the Environment', paper delivered at the 'Beyond Environmental Law Conference', Sydney, 16 and 17 February, organised by the Australian Centre for Environmental Law, Sydney University and the Environmental Defenders' Office.

McKay, J. and Bjornlund, H. (2002) 'Recent Australian Market Mechanisms as a Component of an Environmental Policy', *Property Rights and Responsibilities, Current Australian Thinking*, Canberra: Land and Water Australia.

McRae, H., Nettheim, G. and Beacroft, L. (1991) *Aboriginal Legal Issues*, Sydney: Law Book Company.

Marino, M. and Kemper, K. (eds) (1999) *Institutional Frameworks in Successful Water Markets: Brazil, Spain and Colorado, USA*, Technical Paper 427, Washington DC: World Bank.

Megarry, R. and Wade, H.W.R. (1984) *The Law of Property*, London: Stevens.

Moyle, J.B. (1949) *Imperatoris Iustinani Institutionum* (translated into English), 5th edn, Oxford: Clarendon Press.

Plucknett, T.F.T. (1956) *Concise History of the Common Law*, 5th edn, London: Butterworth.

Sandars, T.C. (1859) *Institutes of Justinian*, 2nd edn, London: Parkes & Son.

Shadwick, M. (2002) 'A Viable and Sustainable Water Industry', National Competition

Council Staff Discussion Paper, Aus Infor, Canberra cited in J. McKay, 'Overcoming Legal Obstacles Associated with Property Rights and Registration to Implement Successful Water Resource Planning Regimes', available at www.unisa.edu.au/waterpolicylaw/documents/IRRpaper.pdf.

Smith, A. (1776, 1937) *The Wealth of Nations*, New York: Modern Library.

Starr, P. (2000) 'The Electronic Commons', *The American Prospect*, 27 March–10 April: 30–4, available at www.prospect.org/print/V11/10/starr-p.html.last (accessed 4 April 2007).

Tan, P. (2002) 'Legal Issues Relating to Water Use', in *Property Rights and Responsibilities, Current Thinking*, Canberra: Land and Water Australia.

—— (2005) 'A Property Framework for Water Markets: The Role of Law', in J. Bennett (ed.) *The Evolution of Markets for Water*, Cheltenham: Edward Elgar.

Tarlock, A. (1988) 'New Commons in Western Waters', in D. Getches (ed.) *Water and the American West*, Boulder, Colorado: Natural Resources Law Center.

Williamson, S., Brunckhorst, D. and Kelly, G. (2003) *Reinventing the Common: Cross Boundary Farming for a Sustainable Future*, Sydney: Federation.

11 Water – fluid perceptions

Tony McAvoy

In the beginning the Rainbow Serpent made its way across the landscape, leaving in its wake the rivers, creeks, lagoons and waterholes that to this day dot the countryside. In most manifestations of Aboriginal religion throughout Australia a spirit being in the form of a rainbow coloured snake is the central feature in the creation stories. The rivers, creeks, lagoons and waterholes, for that reason alone, have a spiritual context that is far greater than that found in a Christian church, for example. The creation spirit personally came to the particular site while travelling through the land.

I do not suggest however, that Aboriginal people have the exclusive rights to real feelings of love and respect for the land. People who have spent time on the land, given birth to children, buried their dead, survived flood and drought, no matter what race, creed or colour, develop a relationship with and an understanding of the land that extends well beyond the physical. That doesn't mean to say anybody who has been through any or all of those trials and tribulations will necessarily comprehend the long-term or broad-scale effects upon the land from any given activity. But there will be an undeniable connection to the land. And, at certain times, for certain people, that connection might take on some elements of the spiritual. But that connection is not and never will be grounded in a religious belief that the earth is one's mother and a gigantic snake brought the rivers into existence.

On the other hand, the NSW Government asserts its ownership of all the water in New South Wales. In 2000, the NSW Government passed the Water Management Act.[1] The purpose of the Water Management Act was to decouple water ownership from land ownership, create a semi-regulated water market, and abolish riparian rights. 'Rivers' are defined in the Water Management Act in the following manner:

> 'river' includes:
>
> a any watercourse, whether perennial or intermittent and whether comprising a natural channel or a natural channel artificially improved, and
>
> b any tributary, branch or other watercourse into or from which a watercourse referred to in paragraph (a) flows, and

c anything declared by the regulations to be a river, whether or not it also forms part of a lake or estuary, but does not include anything declared by the regulations not to be a river.[2]

The objects of the Water Management Act are:

to provide for the sustainable and integrated management of the water sources of the State for the benefit of both present and future generations and, in particular:

c to recognise and foster the significant social and economic benefits to the State that result from the sustainable and efficient use of water, including:

iv **benefits to the Aboriginal people** in relation to their spiritual, social, customary and economic use of land and water.[3]

When we reside in a world where our river systems are managed in a policy framework designed for extractive purpose there is no room for spiritual considerations and it would be naïve for Aboriginal people to think that such a framework has any ability to protect the spiritual aspects of the rivers. It would also be naïve to think that heritage protection, native title or land rights law can protect those spiritual interests.

The spiritual context in which the river systems maintain their relevance is through the use of and access to the flooding, the drying and the ecosystems that once flourished on the floodplains. There are no religious stories about a rising water table and vast tracts of land becoming salt scorched, of rivers silting up or whole colonies of river red gums dying through lack of inundation. Clearly, the existence of stories about spear fishing or netting, finding certain plants or animals in and around the rivers as an incident of that religious connection will not be, and has not been, enough to stop the madness.

The Water Management Act does make provision for Aboriginal people of NSW to exercise their native title rights so long as those rights are limited to the use of water for traditional purposes. Section 55 of the Act provides:

1 A native title holder is entitled, without the need for an access licence, water supply work approval or water use approval, to take and use water in the exercise of native title rights.

2 This section does not authorise a native title holder:

   a to construct a dam or water bore without a water supply work approval, or

   b to construct or use a water supply work otherwise than on land that he or she owns.

3 The maximum amount of water that can be taken or used by a native title holder in any one year for domestic and traditional purposes is the amount prescribed by the regulations.[4]

The effect of the Native Title Act is that where a person has a right obtained through some form of 'valid act', such as a water access licence granted by the Government, that right is protected. However, to the extent that native title is impaired, then compensation is payable. Assuming for a moment that there are Aboriginal people that can make it over the bar set by the High Court in terms of proving native title rights and interests in the waters of a particular river, and that those people could prove that they engaged in aquaculture on a substantial scale, for instance, by the use of fish traps, and that they needed substantial amounts of water of a particular quality for those fish traps to work. That right to have water would be subordinate to the rights of other users who had valid rights. If the rights held by the other users had the effect of depriving native title holders of the use of those waters, then the NSW Government would arguably be required to compensate the native title holders for the water rights given to third parties.

But, of course, money doesn't fix the problem. The loss is not only the fish that are not caught in the fish traps but the damage to the continuation of the culture through loss of use and contextual relevance of the fish traps. The creation of a semi regulated water market is an irretrievable change in the river management landscape. The rights to the water have been sold. The value of the water on the market has increased dramatically, and the only water the government can get back, for purposes other than environmental, is water compulsorily acquired.

There is, however, another way of approaching this dilemma. Aboriginal people are now well acquainted with the notion that the laws do nothing to protect Aboriginal spiritual and cultural beliefs. What was proposed by the NSW Aboriginal Land Council (NSWALC) and the NSW Native Title Services (NSWNTS) when the Water Management Act went through Parliament in 2000, was the establishment of an Aboriginal Water Trust. The schema for the Trust was as follows:

- money was to be paid into a trust;
- the trust would use the money to buy water rights;
- The trust would ensure that for the first ten years the water remained on the market by leasing the water on to users;
- the first ten years of operation would be an accumulation period.
- in the interim Aboriginal communities could access up to 10 per cent of the water for cultural purposes and 10 per cent for commercial purposes (on a subsidised basis);
- at the expiration of the ten-year period the water rights and interests could be divided between the traditional owners, or the trust could continue to manage the water on behalf of the traditional owners.

The theory was, and remains, that in a commodified world the only real power to control exploitation is to own the commodity. If Aboriginal people own significant quantities of water they can then make the decision to use the water, so to speak, by keeping it in the river or by extraction.

The justification for making such payment can be found in the policy underpinnings of the Aboriginal Land Rights Act 1983 (NSW). That Act sought to provide a mechanism for Aboriginal people to be compensated for the manner in which they had been dispossessed from their lands. That Act recognised that Aboriginal people had been dispossessed. What it did not contemplate was the decoupling of water rights from the ownership of land. It had been through the common law imported into NSW that people originally obtained water rights by owning land adjacent to the watercourse, from which they could exercise their riparian rights to take water. From the ancient concept of riparian rights, the water licensing framework, found in the 1912 Water Act, was developed in which a land owner could only apply for a water licence if their land was adjacent to the water course and the water licence then attached to the land.

Because Aboriginal people in NSW had been dispossessed of their land, the opportunity to obtain water licences had not eventuated. Upon the de-coupling of water rights from the land, it was those people who had water licences under the 1912 Water Act who were able to then convert such into water access licences under the Water Management Act 2000. The result was that Aboriginal people were also dispossessed of their water rights.

This argument held some sway with the NSW Government, and Cabinet approved the creation of an Aboriginal Water Trust which would receive an initial payment of $5 million over two years, after which time the project would be reviewed. However, the scheme of the Aboriginal Water Trust, as approved by Cabinet, was markedly different to that proposed by the Aboriginal groups. The Cabinet Office, or the Department of Land and Water Conservation, did not like the concept of an Aboriginal water bank and cited as the reason that the water market was still developing and was thought to be too volatile and, therefore, an expenditure of Government money in such a fashion would be reckless.

As an aside, it was with great interest that the news of the ground-breaking proposal of the Wentworth Group came into the public domain six months after the NSW Aboriginal groups had made the same Aboriginal water trust submission to the Commonwealth for consideration in the National Water Initiative. As you will recall, the Wentworth Group proposed that an Environmental Water Bank be established in which Government money was paid into a trust which could purchase water access licences on the open market and lease the water back to industry for a period of time in order to gain revenue to buy more water licences. The Government thought it was a great idea which gained widespread support.

The Aboriginal Water Trust, on the other hand, never really got off the ground because the Cabinet approval was for a grants program which assisted Aboriginal people to develop water based enterprises, not to buy water licences. That is, an Aboriginal person would be given money to buy a pump or a tank, build a dam or buy a tractor, but the project could not accommodate Aboriginal people amassing water rights. The DIPRN then obtained legal advice to the effect that a grants program could not be a Trust or a charitable trust for tax purposes and, therefore, the Minister could not create the Trust as an interim measure as first proposed. There has been no further development.[5]

Aboriginal people are faced with a world in which water is commodified to the extent that water managers see rivers as water delivery mechanisms. It is a world in which the Rainbow Serpent is having the life sucked out of it and Mother Earth is breaking out in pustules. It is a sad day for everybody in this country when Aboriginal people must claim money for compensation for dispossession of the waters only to use that money to buy back water rights in order to ensure that they have some control over the health of the rivers.

But it is the use of the river that has been commodified, not the spirit. Aboriginal people must have the ability to engage in the water economy not only for economic purposes but because Aboriginal people cannot trust the Government to defend their spiritual beliefs and cultural practices, or make decisions which understand or respect the rivers. It is perhaps timely to remember the words of Ted Strehlow, the anthropologist, who once said that it would only be when we abandoned our search for abstract scientific laws and turned instead to acknowledge the place that their (Aboriginal peoples) spirituality has in our common future with Aborigines, that Australian anthropology would blossom into maturity at last as the true Science of Man.

Notes

1 NSW Water Management Act 2000. Act 92 of 2000: www.austlii.edu.au/au/legis/nsw/consol_act/wma2000166/.
2 NSW Water Management Act 2000, Section 404: *Dictionary*. www.austlii.edu.au/au/legis/nsw/consol_act/wma2000166/sch99.html.
3 NSW Water Management Act 2000, Section 3 *Objects*. www.austlii.edu.au/au/legis/nsw/consol_act/wma2000166/s3.html.
4 NSW Water Management Act 2000, Section 55: *Native Title Rights*. www.austlii.edu.au/au/legis/nsw/consol_act/wma2000166/s55.html.
5 Addendum: On 29 November 2005 the NSW Premier announced the 'Riverbank' programme as part of the City and Country Environment Restoration Program in which the Government allocated $105 million over five years. In late 2005, the NSW Department of Natural Resources called for applications from Aboriginal individuals or organisation for funding grants in respect of 'water-related' business (excluding the purchase of water access licenses).

12 For whom the Fitzroy River flows

A fluctuating analysis of social and environmental sustainability and incremental sovereignty

Sandy Toussaint

The River is alive; the land is alive. It can take your life any time...
(Lucy Marshall, indigenous custodian, Derby, 2006)

The Fitzroy River...? That's why I'm here...!
(Joe Duncan, settler and fisher, Fitzroy Crossing, 2006)

Introduction

The Fitzroy River traverses the Kimberley region of northern Western Australia, variously intersecting along the way with related waterways such as the inland Margaret River to the east, and the Timor Sea on the western coast.[1] At its centre, the Fitzroy River transforms into Geikie Gorge, one of the finest and most renowned gorges in Australia. Joe Duncan's comments – put to me during a conversation about why he had chosen to reside for more than 20 years in a place some distance from his birthplace and homeland – echo those typically expressed by individuals who permanently live near, or visit occasionally, the river, gorge and associated waterways: 'The Fitzroy River...? That's why I'm here...!'

Lucy Marshall, on the other hand, signals the river's benevolent and malevolent qualities. As an indigenous woman whose birthplace, life history and ancestors are intricately intertwined with the river and adjacent areas, her comments – recorded at a Kimberley Tropical Rivers Forum – add another layer of meaning to those expressed by Joe: 'The [Fitzroy] river is alive; the land is alive. It can take your life any time' (quoted in *Environs Kimberley Newsletter* 2006: 9). Elsewhere, Molly Jalakbiya recounts the activities of a Rainbow Serpent or Water Snake, a mythic being regularly credited by local indigenous groups as creating a matrix of water environments:

> [The Rainbow Serpent] rose up again ... He sunk down into the water then for good, and turned to stone. That was downstream, over the other side of the [Fitzroy] river ... he turned to stone downstream, and that is where he is still standing.
>
> (Kimberley Language Resource Centre 1998: 14–17)

Lucy and Molly, like countless other indigenous women, men and children with long-established cultural ties to the area, have a distinct knowledge about, and traditional attachment to, sections of the river[2] through customary law, social connections and keen involvement in a local fishing economy, but their interests do not necessarily contradict or discount those expressed by settlers such as Joe. Indicated in each set of comments is that local representative indigenous and settler groups have equally strong attachments to the same river source.[3] This kind of attachment, as I explain further below, has the potential to ensure the environmental sustainability of the river and the socio-cultural co-existence of local populations, in addition to confusing the long-term implications of sovereignty.[4]

While the Fitzroy River and Geikie Gorge, as with other Kimberley waterways, coastlines and landscapes, continues to define local life-choices, chances and living conditions, as well as support long-term interests and aspirations, water environments are also increasingly attracting national and international tourist attention to facilitate recreational activities such as fresh and saltwater fishing, boat cruises, cultural heritage tours, and camping.[5] Alongside human/water interactions like these, the ebb and flow of the Fitzroy River regularly replenishes the broader environment, including nearby creeks, billabongs, pools and dams, and it provides vital succour for interdependent plants, fish, reptiles and bird species. Notwithstanding the vexed problem of introduced fauna and flora (for example, the ubiquitous and damaging rubber bush and rubber vine [or *calatropis procera* and *crpystostegia madascariens*] that increasingly congregate along river banks) that benefit from the river's water, while often taking valuable nutrients from other species, the Fitzroy River is generally regarded as a large and distinctive water source known widely for its volume and quality (Appleyard 2006; Storey *et al.* 2001; Beckwith and Associates 1999).

There are other ways that the Fitzroy River can be thought of and represented, of course. While the opening remarks in this chapter suggest distinct local images and uses of, and attachments to, the river, from a very different physical, social, environmental and emotional vantage point, the Fitzroy River represents a vast source of water which some parties believe could be of economic, hydrological and political benefit elsewhere, especially in areas where the need for water volume is considered to be urgent. Such a scenario currently exists in many Australian jurisdictions, but in Western Australia government and industry proposals are already canvassing plans to divert the Fitzroy's water south to ease the consequences of diminished water supplies in the agricultural and more densely populated south. Water problems in southern regions are generally regarded as having resulted from poor water management planning in the past (especially in relation to land clearing and irrigation for agriculture), reduced rainfall and the implications of global warming, but an interest in turning to northern rivers for additional supplies of water has been problematically identified as a key possibility to help alleviate these increasingly dry conditions.

One of my primary concerns in this chapter is to investigate this north/south water transport conundrum. I am also concerned with a range of responses to the proposed initiative which I examine more broadly by querying for whom, where and why a river – the Fitzroy River – flows. Mindful of the limitations of a dual or oppositional analysis, and of the need to explore a spectrum of fluctuating perspectives where possible, two fairly distinct positions arise. The first focuses on local indigenous and settler groups (groups represented by individuals such as Lucy, Molly and Joe) who have intimate knowledge and long-term experience of the Fitzroy River and who, in most instances, are opposed to the regulation, diversion or transportation of the river's water; the second is that of government and industry whose personnel, with a few exceptions, have expressed interest in channelling water from north to south as a viable option to offset metropolitan and regional water crises.

I begin with the Fitzroy River, describing further its value and importance to local groups, before turning to an outline of government and industry plans to transport water from the Fitzroy Valley (the broader landscape generally regarded as the Fitzroy River's home) to the State's southern region. Integrating these sections via reference to a selection of media items, commentary, reports and public debate to explore responses to the proposed developments, I then consider whether the Fitzroy River example can be used to explain how shared concerns about social and environmental sustainability might be linked to the long-term impact of sovereignty.

The Fitzroy River environment: fluctuating uses and meanings

Ecologically rich, the Fitzroy River's catchment area covers 85,000 km^2 and extends some distance from Halls Creek (via the Margaret River) in East Kimberley to Derby in West Kimberley (Beckwith and Associates 1999; Storey *et al.* 2001). From local indigenous perspectives, the Fitzroy River and the landscape in which it is embedded, cover the territory of several language groups located along its contours. These groups include speakers from the Ngarinyn, Mangala, Bunuba and Gooniyandi language divisions. As part of a process of forced movement and serial migration since the 1950s from areas often described as southern desert locations, people from groups such as the Walmajarri and Wangkajunga have now also established ties with the river (Toussaint 1999; Toussaint *et al.* 2005). For example, Walmajarri and Wangkajunga women and men describe how their children now have *jarriny* or conception totems affiliated with the Fitzroy River (Toussaint *et al.* 2005: 65).

Evoking aesthetic themes, paintings such as that titled 'Bunuba Water' by Walmajarri artist Nipper Rogers, for instance, evidence how the Walmajarri were encouraged to use water owned, conceptualised and named by the river-related Bunuba language group. As Nipper's painting conveys, it was through this process that Walmajarri people came to 'speak that Bunuba story' (Mangkaja Arts 1991: 21) and, therefore, to establish a more convenient socio-cultural, economic and political co-existence through the river. This type of co-existence, one of practical and symbolic value to local relationships and to social and environmental sustainability of the lands and waterways, is also explained by Walmajarri artist, Daisy Andrews: 'It's really good now how we can all sit down and work together. It's really good, river and desert together, whole lot' (quoted in Mangkaja Arts 2003: 6).

Indigenous narratives generally explicate many other complex aspects of the human/environment relationship and associated water sources (such as the creation, reproduction and maintenance of springs, billabongs, soaks, rains and clouds), as well as river dependent species (fish, birds, plants and so on) and the responsibility humans have to ensure that the health of the river, adjacent areas and dependent wildlife are successively sustained over time for current and future generations (Toussaint *et al.* 2001, 2005; Kimberley Language Resource Centre 1998). Defined this way, the Fitzroy River avoids analysis by reference to topographical data and distinct regional towns, pastoral and industry fences or shire borders only. On the other hand, it demands explanatory attention by way of a body of religion, law and etiquette that privileges indigenous ideas and behaviours despite the broader impact of sovereignty and European settlement.[6]

The Fitzroy River also represents a site of meaning and practical use for settler groups, as indicated above and evident below in the comments of long-term Kimberley resident and co-founder of the Environs Kimberley conservation group, Pat Lowe: 'When we flew over Geikie Gorge and up the [Fitzroy] River ... I felt quite moved to look down on the river and think we had a bit to do with saving it' (quoted in Prior 2006: 15).

It is the case too that the river's riparian environment and associated waterways presents a haven for scientists and researchers such as aquatic ecologists to investigate certain species of fish (Thorburn *et al.* 2004). For pastoralists (including indigenous managers and workers on cattle stations), the river provides a source of water for stock and, during the wet season when the waters swell, for replenishing much needed grasses to supplement feed (Jebb 2002; Marshall 1988). For tourists and for locals, the river represents seductive spots for camping, fishing, and other types of work or recreation, such as kayaking (Hales 2006: 5). From the perspective of medical practitioners and locals, a closeness to the river often results in the stabilisation of client health and wellbeing through direct access to a regular, clean and reliable source of fresh, potable water, and for anthropologists the river involves a research site to be included in environmental studies, native title land claims and cultural heritage projects (Bagshaw 2003; Storey *et al.* 2001; Toussaint *et al.* 2001, 2005; Pannell 2000).

The Fitzroy River also fosters an aquatic garden for the trees and plants that create canopies of high and low shade, and cool riverine habitats for bathing and swimming when and where this is permissible. For instance, some indigenous young people after the enactment of certain rituals cannot enter sections of the river that they once did as children. In this way, water acts as an indicator of sociocultural change in status during their lifetime. The river represents fear, risk and sadness too. It is a reminder of where drownings have occurred, loved ones have died, and a place where fish can be caught when needed for human consumption to replace the intake of beef during mourning periods when food restrictions are imposed on family members of a deceased kinsperson (Toussaint 1999; Toussaint *et al.* 2001, 2005).

During the annual wet season with its pattern of torrential rains, some Kimberley communities and towns become isolated by intermittent or extended river flooding, and lands once travelled regularly as roads or byways become quagmires that disallow even the toughest of four-wheel drive vehicles to get through. Bordered by water and mud, the means to visit loved ones resident elsewhere, the purchase of additional food supplies, and attendance at health clinics temporarily dissolves in these circumstances. As Kimberley residents make clear, the strength and volume of wet season rains combined with the impact of uncontrolled burning is sometimes insufficient to clean up the landscape and renew the conditions for local wildlife and the broader environment to flourish. The consequences of a poor or uneven river flow affect most directly the daily activities and lifestyle of local communities. It is these seasonal or in-between spaces that women, men and children inevitably have to negotiate. The fluid or muddied borders that emerge to restrict their movements do so, however, in a way that pastoral, shire and state borders do not. The former are regarded by most indigenous people as necessary to a vital process of landscape and waterway protection and transformation. As local indigenous woman, Pansy Nulgit, explains:

> The flood water clean up all the country ... like raking up all the rubbish. Cleans the pools out, gets rid of all the *jalgu* [weeds] .... Next year the flood will bring fresh, clean water. Fill up all the *malnganbudu* [billabongs] for the turtles and lilies.
>
> (quoted in Toussaint *et al.* 2001: 58)

The following testimony, from Darnby Nangkiriny, also makes plain the value of the wet season to the river and broader landscape:

> The big *warramba* [wet season rains that cause the river to flood] is good for the country [surrounding landscape] ... he get down *raparapa* side of the river, get all the dry leaves and old water in the river and some in the creek. Have all the water living in the billabong ... Billabongs get their water from the *warramba* ... [there is a Dreaming] story about the big flood because some bad people cause the flood to come. In the *marduwarra* [Fitzroy River] he [rains, flood] finish coming in the cold weather time.
>
> (quoted in Toussaint *et al.* 2001: 58)[7]

The Fitzroy River, as this spectrum of insights indicates, can be defined and valued in different ways. While it sometimes acts as a place for the enactment of co-existence and shared understanding, or presents a kind of distinct or indeterminate border, at other times it does not. Notwithstanding administrative measures, the river's life force pays scant attention to shire and town borders and pastoral fences, it traverses the country of several indigenous language groups, has become a water source imbued with meaning for non-indigenous people as residents or temporary visitors, and during the annual wet season the river's role is to 'clean up' and renew the landscape and associated waterways to ensure environmental sustainability. The river also constitutes a research site for many different disciplines, and it can be regarded as contributing to improved health and wellbeing, including as a preventative measure against the spread of trachoma.

While it is plainly the case that the Fitzroy River has a distinct history, biography and quality of its own, it variously transforms as a place of social and scientific study where water quality can be tested and cultural mapping occur. At the same time, evidence for its origins comes in the active form of indigenous stories and artworks produced by people who continue in many places to maintain and re-produce distinct forms of knowledge and conservation practices aimed at ensuring the river's continuing presence, and accommodating the natural and purposeful logic of its annual environmental flow. In these circumstances, the construction of the Fitzroy River depends on a certain socio-cultural vantage point and a person's, group's, government's, discipline's or season's relationship to it. While the Fitzroy River can be described as linking people and towns, it clearly encompasses a fluctuating matrix of culturally variable categories: the meanings attributed to it are contingent and relational. With these layered complexities in mind, including the view that the river can be understood and interacted with in multiple ways, contemplation of a 2005 Western Australian election campaign and an initiative to dam or divert the Fitzroy River, allows a series of questions regarding the complexities of 'for whom the river flows' to emerge.[8]

River flows, water options…?[9]

In a state dramatically affected by diminished water supplies and associated water shortages, combined with the consequences of salinity and parched landscapes as an outcome of ill-informed farming and firing practices and drought in the agricultural and urban south, the Western Australian Labor Government and Liberal Opposition focused on water issues in a 2005 election campaign. In the lead up to election day, the so-called 'bold' Liberal vision was to build a 3,700 km canal aimed at channelling water from the Fitzroy River to Perth, Western Australia's capital city.[10] The major contender to construct the canal was Tenix Pty Ltd, whose web site included a graphic depiction of the proposed canal, commentary on the water crisis, and the claim that the proposed canal provided a 'completely new solution'[11] for Western Australia's problems:

> The new Kimberley Canal would permit a major switch away from Perth's current reliance on diminishing underground aquifers, and would effectively 'drought proof' the city. It would provide the only long-term, cost-effective, comprehensive, reliable, sustainable and environmentally friendly solution to Perth's water crisis.[12]

On the other hand, the state Labor Government, led at that time by Dr Geoff Gallop, established an 'expert advisory panel' to assess technical proposals to construct a pipeline to divert the river's water, and instigated a series of feasibility studies on the possibility of transporting water south (Government-sponsored item calling for 'Preliminary Proposals', *The West Australian*, January 15, 2005: 56; Appleyard 2006: 7; Pearce 2006: 253–254). Both political parties communicated their visions via public forums, media releases, television interviews and broadsheets inserted into election campaign material. In addition to the pipeline possibility, Labor developed a number of other plans, such as the establishment of a desalination plant, improved irrigation, restrictions on household water use, and a water re-cycling plant for industry. Through the establishment of a 'Premier's Water Foundation', Labor also explained that more research funds would be available to conduct detailed hydrological studies of aquifers and underground water in the State's southwest. While presenting a suite of ideas and activities, however, the focus during the campaign remained firmly on how the Fitzroy River's flow could be diverted or transported to metropolitan Perth.

For a number of reasons, the Labor Government was re-elected on 26 February 2005. One reason, according to a variety of media interpretations, was that the then Liberal leader failed to 'connect with voters'. A more pronounced reason, however, was that the Liberal Opposition's budget for a series of election promises, including for the proposed Kimberley canal, was identified as seriously flawed two days before the election was to take place (Editorial, *The Australian*, 25 February 2005: 14; Mayes 27 February 2005: 41–42, 56–57). After being returned to government, Labor continued to advance water strategies announced during the campaign with diversion of the Fitzroy River from its Kimberley homeland remaining a consistent theme. In this regard, they established an inquiry[13] (at a cost to taxpayers of AU$5 million) soon after being re-elected to assess: 'three possible options for delivering water from the Kimberley, which warranted further assessment by expert consultants. These options were by: pipeline; canal; and ocean transport, using either tankers or towed water bags' (Appleyard 2006: 7).

That both State Government and the Opposition progressed ideas to solve Perth's water problems in the ways described, reveal several lines of inquiry, including an urban-south/regional-north divide, a concern evident in the comments of a Kimberley resident:

> I am a resident of the Kimberley who has fished the mighty Fitzroy River. Every person I talk to in Broome is against a canal.... All of the talk by the Opposition Leader and the media is about how much will the canal cost, how long will it take to build ... and the benefits for Perth residents.... However, there is one question that has not been asked or talked about.... What will the Kimberley get out of it? ... Are we going to get funding for extra hospitals, schools and police? Halls Creek doesn't have a swimming pool, yet you want to take its water.... The North-West has learnt to live in

> dry conditions.... In Broome we now have a beautiful green golf course and oval due to watering with grey water. Sure, it may stink, but the residents put up with that to save water. I wonder whether the residents of Perth would put up with the same smell to protect their water. It seems unlikely.
>
> (Taylor 10 February 2005: 20)

Of interest here too is the opinion of local Liberal candidate, Mr Ron 'Sos' Johnston, whose comments reflect the diversity of views in his own party about the canal:

> At his campaign office in Broome, Mr Johnston admits to having had a frank exchange of views on the issue with his Perth Liberal colleagues. 'If this [the canal] is solely for the rose gardens of Perth then it's a complete waste of time,' he said. 'At the moment we're paying more for water up here than the people of Perth when we've got plenty of water in the Kimberley.'
>
> (Dodd 9 February 2005: 7)

Another line of inquiry concerns how knowledge about the issue was created and re-produced during the campaign and how the river came to be represented and by whom. For example, while the issue affected water for personal consumption as one point of entry, at another, industry and agricultural groups were affected, including environmental groups concerned about conservation and sustainability issues. In other words, a range of divergent groups were engaged.

The two major sectors that took carriage and authority of the debate during the campaign and its aftermath were (i) environmentalist and conservation groups, and (ii) government and industry groups. Notably, Kimberley indigenous groups were hardly visible throughout the campaign, despite a number of attempts to explicate their concerns. The Broome-based environmental group Environs Kimberley campaigned against the proposal, and sometimes referred to the importance of indigenous rights and interests in the Fitzroy River,[14] but local Aboriginal culture, in particular, and everyday social and cultural life and human/water interactions more broadly, were under-represented. Of concern in such representation is a failure to consider the diversity and complexity of human activities, the value of understanding people's relationships to, and interactions with, the river, and the importance of social sustainability.

A way to assess the claim that local, especially indigenous, concerns were largely absent from public debate is by examining how sectors of the media represented the issue. Clearly one source of data only, what is of value in canvassing media items is that they represent the sorts of information and emphases readers and consumers received about the proposal (via press releases, industry and government statements), as well as how certain readers responded to that information (in letters to the editor, feature articles). Drawing on selected data from items published in *The Australian*, *West Australian* and Western Australia's *Sunday Times*[15] seven weeks prior to election day, only three items out of a total of 61 drew attention to indigenous river concerns (two of these focused on native title issues, a matter that still tends to attract a certain amount of controversy). Only two (including the letter by Taylor, quoted above) addressed the concerns of non-indigenous locals.[16] In addition to the absence of attention paid to human beliefs, ideas and practices as these related to the use, meaning and management of the Fitzroy River, was that in the 61 items evaluated the emphasis was squarely placed on environmental, political, engineering and economic issues as though these were somehow devoid of consequences for local populations.

While there is not the scope in this chapter to address fully settler relationships with the Fitzroy River in addition to canvassing how and to what extent these might coincide with or differ from those of an indigenous kind, what emerges from analysis of the media items during 35 days in the State's election campaign is that minimal consideration was given to local and tourist activities along the river (fishing, boating, swimming, camping, painting, relaxing, walking and so on) or to people's social, economic, physical, aesthetic and emotional relationship with the nearby waters and lands. And despite the wealth of extant material on indigenous custodianship, almost none was directed to indigenous socio-cultural affiliations with the river and associated waterways.[17]

Knowledge privileged during a campaign that was conducted, coincidentally, in an era often referred to as one of indigenous and settler reconciliation, related to issues not directly relevant to the maintenance and reproduction of indigenous values. For environmentalists, some of whom had geographically distant relationships with the Fitzroy River and with local indigenous custodians,[18] it was the river environment and not the people or the local culture that mattered most. For the politicians (a few of whom lived in the region)[19] it was the metropolitan voters, employment issues and economic development that mattered most.[20] Sentiments such as these were eerily replicated in the work emphases of the expert advisory panel, as the following reportage indicates:

> The panel assessing the viability of transporting water from the Fitzroy River to Perth is concerned there may not be enough time to do the job properly. The cost of engineering factors for the project have been the initial focus of the study. If the concepts were not feasible from an infrastructure and cost perspective then panel head Professor Reg Appleyard said there would be no point investigating the environmental and social impact.
>
> (Doyle 2005: 5)

In November 2006, the expert advisory panel released its report titled *Options for Bringing Water to Perth from the Kimberley: An Independent Review* (Appleyard 2006). In a detailed 90-page (plus appendices) report, their recommendation to government was that, while their review had revealed there were several technical options available to transport water from the Fitzroy River (such as supplying water by pipeline, canal or ocean transport), the cost would be prohibitive. It was concluded that:

> Given the cost of the water from either a pipeline or canal (about 100 to 200 times more expensive than current prices for irrigation water) it could not be economically justified to use this water for any irrigation development along the proposed routes.
>
> (Appleyard 2006: 9)

Commenting in the Executive Summary on 'Social Issues', it was also stated that (i) local indigenous communities did not 'support taking water from the region', and (ii) native title issues could delay the possible development of canal or pipeline options (Appleyard 2006: 9).[21]

Post its release these findings attracted further attention in media forums where the emphasis on structural and environmental issues remained dominant. Less privileged were the concerns of Fitzroy River locals who continued to express concern that the river was vulnerable to outside interests.[22] As indigenous woman Puruta Kogolo expressed it during a telephone conversation about the advisory panel's findings:[23]

> When the government mob came to tell us that they weren't taking our river, everyone was happy. But when they were leaving the meeting, one old man called out, 'so when you going to take our water…?' And we all knew what he meant. We're still worried here…

For whom the river flows…?

How the Fitzroy River was conceptualised and embedded with meaning during a state election campaign and a government initiated inquiry after the results of that campaign, demands further analysis, including in relation to the topics of sovereignty and sustainability. Keeping in mind that Western Australia was colonised in 1829, and that it was not until over one hundred years later that the cultural and ecological footprints of the colonisers began to impact on Kimberley peoples, waterways and landscapes, it is clear that sovereignty has been incrementally consolidated since that time. The possible regulation, selective transportation and/or diversion of water from the Fitzroy River to populations and lands in southern Western Australia prompts an intriguing case, in part because a selection of data shows how indigenous groups were largely excluded from government and industry initiatives, and from broader environmental debate.

The Fitzroy River, while life- and environment-sustaining, is less well recognised as central to local, everyday and long-term cultural life, not only with regard to indigenous groups but also to more recent settler migration. In an ironic and complex twist that might not have been foreshadowed 20 years ago, it is evident with regard to the Fitzroy River example that most indigenous and non-indigenous Kimberley groups opposed government and industry proposals to tamper in any way with the river, a cooperation that helped to reduce current threats and sustain local sociality and co-existence. At the same time, however, media coverage and public debate about the issue tended to consolidate Australian sovereignty in a way that clearly minimised indigenous people's demonstrated, long-term relationship to the river. The question of 'for whom the river flows...' thus remains open to further investigation, as do questions surrounding what constitutes environmental and social sustainability, especially when each of these have the transformative power to evolve over time into something seemingly new.

Notes

1 There are several Fitzroy Rivers in Australia, including northern Queensland's Fitzroy River. As evident in this chapter, my focus is on the Fitzroy River in northern Western Australia's Kimberley region. The Fitzroy River's environmental flows include high wet season levels, and low dry season levels where the volume of water is markedly reduced. That the river washes into the Timor Sea (and the Indian Ocean) is central to natural fresh and saltwater re-cycling and regeneration, and therefore beneficial to the ecology and interdependent species, such as the health and reproduction of fish stocks. That the river's water is useful rather than wasted when it washes into the sea is not widely understood.

2 While I refer throughout this chapter to the Fitzroy River, local indigenous groups with cultural affiliations to the river conceptualise and refer to it as a series of sections rather than a whole. See, for example, the maps included in Marshall 1988: 164, 165 which show a number of river section names.

3 The term 'settler', while not wholly satisfactory, is used generically to refer to non-indigenous people.

4 Other chapters in this volume consider in greater depth the legal implications of sovereignty, especially with regard to freshwater sources and saltwater oceans across and within nation states. It is important to note here, nonetheless, that on the 3 June 1992, in the case known as *Mabo* v. *the Commonwealth (No. 2)*, the Australian High Court found in favour of the Meriam people, custodians of the Island of Mer in the Torres Straits, in a landmark decision which led one year later to implementation of the *Native Title Act*. Native Title Claims are now mediated by a National Native Title Tribunal where indigenous claimants have to prove a continuing link with the land consistent with traditional usage. The High Court did not consider the matter of Aboriginal sovereignty and, in many ways, agreed with the 1979 Decision in *Coe* v. *the Commonwealth* where Justice Lionel Murphy maintained that to formally recognise Indigenous sovereignty would be for the Australian court to deny (or contradict) its own authority. Many years later, in the 1992 judgement, however, the High Court argued that it used Australian sovereignty to recognise Native Title in order to ensure that some Indigenous peoples would be assured of the right to lodge a claim to land. In some quarters, the matter of Indigenous sovereignty remains contested ground. Toussaint (2004) and the National Native Title Tribunal web site (www.nntt.gov) provide further details and links; see also Hookey 1984 for an outline of the 1979 Coe case.

5 Tourist Bureaus in West Kimberley towns such as Broome, Derby and Fitzroy Crossing increasingly boast substantial information on tourism activities and services. See, for instance, the 2005 *Derby & Fitzroy Crossing West Kimberley: Information Directory* for details.

6 Sovereignty is generally regarded as having occurred in Australia in 1788 when the British landed at Sydney Cove. Western Australia was not colonised until 1829, when the Swan River Colony was established in the southwest of the State. The northern Kimberley region did not become attractive to government, pastoralists, missionaries

and miners until the latter part of the nineteenth century. Jebb 2002, Choo 2001, Kimberley Language Resource Centre 1997 and Toussaint 1995 discuss different aspects of Kimberley history.

7 Both these narratives were recorded by Sarah Yu.

8 A reference to damming the Fitzroy River is included here in recognition of an earlier government and industry initiative to dam the river at one of its gorges (e.g. Dimond Gorge known also as *Jijidju*) to establish irrigation for cotton production. There was strong resistance to the initiative from local indigenous, settler and pastoral groups and the proposal was later withdrawn. Toussaint *et al.* 2001: 7 provides further detail and references; see also Strickland *et al.* 1993.

9 This title is adapted from the cover of the report titled *Options for bringing water to Perth from the Kimberley: an independent review*, Appleyard 2006.

10 A series of media items carried stories about the proposed canal. Too numerous to mention here, examples can be found in *The West Australian*, 23–25 February 2005, *The Australian*, 24–25 February 2005, *Sunday Times*, 27 February 2005.

11 This was not, however, the first time that the idea had been promoted. Former Labor Minister for the Kimberley, Indigenous man Ernie Bridge, proposed the harvesting of Fitzroy River waters in 1993. His initiative was not backed by the then Liberal State Government led by Richard Court (Trott 2005: 16; see also Pennels 2005: 1, 19 which includes commentary from former Liberal Premier, Sir Charles Court, who argued that the water should remain 'up north' (p. 1).

12 Information from a one-page advertisement placed by Tenix in *The West Australian*, 21 February 2005, p. 8.

13 Members of the panel commissioned to conduct the inquiry had a mix of environmental, economic, legal and engineering backgrounds. They were Professor Reg Appleyard (Chair), Professor Ian Lowe, Dr Don Blackmore, and Dr Beverley Ronalds.

14 For example, in a submission to the expert advisory panel established to assess water options from the Kimberley, local group Environs Kimberley noted that 'The Community and Traditional Owners have previously made their views on damming the Fitzroy River known. There is widespread community opposition to impounding the waterways of the Fitzroy River and the wild rivers of the Kimberley' (2004: 2).

15 Data referred to here is from a larger Australian Research Council Discovery Project titled 'Under Water: a comparative ethnographic analysis on the use and management of water and natural resources in Queensland and Western Australia', awarded to Veronica Strang and me in 2003.

16 Further illustration of the lack of attention paid to people and culture is that in a number of events organised by environmentalists in Perth to put the case against the proposed canal, including one by the Western Australian Conservation Council, Joe Ross, a Kimberley Bunuba man with cultural affiliations to the river inherited through his mother, was listed as the last speaker (after an environmentalist, fish specialist and historian) in a program ironically titled 'Canal Dreaming: is it worth the price the environment will pay?' (Conservation Council of WA Flyer, 24 February 2005, Perth).

17 As indicated above, indigenous relationships to the Fitzroy River have been identified as part of several ongoing native title claims, e.g. Bagshaw 2003. Ethnographic and environmental reports documenting Indigenous knowledge were commissioned by the State's Water and Rivers Commission (Toussaint *et al.* 2001; Storey *et al.* 2001). A series of ethnographic and documentary films (for example, Hughes 1998, 2000; Hughes and Kinnane 1999) explaining Indigenous attachments to the river, and art exhibitions highlighting the river through visual and narrative vantage points (*Martuwarra* and *Jila: river and desert*, 2003), highlight relationships with local river and desert migrant Indigenous groups.

18 'Custodians' is used here and elsewhere as an alternative to 'Traditional Owners', even though both terms are contextually appropriate.

19 Carol Martin, the local Labor Kimberley Member and an Indigenous woman from southern Western Australia, is an exception here. She consistently expressed her opposition to the proposal in parliamentary debate and media commentary.

20 Notable also in the campaign was the inadequate attention paid to alternative means to assist the problem of diminished water supplies, such as re-cycling and 'green' technologies. Since that time, however, re-cycling has been increasingly promoted by government, and a desalination plant to service the urban and regional south has been opened, albeit with mixed responses from environmentalists.

21 Social Issues are briefly dealt with in other sections of the report, such as on pages 70–74 where reference is made to a 2005 meeting organised by the Kimberley Land Council, the Australian Conservation Foundation and Environs Kimberley.

22 Notable too is that in a recent weekend edition of *The West Australian*, a feature article returned to possible transportation of water from the Fitzroy River to ease problems in the State's south (Parker 2007: 1, 8.)

23 Puruta Kogolo is a Walmajarri woman who currently works for Karrayili Adult Education in Fitzroy Crossing. This conversation took place during a phone call a week after the report's release.

Bibliography

Appleyard, R. (2006) *Options for Bringing Water to Perth from the Kimberley: An Independent Review*, Perth: Department of Premier and Government, Western Australia.

Bagshaw, G. (2003) *The Karajarri Claim: A Case Study in Native Title Anthropology*, Oceania Monograph, Sydney: University of Sydney.

Beckwith and Associates (1999) *Kimberley Water Allocation Planning: An Overview of Stakeholder Issues*, report for the Western Australia Water and Rivers Commission.

Choo, C. (2001) *Mission Girls: Aboriginal Women on Catholic Missions in the Kimberley, Western Australia, 1900–1950*, Nedlands: University of Western Australia Press.

Conservation Council of Western Australia 'Flyer', 24 February 2005, Perth.

Derby Visitor Centre (2005) *Derby & Fitzroy Crossing West Kimberley: Information Directory*, Derby.

Dodd, M. (2005) 'West Australian Poll', *The West Australian*, 9 February.

Doyle, M. (2005) 'Time a Concern for Water Study', *Broome Advertiser*, 1 December.

Environs Kimberley (2004) *Submission to the Kimberley Expert Water Supply Panel*, Perth: Western Australian Government.

Hales, R. (2006) 'Kayaking on the Fitzroy River', *Environs Kimberley Newsletter*, Bulletin No. 37.

Hookey, J. (1984) 'Settlement and Sovereignty', in P. Hanks and B. Keon-Cohen (eds) *Aborigines and the Law*, Sydney: Allen & Unwin.

Jebb, M.A. (2002) *Blood, Sweat and Welfare: A History of White Bosses and Aboriginal Pastoral Workers*, Nedlands: University of Western Australia Press.

Kimberley Appropriate Economies Roundtable (2006) Forum Proceedings published with support from the Australian Conservation Foundation, the Kimberley Land Council, and Environs Kimberley, Cairns, the Australian Conservation Foundation.

Kimberley Language Resource Centre (1997) *Moola Bulla: In the Shadow of a Mountain*, Broome: Magabala Books.

—— (1998) *Thangani Bunuba – Bunuba Stories*, Halls Creek: Kimberley Language Resource Centre.

Kogolo, P. (2006) Personal communication.

Mangkaja Arts (1991) *Karrayili: An Exhibition of Works by Students of Karrayili Adult Education Centre, Fitzroy Crossing and Bayulu Community, Kimberley, Western Australia*, Exhibition Catalogue.

—— (2003) *Martuwarra and Jila: River and Desert*, Exhibition Catalogue, Mangkaja Arts and the University of Western Australia, Nedlands.

Marshall, L. (2006) 'Tropical Rivers Forum', *Environs Kimberley Newsletter*, Bulletin No. 37: 9.

Marshall, P. (ed.) (1988) *Raparapa: Stories from the Fitzroy River Drovers*, Broome: Magabala Books.

Mayes, L. (2005) *Sunday Times*, 27 February, pp. 41–42, 56–57.

Pannell, S. (2000) 'Upper Fitzroy Valley: Identification of a Nationally Significant Historical and Cultural Landscape', unpublished report for the Kimberley Land Council, Fitzroy Crossing.

Parker, G. (2007) 'Feature Article', *The West Australian*, 13 January.

Pearce, F. (2006) *When the Rivers Run Dry – What Happens when our Water Runs Out?* London: Transworld Publishers.

Pennels, S. (2005) 'Opinion', *The West Australian*, 17 February.

Prior, P. (2006) 'Back to Mornington', *Broome Happenings*, Issue 79, 16–29 June.

Storey, A., Froend, R. and Davies, P. (2001) 'Fitzroy River System: Environmental Values', unpublished report for the Water and Rivers Commission, Perth.

Strickland, G., Fitt, G., Thomson, N. and Constable, G. (1993) 'The Potential for Sustainable Cotton Production in the Kimberley', unpublished report, Western Australian Department of Agriculture and the CSIRO.

Taylor, P. (2005) 'Broome Letters', *The West Australian*, 10 February: 20.

Thorburn, D., Morgan, D. and Gill, H. (2004) 'Biology and Cultural Significance of the Freshwater Sawfish (*Pristis microdon*) in the Fitzroy River, Kimberley, Western Australia', unpublished report for the Centre for Fish and Fisheries Research, Perth: Murdoch University.

Toussaint, S. (1995) 'Western Australia', in McGrath, A. (ed.) *Contested Ground: Australian Aborigines Under the British Crown*, Sydney: Allen & Unwin.

—— (1999) 'Kimberley Aboriginal Peoples', in Lee, R. and Daly, R. (eds), *Foraging Peoples: Contemporary Hunters and Gatherers*, Cambridge: Cambridge University Press.

—— (ed.) (2004) *Crossing Boundaries: Cultural, Historical, Legal and Practice Issues in Native Title*, Carlton: Melbourne University Press.

Toussaint, S., Sullivan, P., Yu, S. and Mularty, M. Jr (2001) 'Fitzroy Valley Indigenous Cultural Values (a Preliminary Assessment)', unpublished report for the Water and Rivers Commission, Perth.

Toussaint, S., Sullivan, P. and Yu, S. (2005) 'Water Ways in Aboriginal Australia: An Interconnected Analysis', *Anthropological Forum*, 15(1): 61–74.

Trott, P. (2005) 'News Election 2005', *The West Australian*, 10 February.

Yu, S. (2000) 'Ngapa Kunangkul: Living Water', report on the Aboriginal cultural values of groundwater in the La Grange sub-basin, for the West Australian Water and Rivers Commission, Perth.

Film

Costin, R. (2003) *Heart of the Kimberley: Wildwater Country – A Film by Richard Costin*, Kimberley Media, www.kimberleymedia.com.au.

Hughes, J. (1998) *A Conversation with Butcher Cherel*, Fitzroy Crossing: Mangkaja Arts.
—— (2000) *Willigan's Fitzroy*, Sydney: Film Australia and the Australian Broadcasting Corporation.
Hughes, J. and Kinnane, S. (1999) *River of Dreams*, Canberra: Australian Institute of Aboriginal and Torres Strait Islander Studies and SBS Independent.

13 Salt Pan Creek

Rivers as border zones within the colonial city

Heather Goodall and Allison Cadzow

When Joe Anderson became the first Aboriginal man to use the cinema to demand recognition for his people in the 1930s, he did so by standing at his riverbank home in the centre of Sydney. The role of the river was crucial in Joe's challenge to white Australia. This chapter is a close study of a river community in Sydney, Australia, to investigate how an urban area which was densely colonized could nevertheless shelter a nucleus of indigenous and undefeated people who eventually reasserted their right to be heard in their own country.

The 1933 Cinesound News broadcast reached audiences across the nation. Joe Anderson refused to be depicted as a relic from the past, unlike earlier filmed Aborigines, nor did he make any concessions to the British who had invaded his country nearly 150 years before. Instead he made it clear that he was from the very contemporary present, standing in his own heavy greatcoat in front of the tea trees where he lived at Salt Pan Creek, on the Georges River in southwest Sydney. Looking directly at the camera, he began his dignified and impassioned plea to the audiences beyond:

> Before the white man set foot in Australia, my ancestors had kings in their own right, and I, Aboriginal King Burraga, am a direct descendant of the royal line...
>
> (*Cinesound Review* 1933)

His message was urgent: he and his family were under immediate threat of eviction from their traditional home. The local Progress Association in this densely populated district did not want the potential for housing expansion to be disturbed by a 'blacks' camp' and had petitioned local government to force the Aborigines to 'move on'. The Progress Association was acting on the assumption that the Andersons were newcomers, describing them as being 'from elsewhere', although they never bothered to find out where. Joe Anderson knew better: his grandmother was Biddy, a Gweagal woman from the northern shore of the river who was living at Mill Creek in the 1860s, just opposite the entrance to Salt Pan Creek, and who continued to live on the river until her death in the 1890s. His grandfather was Burragalung, a Dharawal man whose country stretched from north of the Georges River to south of Thirroul. Their daughter, Ellen, maintained Biddy's commitment to the river. Despite being forcibly moved with many Sydney Aboriginal people to the Murray River in the 1880s, Ellen returned and purchased land on Salt Pan Creek in the 1910s. There she and her husband, Hugh Anderson, raised Joe.

Salt Pan Creek was central to Joe's life and to the story of Aboriginal re-assertion in Sydney over 200 years. It was no accident of geography that the site for such a rich tradition of resistance to the colonial enterprise should have been a watercourse. Rivers, creeks and waterholes have not only been key sites of conflict because their resources were necessary to both settlers and Aboriginal people, they have also been seen by settlers as the means to mark out the dividing lines between them and the conquered peoples.

In townships around rural Australia, settlers tried to make rivers into the borders which separated the orderly grid patterns of the town's society and economy from the disorderly 'blacks' camp' which was always 'over the river', in the symbolic as well as physical sense. The Aboriginal people of the camp might fulfil lowly cleaning jobs in the town but they were not permitted to live closer than the camp, which was confined to the more flood-prone low bank of the river, isolated from the stores and schools, always cut off during a flood and easily cordoned and quarantined in times of illness or unrest (Rowley 1971). Simon Schama has pointed out that Europeans – and particularly those in the 'new world' colonies like the United States – have often tried to embed their visions and desires into the natural surroundings to which they had laid claim (Schama 1996: 17). By doing so colonizers have sought to recruit Nature to bring authority and certainty to their newly imposed control over land and people. Goodall has shown how white Australian residents of Brewarrina, a town on the upper Darling River in pastoral country, used the river to control the Murri camp, located 'over the river' at Billy Goat Bend (Goodall 2006). As the Aboriginal population at the camp grew in the 1930s, with Aboriginal parents demanding enrolment for their children at the town's public school, the municipal council exploited the spatial power which this 'over the river' banishment allowed. Although there was no legislative basis to do so, the Council ordered the police to impose a curfew on all Aboriginal people by closing the bridge into town after 6 pm, refusing them entry into the town and arresting anyone still lingering in the streets on charges of drunkenness, which were impossible to disprove (Goodall 1982, 1996).

Yet Australian rivers betrayed this settler hope: they were not the well-behaved rivers of Britain and Europe. Instead, their banks were steep, gullied with incoming streams, thick with fine black mud, which turned to a quagmire when wet, and thickly covered with entangled gum tree roots. They offered retreats where Aboriginal people could shelter in safety from pursuing troopers on horseback, and later even from police in four-wheel drives. Australian rivers are characteristically variable in their flow – droughts leave the banks exposed as plunging ravines, while floods swell the waters until they expand far beyond the narrow river bed into a wide, trackless marsh, an experience which had bewildered early colonial explorers. Once the floods subside, the river's bed might have altered or the billabongs and overflows which run parallel to the main bed might continue to be full and impassable for months. This could be no simple border. Eventually, in Brewarrina, a major flood in 1974 became the occasion for a dramatic confrontation between the white town authorities and what had become an articulate and nationally connected Aboriginal community. A breach was finally opened in the town's segregation (Goodall 2006).

This has been the general Australian experience: rivers have proved to be unreliable allies for colonizers and settlers, and the climatic and hydrological eccentricities of the Australian landscape have favoured sustained Aboriginal presence. This has meant that rivers were not firm barriers between colonizer and colonized. Instead they have been liminal zones, allowing not only the continued presence of the colonized but also their unregulated interaction with settlers in illicit social and sexual encounters, which meant in practice their subversion of the orderly life of the township. Eventually these unreliable border zones allowed Aboriginal people 'across the river' to reassert their sovereignty over the river lands and, more broadly, their right to be heard in the town itself.

However widespread this has been in rural areas, such a pattern has not been considered in relation to Australian cities, where Aboriginal people were assumed to have disappeared rapidly after the initial invasion. Yet Joe Anderson's story suggests that city rivers might prove to have been just as unreliable as rural ones in shoring up settler control. This chapter will trace the history of one of Sydney's most heavily populated and industrial waterways, the Georges River, to uncover a history of ambiguous border lands, riverbanks shared in de facto commons with working class and outlawed settlers and, eventually, a reassertion of Aboriginal sovereignty in the centre of the colonial city.

The Georges River is a long river, rising in high country and running north to the Cumberland Plains, where it drops its silt burden as it swings east at Liverpool to carve its way through rising sandstone cliffs towards Botany Bay. Its fresh water begins to mix with the salt water in the bend at Liverpool, becoming tidal as it flows past Salt Pan Creek and on into the Bay. The river flows from relatively open plains into steep escarpment country, leaving it with only narrow banks at the Salt Pan junction. These banks had a sequence of salt tolerant vegetation, ranging from fringing mangroves to salt marshes and reed beds, to stands of casuarina on higher ground. The cliffs are steep and the mangroves grow thickly on some narrow littoral areas, but in others the salt marsh zones are wider, giving the impression of open spaces running down to the river. Importantly, there are freshwater springs on the tidal saline estuary, including at Salt Pan Creek, and these guaranteed drinking water to the indigenous communities who regularly camped there on their journeys along the river, from coastal camps to the wooded hinterland.

This country was heavily populated before the British invasion in 1788. The southern bank of the estuary was Dhawaral people's land, which stretched from Liverpool in the west to Botany Bay in the east and as far south as Wollongong and Thirroul.[1] The Gweagal people held responsibility for the Kurnell Peninsula, around the southern edge of Botany Bay, while the area to the north along the Cooks River was Bidjegal land. Both Gweagal and Bidjegal people shared responsibility for Kamay, the Indigenous name for Botany Bay (Williams 2005). Northwest of the river were the extensive lands of the Dharug peoples which included the Parramatta River, while to the southwest, on the headwaters of the Georges and Nepean Rivers in the southern highlands, were Gandangara peoples. There appears to have been a high degree of movement between these language groups' areas, both seasonally and on ceremonial occasions. Besides their neighbours, each language group would be in communication with and connected to larger trading and ceremonial cycles which stretched along the coast and over the Blue Mountains to Wiradjuri and Gamilaraay country. The river was intensively used: the tops of the escarpments show the remains of tool-making sites, and along the cliffs and overhangs there are charcoal-blackened hearths and extensive middens with traces of mussels, oysters and birds. The surrounding bush yielded possums, wallabies and goannas as well as honey and eggs. The overhanging caves of the sandstone escarpments have many beautiful art sites overlooking the river, like the stencil gallery above Sandy Point, where the vivid prints of many hands point to large gatherings of people over centuries.

The early years of the British invasion caused as much illness as violence for local Aboriginal people and this decimated the population of the river lands for some decades. Although Aboriginal people remained on the Georges River, an 1843 map of Bankstown shows that most of their lands had been alienated to private British owners by grant or sale within a few years.[2] The way the settlers could use these river lands depended on the soils. The shale-based soils, like the alluvial flats along the narrow floodplains, were fertile enough to support settler agriculture so that farming proliferated especially where fresh water was plentiful. There were, however, wider areas of sandy soil found particularly on the lower saltwater reaches of the river. Although rich in iron and allowing a riot of colourful wildflowers in spring, the sandstone soils were far less fertile and retained little water, making settler farming impossible.

The sandstone areas became increasingly obvious on the parish maps onto which the clerks of the Lands Department carefully pencilled in each new subdivision and its new owners whenever land was sold. The infertile areas were never annotated because they never changed hands. Yet the fact that no one wanted to buy them did not mean that those areas were not used. The initial settlers were a mixture of English military supervisors and convict workers, many of whom were Irish. The economy they developed mixed a formal inflow of cash wages from working on the larger agricultural properties with an informal income from the domestic produce of household gardens and chickens within the residential areas but also from fishing and shooting, especially rabbits, as they harvested the adjacent sandstone country. The water's edge itself proved to be lucrative: the best alkaline ash for soap making came from the mangroves (Bird 1982: 274–80). Salt Pan Creek gained its English name from the shallow pans built by the first settlers on its shores in which water would be evaporated to leave a residue of salt which could be sold for ready cash.

While there were no formal records of the sandstone use, there were many tracks worn through the undergrowth as people travelled from one place to another to fish, hunt or gather firewood from the scrub. Along with their economic motives, there were social motives as well. Local people went into the scrub seeking privacy and discretion for many reasons, from secret sexual dalliances to illegal coursing and gambling (Davies, Mulholland and Pipe 1979; Haworth 1995: 37–8). The first aerial photographs in 1930 show the presence of these foot tracks, some worn deeply into the earth, reflecting the generations of working people who had gone about their livelihood and their leisure in the bush (Haworth 1995). These areas on the map were not 'blank': they were merely invisible to the law, the surveyors and the property market.

The river environment had always been a dynamic one shaped by Aboriginal harvesting over many centuries. But the pressures on it accelerated with the first impacts of European settlement, including clearing, erosion and siltation as well as introduced species, all of which were indicated by changes in the river banks. Changing land use reshaped the river bed below the surface too, and it was fishing people casting nets and launching boats who began to notice the new underwater banks and shoals, while swimmers and picnickers were acutely aware of the changing ratio of sand to mud and the altering view from land to river.

The complex effects on riverbank mangroves were an example. The impact of soap making on the mangrove stands was significant, causing them to retreat in many areas where the harvesting was most intense (Bird 1982). Just as significant may have been the changes in native grazing pressure on the shore and wetland vegetation: swamp wallabies grazed on both mangroves and saltmarshes, but caused greater impact on the mangroves. Aboriginal hunting of wallabies may have declined with severe population loss from violence and illness, but on the other hand European hunting was increasing. The shifting balance between the two, and the varying numbers of wallabies, meant that the relationship between mangroves and saltmarshes became unstable. This may have led to mangrove retreats in some areas and in others to mangrove expansion into the saltmarsh area (Haworth 2002: 99). Another major impact on the shores was the effect of the extensive clearing for agriculture on the middle and upper reaches of the river. As soon as clearing commenced, erosion began to increase, leading to a greater burden of silt being washed down river with any rain. Such changes in riverine sediments further destabilized the relationships between bank vegetation types, often leading to the expansion of mangroves either at the expense of the inland salt marshes or, in rare cases, into the water on broadening silt sediments (Adam and Striker 1989: 11–13; Dunstan 1990: 1–6; Haworth 2002: 99).

Yet despite the continuing impacts on the river, Aboriginal people closely connected to it kept on living there and travelling through this area. The earliest Aboriginal evidence is the testimony of a Botany Bay man, Mahroot, answering questions at a Parliamentary Inquiry in 1845.[3] Mahroot said that few of his people had survived the early years around Cooks River and Botany, but there had been a more substantial surviving population on the Georges River around Liverpool. These people spoke a distinct language from that of his own people and he called them Cobrakalls, associating them with a prized delicacy, *cobra*, the long estuarine worms which taste like rich oysters and live in submerged wood in brackish water. Mahroot explained that although only a handful of speakers of his own language remained, these other Aboriginal people had moved into the Botany area to live with them. In those days when the British settlement was still very limited, he described the Liverpool area from which they came as 'the country', but he explained that while these 'other' people did not 'belong to Botany', they nevertheless had a connection to his place: they were 'different people raised up here [Botany] in former times come [back]'.

Mahroot's explanation that the incoming 'other' people had earlier links to Botany is consistent with what was learned in later-settled areas, which was that knowledge of and formal responsibilities for adjacent people's lands were protected in ceremonial relationships which stretched across substantial areas of land. This broad network allowed neighbouring peoples to take up responsibility for land if it became necessary due to death or disaster, so while the colonial settlement may have brought far more rapid and greater changes than before, it could still be met with responses grounded in familiar cultural patterns.

As well there continued to be local people travelling and camping regularly along the Georges River. In the 1840s a well-known group, led by 'King Bungerry and his wife Betsy', were regularly seen travelling around Bankstown and camping at the Salt Pan Creek, because of the freshwater spring and the plentiful possums and other game.[4] Bungerry was a Bidjegal-speaking man from the northern bank of the Georges River, with affiliations to Prospect Creek. This would align his country with that of the Cobrakalls of whom Mahroot spoke at around the same time (Flynn 1997; Brook and Kohen 1991: 91–2).

Two decades later, Biddy, was first recorded as living at Mill Creek. She was a Gweagal woman, born probably in the early 1830s. Although she may have been betrothed as an adolescent to Kooma, an elder of the Georges River country, Biddy left this relationship as a young adult to marry Paddy Davis Burragalung, from the southern Dharawal communities around Thirroul and Wollongong, and on this basis she was remembered by whites as a princess of the Wollongong tribe.[5] Ellen's son, Joe, Biddy's grandson, wrote in 1936 that the language and land of Burragalung, his Dharawal grandfather's people, extended even further, from Wollongong in the south to Port Stephens, well beyond Sydney, in the north.[6]

Biddy later married a white man, Billy Giles, and in the 1860s was living with him on Mill Creek which runs into the Georges River on its southern bank. This relationship brought Biddy to the attention of whites seeking to make small adventurous 'exploration' trips, or to hunt and fish on the southern side of the Georges River. This area was undeveloped until the 1880s, when Thomas Holt's pastoral concern was established. A cluster of settler memoirs published in 1904, 1907 and 1911 describe Biddy's knowledgeable guidance and her active engagement with white people in the area. As S.B.J. Robinson recalled, Biddy and Billy,

> ...acted as guides, philosophers and friends to a party of us who, in 1866 ... came down the Georges River from the Liverpool Dam.... And such fishing! It seems to me now as if, no matter what hour of the day it was, or what was the state of the tide or what kind was the weather, 'Biddy' could put us 'on' to the fish.
>
> (*St George Call*, 8 April 1911)

Biddy guided and cooked for another party, who described her stringybark-lined boat (*St George Call*, 17 August 1907: 3) and for yet another group, this time on a shooting trip, whom she not only took on productive hunts but to whom she told creation stories and explained rock engraving sites (*St George Call*, 6 April, 20 April, 11 May 1907: 3). Long after her Billy's death, Biddy remained in the area, moving along the river from Mill Creek east to Sylvania, where she was photographed in the 1880s some years before her death.[7]

These settler memoirs allow us a window into the social network which existed along the banks of the Georges River throughout the second half of the nineteenth century. Biddy was not the only Aboriginal person on the river, although she is one of the few mentioned by name as having been there in the 1860s. Yet the settler memoirs are peppered with references to the way Biddy organized her guided trips by travelling between the camps along the river in which both Aboriginal and non-Aboriginal people were living. At times those Aboriginal people were described but not named and at other times they appeared as transient figures with names like Yellow Nancy. The whites visited in these accounts were invariably reclusive eccentrics and were fishermen or small farmers and oysterers living isolated lives. In all, there are enough glimpses here to see a continuing presence of Aboriginal people in a range of different situations, virtually all of them interacting with the margins of the settler society which was consolidating more substantially on the northern side of the river. By the 1880s, there were more detailed recordings as the NSW State government established a formal system of administration, ironically called 'Protection'. In 1882, the Protector recorded the frequent and regular movement of Aboriginal people between Wollongong in the south and the Burragorang Valley, in the west, along the length of the Georges River to and from the government reserves at Botany and La Perouse at Botany Bay (Report of Protector of the Aborigines, 1882: 7). These reports confirmed the presence of groups of Aboriginal families living at Holsworthy near Liverpool at the upper tidal point. At the lower end, near the junction with Botany Bay, there were camps at Kogarah Bay, Weeney Bay and at the Holt property at Sylvania. The Protection Board continued to report on the communities of Aboriginal people in an annual census. These figures suggested that although the outlying communities like Windsor and the Burragorang Valley had more people, there were sustained groups of Aboriginal people living on whole length of the lower Georges River, and there was continuing contact between these smaller communities and the more closely government-controlled settlements at La Perouse on Botany Bay itself. Furthermore, most of the Georges River groups were living largely independently of the Board, with one extended family at Holsworthy managing a profitable farm and the nearby Liverpool group receiving only the occasional symbolic blanket issue, but otherwise supporting themselves entirely from a mixture of cash employment and traditional subsistence fishing, hunting and harvesting wild honey (Report of Protector of the Aborigines 1882: 12–13).

Georges River people had not only embedded themselves in particular blocks of land like the Holsworthy farmers. Many, like Biddy, were on the move, using the waterways as inexpensive and simple ways to travel, exactly as traditional societies had for centuries. William Rowley was a Gweagal-Dharawal man who had been born at Pelican Point near Weeney Bay, where the Georges River empties into Botany Bay. He was at the La Perouse reserve in the 1880s, and was one of five men who wrote to George Thornton, the Chief Protector, in 1883, to express their thanks for the issue of a fishing boat and occasional rations (Report of the Protector of Aborigines 1882: 9). He moved along the river, working on the large Holt estate at Sylvania as well as fishing at Weenie Bay. In the early years of the twentieth century he made his way to Salt Pan Creek and settled there in the 1910s.

Yet although many of the people on the river by the early years of the twentieth century had their ancestral roots on the river, there were also many Aboriginal people who had come across the state and beyond to work and live there. Many of Rowley's fellow workers on the Holt Estate, for example, like Jimmy Lowndes, had come from western NSW to work as stockmen on the pastoral concern and stayed on as bullock drivers or general hands once Holt's interest turned to oysters. The story of Biddy Giles's daughter, Ellen, is important in understanding how the river Aboriginal communities became ones of great diversity at the same time as they maintained a link with the traditional owners.

Ellen was among the young Sydney Aboriginal people who had been forced to move to the missionary establishment at Maloga on the Murray River in 1881 (Report of Protector of the Aborigines 1882: 4–8; Nugent 2005: 48). There she married Hugh Anderson, from one of the families who were the stalwarts of the Cummeragunja Yorta Yorta community, which campaigned for control over their land against the NSW Protection Board. Anderson was an outspoken advocate for better conditions for Aboriginal people, writing for the local newspaper and speaking in public about the need for justice. Ellen and Hugh's travels in their early married life took them from Cummeragunja to Kangaroo Valley, to Wollongong, down to Salt Pan Creek and then all the way back.[8] Some of Ellen's children, like her oldest son Joe, were born at Wollongong, others, like her youngest daughter Dolly, at Cummeragunja. Their by-then grown children were with them when Ellen and Hugh settled down to live at Salt Pan Creek sometime around 1910. So Gweagal and Dharawal people continued to live around the river, socializing with settlers as well as their own community, working for local land owners like Holt and living from a mixture of their cash earnings along with fishing, hunting and guiding. Other Aboriginal people had been drawn there by work, like Jimmy Lowndes, or by marriage, like Hugh Anderson. All this while, much of the land they used along the river for their informal economy of hunting and subsistence gathering, to supplement working for cash, was land which seemed to be 'vacant' on the maps. Although legally in private hands, it had been undeveloped because it had proved unsuitable for either agriculture or housing, having no capacity for domestic gardens. In effect, these areas continued to function as a de facto commons.

Behind these sandstone riverlands, in the early decades of the twentieth century, local suburban residential populations were consolidating, although their expansion had been slowed by the loss of large numbers of men during the First World War. However much of the compensatory land settlement for returned servicemen was also located in this area, including the subdivision of large blocks of market gardens at Milperra, Hillview and Chipping Norton. These soldiers' settlements were seldom successful commercially but, at least initially, they increased the population and added to the pressure to subdivide and clear agricultural areas, increasing siltation and moving housing steadily out towards the sandstone. The penetration of factories onto the Georges River from Liverpool to Bankstown in the 1920s further increased employment opportunities, although adding a burden of toxic industrial pollution to the river at the same time as the increased amount of cheaply built, unserviced housing needed for workers' accommodation added major flows of untreated sewerage (Kass 2005; Rosen 1996).

The sandstone areas were still largely intact however when Ellen and Hughie Anderson first came back to settle down at Salt Pan Creek around 1911. They were just a mile or two downstream from Mill Creek and opposite Alfords Point, both places where Ellen's mother, Biddy, had lived. In the 1920s they purchased a block in Ogilvy Street on the eastern side of the creek near the junction with the Georges River[9] and Hugh made a living by fishing (*Propeller*, 24 August 1923). William Rowley, the Gweagal man from more easterly parts of the river, purchased the block next door and their blocks became a nucleus for a new consolidation of the Aboriginal population.[10] This part of the river remained largely undeveloped and their neighbours, although not Aboriginal, were initially people from the same social stratum who had little income and made precarious livings from selling locally grown produce or fish. The young Eric Dickinson, a white boy visiting his aunt on the western side of Salt Pan Creek in 1913, remembers it as a clear, unpolluted stream whose banks were sandy rather than choked, as they later became, with invasive local mangroves expanding into what became a polluted and silted channel.[11] Dickinson's visits there were always 'an adventure' because of the Aborigines living there (Dickinson 1984). Ellen and Hugh's home expanded: by the mid 1920s they had built three weatherboard cottages and some sheds, one large enough to be used as a church. Other visitors camped in tents. There were around 30 people living at Ogilvy Street in 1926 (*The St George Call*, 7 May 1926; 30 December 1927: 2).

The Andersons were closely involved with the Anglican Inland Mission. They were mentioned in the AIM newsletter, held church services on their land and encouraged one of their sons when he became a missionary for the organization in other parts of the state. At the same time, the State government had intensified its control over Aboriginal people, gaining new powers to remove people from long established rural camp sites where they had been farming, as well as gaining the power to remove Aboriginal children from their families. Many Aboriginal people found the networks they had developed through missionary activity offered them a new strategy for objecting to this increasing State pressure. Just a few suburbs away from Salt Pan Creek, one white member of the AIM, Elizabeth McKenzie Hatton, had begun organizing with Aboriginal activists like Fred Maynard, and in 1924 she established a home for girls who had been removed from their families by the Protection Board but had then escaped Board control (Maynard 2005: 3–27). The Salt Pan Creek community was in touch with this movement and its currents were reflected in the way the community developed.

As Ellen Anderson and William Rowley owned their land outright, there had never been any control by government over this camp, nor over the other Aboriginal families who might have been living either in private rental accommodation nearby or on the 'common' sandstone areas. So as the State government pressure became ever more oppressive, the Salt Pan camp became a beacon as a free community, attracting those who refused to live under Protection Board control. One such person was Tom Williams Senior, a Gamilaraay man from Coonamble who had served overseas in the Australian Infantry during the War and, on his return to Australia, refused to live under the Board. His children remember that even in the worst days of the Depression, when Tom had lost work and faced eviction, he moved his family to a tent on Ellen's block, telling them that he would 'rather take them to live in a bag hut than go to live on a (government) mission with a manager standing over them!'[12]

While there were conflicts with the white neighbours, there were also close relationships, with many local memoirs recalling frequent interactions between Aboriginal and Anglo residents, like those of the Webb family, whose children remember being taught to throw boomerangs and blow gum leaves to play music by the Anderson brothers at the family store.[13] When the store owner, L.C. Webb, died in a car accident, the Aborigines from Salt Pan were the first to arrive at his funeral, walking overland to reach the cemetery at Woronora, and their 'lovely wreaths, sprays of native flowers and beautifully handwritten note were greatly appreciated by the Webb family'.[14]

The interactions between both Aboriginal and Anglo children, particularly, have left memories about the informal economy of the riverbanks. Families from both communities fished, netted for prawns and gathered oysters on the creek, although it was usually only the Aboriginal families who caught eels and mussels. And it was only the Aboriginal families who did the more specialized work based on Aboriginal traditional skills. Tom Williams Senior, for example, as his daughter Ellen Williams (now James) remembers, supplemented his wages in the 1920s by rowing down the river in the family's small boat, searching for 'elbows' of mangrove wood which would have just the right shape for carving boomerangs to sell for 'pocket money'. Ern Blewett, a local Anglo resident, remembers as a boy watching while Tom carved the boomerangs and then burnt delicate ornamental patterns into the wood with a hot poker. Younger men from La Perouse eagerly rowed up the river to Salt Pan to take advantage of Tom's knowledge of the best places along the riverbank to get the wood for the boomerangs and other artifacts they carved for sale to tourists at La Perouse.[15]

Just as important for cash income was the gathering of the prolific wildflowers, including those known to the settlers as Christmas Bells, as well as the vivid red new gum tips, which would be sold door to door locally or taken into the city markets on Friday nights. A young Ellen Williams (Tom and Dolly's daughter) was frequently taken in the 1920s by her grandmother, Ellen Anderson, into the surrounding bush to gather flowers and gum leaves, with Granny Ellen teaching her granddaughter as they went about the medicinal uses for the plants and insects they encountered. At the same time Granny Ellen explained the stories for the country there, the traditional myths which showed how the plants, animals and people were related to the landscape of the river (James 2005). Thus both traditional economies and traditional knowledge were being brought into the contemporary lives of young Aboriginal people growing up along the river. Ellen Anderson retold some of these stories to W.C. Peck, a local small businessman who collected Aboriginal narratives. She had seen his newspaper articles and sought him out, becoming the major informant for his 1933 edition of *Aboriginal Legends*, published after Ellen's death but in which Peck describes his meeting with her (Illert 2003).

It was a common situation for Aboriginal people in the mid-twentieth century to be working in these mixed environments. Whether employed for wages and attending the Returned Servicemen's League, like Tom Williams, or owning land freehold and selling gum tips for cash, like Ellen Anderson, they were active in the market economy and they interacted with the growing non-Aboriginal society in the area. Yet, simultaneously, whether carving boomerangs, as Tom did, or taking her granddaughter to find bush medicine plants, as Ellen did, these Aboriginal people were drawing on a heritage of traditional values and skills to weave a life for themselves which contained all these varied and sometimes conflicting elements.

The rising numbers of Aboriginal people living at the Salt Pan camp and in the surrounding area by the late 1920s were no accident. This was a time of intense turmoil among Aboriginal people as the Aborigines Protection Board tried to impose its new powers to disperse Aboriginal communities across the state, which it did by first driving people off their independent farmed reserves, and second by separating children from their families – both strategies aimed at undermining community identification (Goodall 1996: 126–36; Read 1988). The Board's first intervention had been at Cummeragunja, Hugh Anderson's home, followed by pressure on other communities, starting in the northwestern areas, including Brewarrina and Coonamble, then moving to the north and south coasts of the state. Those who protested, like the south coast families and the Cummeragunja people, found that they needed to escape Board control. The Salt Pan camps were an important resource because they were not on reserved land and had little surveillance from the authorities. By the early 1920s, the Board had escalated its campaign to take children, so the numbers of people fleeing the Board increased greatly, as families left either to prevent the loss of their children or because they resisted their removal and feared punitive consequences. Further intervention in independent farming dispossessed still more families who moved to safe areas like Wolli Creek, Lugarno and Oatley. However the Salt Pan Creek camp attracted the most militant of the refugees (Goodall 1988a; Goodall 1996: 145–6; Blewett 1981).

Young Ted Thomas, about 16, arrived in the Salt Pan community around 1924, after walking up from Wallaga Lake, 'with a spear and me swag on me back'.[16] He moved in with Joe Anderson in his small camp on the block owned by Ellen and Hughie, and went to Brighton-Le-Sands with Joe and some of his brothers to busk there with a gum leaf band. Young Ted took the hat around for money from their audiences. Ted remembered, 'They were great blokes on politics too!' (Campbell and Thomas 1980). Other men from the South Coast included Paddy Pitman and Jimmy Lukum, who had good reason to avoid any interference by the Protection Board: 'That's the time when they got hunted off Roseby Park for shit stirring with the manager!' (Campbell and Thomas 1980).

Jacko Campbell came from Kempsey to Salt Pan in 1926 when he was about ten. His family had escaped from the Burnt Bridge reserve to avoid the 'kidnapping' of their children by the Protection Board Inspector, Donaldson, who was in charge of the 'collection' of children to be 'disposed of' into the Board's Homes and into its indentured labour or 'apprenticeship' system. Jacko's mother had fired a shotgun over Donaldson's head, so the family had escaped before the inspector came back (Campbell 1980). They sailed down the coast in Jacko's father's fishing boat to the Georges River, where Jacko's sister was already living. The Campbells lived for a while next to Joe Anderson's camp and Jacko described the camp as a mixture of structures: Ellen Anderson and her family, and old Bill Rowley, had nice houses, he remembered, but others lived in little mia-mias and bag huts. After a while, the Campbells moved to a rented house owned by an Italian market gardener. Like Ted, Jacko remembered Joe Anderson and his brothers busking with the gum leaf band or selling the introduced blackberries and gooseberries or native gum tips and wildflowers like boronia, Christmas Bush and flannel flowers around Hurstville, Penshurst or Mortdale. At the Salt Pan camp there were the north coast Kelly family and the Glass family from Cowra. Another important group were the Onus and the Patten families from Cumeragunja who had histories of forthright outspoken criticism of the Protection Board. All these families and individuals were seeking refuge from the coercive intrusions of the Board into their lives and their families. Salt Pan represented freedom to them.

Related to Tom Williams were the Groves family, from Walhallow, led by Bob Groves and including his son Bert. Ted and Jacko remembered the Groves well because they moved into the house which the Campbells had rented from the market gardener. As they recalled the atmosphere they experienced at the camp as youngsters in the later 1920s and early 1930s, there was always talk of politics:

JACKO: All them old fellas used to live out there, the Pattens and all them others. You'd see them old fellas sittin around in a ring, when there was anything to be done.

TED: They were well educated! They could talk on politics!

JACKO: They always DID! .... Around the kids! ... No matter where they went! ... Specially when there was anything to do about the Aborigines Protection Board! There was talk about writing a petition. That was always goin' on! Joe Anderson said he'd be talking to the Duke of Gloucester!

(Campbell and Thomas 1980)

The Salt Pan Creek community was a vibrant and active place in the 1920s and even during the Depression in the 1930s. Jacko Campbell remembered that many of the Salt Pan Creek men would take the opportunity to 'spruik' at Paddy's Market while selling their gum tips or busking.[17] A well-known member of the Aboriginal community, Monty Tickle, was a nightwatchman at the Markets and he made sure that Jacko got 'to see these fellas on the butterbox' down there.

JACKO: Every Friday night they used to be spruiking at Paddy's Market. Jack Patten, Bill Onus, Bob McKenzie from Woolbrook, old Joe Anderson, they all lived at Salt Pan ... They'd only be spruikin' on land rights, that's all, on land rights ... You know: 'Why hasn't the Aboriginal people got land rights?' That was always the [thing] ... That paper come out, the *Aboriginal Warcry*. It was the first and then the *Abo Call*.[18]

HEATHER: They wouldn't have used those words would they? Did they actually say 'land rights'?

JACKO: They actually said: 'The Aboriginals cryin' out for Land Rights' and they called it the *War Cry*....

HEATHER: What sort of land were they asking for?

JACKO: Aboriginal land! They were asking for the land they were on! That's when they were chuckin' 'em off. There's places round Nowra, 'bout 35 or 40 acres, 60 acres, what Aboriginal people was ON. And they [whites] went into 'em, run their cattle through 'em, mob of cattle through 'em, through their crops and that! They only had dogleg fences then. That was the Stewarts and Bollaways at Tullanger ... they was pushin' Lang at that time for Land Rights. That was what it was all about. And to break up the Aborigines Protection Board!

(Campbell and Thomas 1980)

This was a powerful induction to the world of political activism and it showed in the later careers of the young men who experienced it. In the 1930s, two of the Patten sons, Jack and George, made interstate headlines leading the protest walk off from Cummeragunja in opposition to the Board. The quiet Bert Groves became a powerful leader of the Aboriginal political movement through the tough years of the 1950s and 1960s. By the 1970s, Tom Williams had become an organizer at La Perouse and across Sydney. Both Guboo Ted Thomas and

Jacko Campbell became key figures in a renewed national and state land rights campaign through the following decade (Goodall 1996: 335–51). But for Joe Anderson, his time was to be there and then.

From 1931 numbers of Aboriginal residents at Salt Pan Creek increased as Aboriginal workers, initially included in the new Unemployment Relief benefits, found that they had been excluded in a bureaucratic attempt to cut costs. Aboriginal unemployed were told to find their way to a Protection Board station and submit to managerial control in order to be given a small fraction of unemployment relief. Such unwelcome pressure pushed many towards the free camps like Salt Pan, and was spurned by those living there who were doing so already to keep away from Board control. Some of the men got Relief Work building the railway line to East Hills: Jacko Campbell's older brother, supporting the family of 16, had two weeks on and one week off, but a single man only got one week on and then three weeks off. But at least while they could stay at Salt Pan Creek, they were safe from Board intervention and the children could be sent to school. A former white pupil at Peakhurst Public School remembered the influx of new Aboriginal faces at this time. The sense of increasing turmoil was reflected in this man's uneasy memories that these new pupils 'were regarded as outsiders.... not merely by the white kids but also by the black kids.' (Hatton 1981).

Many white neighbours were even less welcoming of the rising Aboriginal population in the area. This was precisely the period when local and largely Anglo-Irish community organizations were emerging and seeking to shape the suburb's social and physical environment. Such hopes were fuelled by the expansion of the rail network, which led to subdivision of large gardening properties and, like the earlier Soldier Settler agricultural programs, significantly increased the population in the area.[19] The need for a productive domestic garden, 'to produce food as a safeguard against hard times', was still a powerful factor in land sales, leading to ever more densely packed residential areas on the shale soils near the centre of the townships (Haworth 1995: 35). This dense pattern of settlement fostered close-knit communities. The progress associations both expressed and shaped the local sense of these emerging communities. There was a strong, vocal contingent of local businessmen, including established market gardeners, poultry farmers and storekeepers in the developing shopping centres. The Depression briefly slowed this process of community assertion but it soon re-emerged. This sense of community was racially limited and class defined, despite the presence of Italian and Chinese market gardeners in the area, as the Anglo-Irish component of the population was self-consciously flexing its remaining demographic strength to exert control over the directions in which their community might develop.[20]

Although there had been some complaints by local white residents to Hurstville Council in 1926 that the Aboriginal community at Ogilvy Street was unsanitary and created disturbances in the area, the Health Inspector had found that the Anderson's sturdy weatherboard cottages were 'surprisingly clean and well-kept' with 'tidy' surroundings. This Inspector argued that there was little the Council might do without more substantial cause since the Andersons and

Rowley owned the blocks (*St George Call*, 7 May 1926). But the community's defence was about to disappear: Hugh Anderson died in July 1928 and by November 1930, under Depression pressures, the Andersons had sold their Ogilvy Street block, forcing Ellen Anderson and her community, which now numbered around 40 people, to move into more secluded bushland, closer to the creek, over which they had little or no tenure (*Propeller*, 15 May 1931: 7; 21 November 1930: 4). A rowdy Christmas followed by police visits to the new camp coincided with more formal resident protests, including one from the Herne Bay Progress Association to Hurstville Council, complaining about unsanitary conditions, noisy disturbances and the inappropriateness of 'a blacks' camp' in this 'growing district'. The residents' organizations, with no comprehension of the long established relationships between the land and the Dharawal people who formed the nucleus of the camp, argued that these Aborigines 'were not the original ones who had camped at Peakhurst, but were newcomers from Wollongong, La Perouse and other places' and that they should be 'removed to the compound at La Perouse' where they could be properly 'supervised' and 'protected' (*Propeller*, 16 January 1931: 3).

With Ellen's death in May 1931, Joe was left to defend the community as the senior member of the Anderson family. He was a well-known identity in the area and in the press, regarded as a jovial local 'personality', frequently photographed at the camp with local storekeepers and posing good humouredly in kangaroo skins with dead wallabies to convey traditional lifestyles.[21] Despite this patronizing and occasionally cynical attitude of the white press, Joe was passionate about the evictions and dispossessions of his countrymen over the last decade. Jacko Campbell remembers Joe Anderson 'spruiking' about land and dispossession to the crowds at the Sydney Markets on Friday nights, at the same time his family was under increasing pressure. So when he was able to gain time on the *Cinesound Review* in 1933, Joe Anderson chose to voice his outrage.[22] He drew on the authority of his country, calling himself King Burraga after his grandfather, choosing a name that resonated through Dharawal and Gandangara country from the Burragorang Valley in the west to the inlet called Burraga on the coast at Botany Bay. Speaking directly to the camera and the audience beyond he said:

> The black man sticks to his brothers and always keeps their rules, which were laid down before the white man set foot upon these shores. One of the greatest laws among the Aboriginals was to love one another, and he always kept to this law. Where will you find a white man or a white woman today that will say I love my neighbour.... It quite amuses me to hear people say they don't like the black man.... but he's damn glad to live in a Black man's country all the same!
>
> I am calling a corroborree of all the Natives in New South Wales to send a petition to the King, in an endeavour to improve our conditions. All the black man wants is representation in Federal Parliament. There is also plenty fish in the river for us all, and land to grow all we want.

> One hundred and fifty years ago, the Aboriginal owned Australia, and today, he demands more than the white man's charity. He wants the right to live!
>
> (*Cinesound Review* 1933)

Joe Anderson's challenge was heartfelt, but it only staved off the pressure at Salt Pan Creek for a short while. The family faced eviction again in 1936 and Joe once more began recruiting support, inviting a press interview in the Sydney papers; writing to the newly appointed Governor, Sir Murray Anderson, in his role as King Burraga, and writing also to the Society for Protection of Native Races, chaired by the up and coming policy broker, A.P. Elkin. Joe Anderson's letters to them stressed that there were resources for all and that Aboriginal people needed to have justice, not charity.[23] He kept on organizing, linking up with the emerging political movement, led by his young friends, Jack Patten, Pearlie Gibbs, Bill Ferguson and Bert Groves. Joe attended the 1937 hearings of the NSW Select Committee into the Aborigines Protection Board, interacting with the new leaders and, as King Burraga, meeting white supporters like Joan Kingsley Strack, who was delighted to receive a carved hatpin in the shape of a boomerang (Haskins 2005).

But once the worst of the Depression was over, the local white residents' organizations repeated their demands that the camp and its community be removed. By 1939, their complaints included 'spoiling the beautiful bush area' (*St George Call*, 3 March 1939; *Propeller*, 23 February 1939) as well as the allegedly poor hygiene and noisy disturbances of the camp, and the needs of the expanding population of the 'growing' suburb. Most of the camp were forced to move to La Perouse in 1939. Yet this did not mean that Aboriginal people left the area. A number of the camp residents moved slightly to the north, closer to the rail line, and set up camp on unoccupied land known as Doctor's Bush, which later became a Housing Commission estate, while others camped round Peakhurst Park near Jacques Avenue. Before long, there were further dislocations as a large US military hospital was constructed on Doctor's Bush, but ultimately, as these buildings became migrant and then Housing Commission homes, Aboriginal people from rural areas in New South Wales began to move in, drawn by the promise of jobs and better education in the city than they could find in conservative country areas. These incoming families came to the same Salt Pan Creek, into the Housing Commission hostel set up on Doctor's Bush. As they settled in they often moved along the Georges River, to Green Valley, just west of Liverpool, but they too adopted the river as home and, before long, they met up with the old timers of the Salt Pan Creek camp. Bert Groves came back to live in the area, and Jacko Campbell visited often, while Tom Williams Junior, Tom and Dolly's son, along with his family, kept the Anderson spirit alive just along the river at Botany Bay. The river continued to be a shaping force in the way Aboriginal people made lives for themselves and their communities in the city.

Conclusion: the river as fruitful borderland

This chapter has argued that rivers have offered safe and fruitful places for colonized Aboriginal people to remain even while other areas of their traditional country have become too difficult for them to access. The geology and hydrology of the area were important in allowing a substantial area of sandstone which could not be profitably cultivated but which offered a broad expanse of de facto commons to be used by the rising working-class population but also to continue to sustain the colonized Aboriginal population. As Maddison has pointed out, in British colonies all commons land, official and unofficial, was ambiguous: although formally in settler hands, the active cultural and economic presence of colonized peoples reflected a continuing assertion of underlying sovereignty (Maddison 2008). Yet the riverbanks offered more – access to rapid transport, fruitful harvesting and rich cultural expression as well as a space in which to live safe from settler expansion for long after initial invasion and settlement.

There was a continuing presence of Aboriginal people in the area, from very early in 'settlement' history, which became a community of traditional owners who interacted with other indigenous communities and had wide and active networks. The economic independence of the area, based on traditional resources and waged and cash labour, freed Aboriginal people from institutional control and surveillance, fostering a spirit of resistance. The traditional owners used their local knowledge to engage with activists and political refugees from other areas. At the same time, the urban setting allowed the interaction of Aboriginal people with working-class community and political activists in a marginal suburb where dissent was a common orientation. The building pressures in the interwar period eventually led to the dislocation of the core of traditional owners but younger members of these extraordinary communities remained in, or in contact with, the continually expanding Aboriginal population of the industrializing river lands after the Second World War. The experience of independent and vigorous community life in this urban borderland had generated a visionary and committed leadership which has continued to shape Indigenous politics in Australia to the present day.

Notes

1 The land responsibilities of the Aboriginal people in this coastal area were not well understood by early European observers, and as a consequence the remaining documents show many variations in the detail of which language group was responsible for which precise area. To see the discrepancies in the secondary sources based on these ambiguous documentary records, compare Willey, Flynn, Brook and Kohen, Davis, Barani [City of Sydney] and Nugent. The generally understood Australian tendency of language speakers to be highly knowledgeable about the language and land responsibilities of their neighbours probably held for this area as it did in all others and so it is likely that highly flexible and negotiable responsibilities were the rule for much of the time, particularly in resource rich liminal areas like the rivers. The most reliable indicator of traditional affiliations remains the memories and practices of the ongoing Aboriginal families in the area who are most closely descended

from the traditional owners. Consequently, this chapter will follow the approach to language affiliation which is held by family researchers of the Anderson family [Shayne Williams] and others, which are based on extensive reading and discussion about the archival sources in the context of family memory and known current family practice.

2 Map of Bankstown, 1843, reproduced in Rosen 1996: 45. Original held at Mitchell Library.

3 NSW Parliamentary Papers of the Legislative Council: Minutes of Evidence before the Select Committee on the Aborigines, 1845: 943–7, Questions 44–55.

4 Mrs Michael Ryan, 1845, quoted in S. Fraser 'Souvenir of Bankstown', Bankstown 1922.

5 Ellen Anderson to C.W. Peck, reported in 'Prelude: A Princess', 1933 edition of Peck's *Australian Legends: Aboriginal Folk-Lore*, originally published by Stafford and Company, Sydney, 1925. The 1933 edition is reproduced on the web at: www.-sacred-texts.com/about.htm and the 'Prelude' section at: www.sacred-texts.com/aus/peck/peck02.htm. See also *St George Call*, 17 Aug 1904. A later and much less direct reference suggests Biddy had originally 'come from' Broughton Creek, somewhere on the south coast, but the source is not specific, *St George Call*, 11 November 1929, 'Early memories of Captain Cook Lodge' by P.G. Bro F.G. Gates. For the recollections of white men about King Kooma and Biddy, see *St George Call*, 9 January, 23 January, 30 January 1904; 11 May 1907 (this last is the only reference where Biddy is said to have actually passed on the name of her former husband herself as 'King Kooma'). For the naming of Biddy's husband and Ellen's father as Paddy Davis, see Ellen's death certificate, 14 May 1931, and for Paddy's language name of Burragalung, see his grandson's letter of 16 January 1936. Joe Anderson, King Burraga, to A.P. Elkin, APNR, 16 January 1936, quoted in Attwood and Markus 1999: 74–5. Shayne Williams, Ellen Anderson's great grandson, understands that Paddy Burragalung worked for a white man called Davis and may have therefore been on occasions referred to, as was customary, as Paddy 'Davis'.

6 King Burraga, Joe Anderson, to A.P. Elkin, APNR, 16 January 1936.

7 See photo by J. Robinson which appeared in *St George Call*, 14 May 1904: 1. See also AIM pictorial collection, ca. 1860–1909 PXA 773/Box 6#42m, Mitchell Library.

8 Moama: Registrations of Births, Deaths and Marriages, in *Riverina Aboriginals: 1874–1975*, Don J. and Beverly F. Elphick, Canberra, 1997, Shayne Williams, personal communication, October 2005.

9 Title Deed, Lot 126, transferred 1925 to Ellen Anderson, copy held by Shayne Williams.

10 Title Deed, Lot 127, transferred 1929 to William Rowley, copy held by Shayne Williams.

11 Photographs reproduced in Molloy 2003: 34, 163 from Salt Pan Creek in 1914 show open space and a lack of mangroves.

12 Ellen James, Interview 21 October 2005, conducted by Shayne Williams, Ellen's nephew, at Ellen's home in St Georges Basin, with Heather Goodall and Ellen's husband, Frank James, also present.

13 See photo reproduced in *St George and Sutherland Shire Leader*, 3 August 2000: 13 of Joe Anderson buying bread, *Sydney Sun*, 1931.

14 Cited in D.J. Hatten 'Salt Pan Creek Aborigines' *Hurstville Historical Society Newsletter*, April 1984: 2n79, Aborigines, Volume 2, LHVF, Hurstville LS.

15 Ellen James (née Williams). Interviewed by Shayne Williams and Heather Goodall, 21 October 2005, St Georges Basin. Ern Blewett Interview 2005.

16 Ted was born 1909 and so was around 15 or 16 when he came up to Sydney. Interview 24 September 1980, Glebe, with Jack Campbell, Ted Thomas, Kevin Cook, Paul Torzillo, William Kennedy. Interview conducted by Heather Goodall. Audiocassette recording and transcript in author's collection (to be deposited in State Library NSW).

17 Jacko Campbell interviewed by Heather Goodall, 1980. Attwood and Markus 1999: 5–6 have questioned whether terms such as 'land rights' would have been circulating in the 1920s or 1930s. However, as this transcription indicates, Jacko was queried about his use of the 1970s terminology and insisted that this was the term used by Anderson and others. What is of greatest interest is the fact that Jacko saw an identical meaning in the demands of this grassroots campaign to the one he was a leader of in 1980. He was insisting on that consonance of meaning as much as he was on his emphatic assertion of the 1930s speakers' literal use of the phrase 'land rights'. Attwood and Markus' implication that Jacko's memory was 'coloured' by the present is no argument against such a consonance, and indeed there are many examples of the use of comparable terminology, not in the documents of the 1930s movement but in those of the 1920s movement. See Goodall 1988b: 181–97. Jacko's reference to Jack Lang, the Labor Party Premier, dates this memory to the years before mid 1932, when Lang was famously dismissed by the Governor because, in the depths of the Depression, he refused to use State money to pay the interest on British loans.

18 We haven't been able to trace this earlier form of a paper representing these views. The title is certainly consistent with the sense of the title of *The Abo Call*. Jacko suggested it had something to do with a religious group, and may have related to support the Andersons gained from the AIM, with whom Ellen was closely associated. However, it seems from Jacko's account that its content would have been more consistent with the campaigns of the AAPA in the 1920s, and the alliance between the north coast nationalists, like John Maloney, and the Aboriginal farmers at Kempsey, land owners whom Jacko knew, like John and Percy Mosely, with which the AAPA was able to form strong links from 1925 to 1927.

19 Rosen 1996: 94–5, 98; a soldier settlement in Bankstown was the subject of comment in the 1922 NSW Select Committee on Soldier Settlements.

20 Not only were these Progress Associations to object to Aboriginal residents (Herne Bay, 1930) but to gypsies (Padstow Progress Association, 1941); Molloy 2003: 24 citing PPA minutes of request to Bankstown Council.

21 See report in *St George and Sutherland Shire Leader*, 3 August 2000, pp. 13, 17, with photos of Anderson, sourced from *Sydney Sun*, 1931. This is not however the correct source, although the date may be correct. The photo of Joe Anderson dressed in skins and carrying a wallaby is from *Man*, January 1938. p 101.

22 The precise location for this filming is not known but Jacko Campbell was adamant that it was among the tea trees at Salt Pan Creek and close to the camp he had lived on. The Anderson family had been forced away from Ellen and Hugh's block by 1933. They were living close by, however, in slightly more secluded bush land to the north and nearer Belmore Road. So the film may have been shot at the old block itself or a short distance away.

23 Newspaper article 'Evicting a King', undated but referencing the recent appointment of the new Governor, August 1936; King Burraga to A.P. Elkin, Society for the Protection of Native Races, 16 January 1936, reproduced in Attwood and Markus 1999: 74–5.

Bibliography

Adam, P. and Striker, J. (1989) *Wetlands of the Sydney Region: Inventory*, National Estate Grants Program 51, Sydney: Nature Conservation Council of NSW.

Attwood, B. and Markus, A. (1999) *The Struggle for Aboriginal Rights: A Documentary History*, Sydney: Allen & Unwin.

Bankstown Local Studies Collection, Bankstown City Library, Sydney.

Bird, J.F. (1982) 'Barilla Production in Australia' in D.J. and S.G.M. Carr (eds) *Plants and Man in Australia*, Sydney: Academic Press.

Blewett, Ern and Ethel (2005) Interview by Heather Goodall on audiocassette, November 2005.

Blewett, G. (1981) 'Salt Pan Creek Aborigines', *Hurstville Historical Society Newsletter* 2: 49, July.

Brook, J. and Kohen, J.L. (1991) *Parramatta Native Institutions and the Black Town*, Sydney: UNSW Press.

Campbell, J. and Thomas, T. (1980) Interview by Heather Goodall on audiocassette, 24 September 1980.

Cinesound Review (1933) 'Australian Royalty Pleads for his People: King Burraga, Chief of Aboriginal Thirroul Tribe, to petition King for Blacks' Representation in Parliament', No. 100.

City of Sydney (2002) *Barani: Indigenous History of the City of Sydney*, www.cityofsydney.nsw.gov.au/barani

Davies, J. Mulholland, D. and Pipe, N. (eds) *West of the River Road*, Sydney: Towrang Publications.

Davis, P. (1986) *The Hurstville Story: A History of the Hurstville Municipality 1887–1987*, Sydney: Hurstville City Council and Marque Publishing.

Dickinson, E. (1984) 'Salt Pan Creek about 1913', *Bankstown Historical Society Journal*, December.

Dunstan, D.J. (1990) 'Some Early Environmental Problems and Guidelines in New South Wales Estuaries', *Wetlands (Australia)* 9(1): 1–6.

Earnshaw, B. (2001) *The Land Between Two Rivers: St George in Federation Times*, Sydney: Kogarah Historical Society.

Flynn, M. (1997) *Holroyd History and the Silent Boundary*, Sydney: Holroyd City Council.

Garside, M. (2001) *Padstow Park Progress Association History, 1913–2001*, Sydney: Padstow Park Progress Association.

Goodall, H. (1982) *A History of Aboriginal Communities in NSW, 1909–1939*, unpublished PhD thesis, University of Sydney.

—— (1988a) 'King Burraga and Local History: Writing Aborigines Back into the Story', *Bridging the Gap: National Issues in Local History*, Proceedings of the Royal Australian Historical Society's Annual Conference.

—— (1988b) 'Cryin' Out for Land Rights' in V. Burgmann and J. Lee (eds) *Staining the Wattle*, Volume IV, *The People's History of Australia*, Sydney: Penguin McPhee Gribble.

(1996) *Invasion to Embassy: Land in Aboriginal Politics*, Sydney: Allen & Unwin and Blackbooks.

—— (2006) 'Main Streets and Riverbanks: The Politics of Place in an Australian River Town', in R. Hood-Washington and H. Goodall (eds) *Echoes from the Poisoned Well*, Lanham, MD: Lexington Books.

Graham, B., Ashworth, G.J. and Tunbridge, J.E. (2000) *A Geography of Heritage: Power, Culture and Economy*, London: Arnold.

Haskins, V. (2005) *One Bright Spot*, London: Palgrave Macmillan.

Hatton, D.J. (1984) 'Salt Pan Creek Aborigines' *Hurstville Historical Society Newsletter*, 2: 79, April.

—— (1981) 'Salt Pan Creek Aborigines' *Hurstville Historical Society Newsletter*, 2: 48, April.

Haworth, R.J. (1995) 'Bush Tracks and Bush Blocks: The Aerial Photography Record from South West Sydney, 1930–1950', *People and the Physical Environment, Research Paper* 49: 32–42.

—— (2002) 'Changes in Mangrove/Salt-Marsh Distribution in the Georges River Estuary, Southern Sydney, 1930–1970', *Wetlands (Australia)* 20n.2: 80–103.

Hood-Washington, S., Rosier, P. and Goodall, H. (eds) (2006) *Echoes from the Poisoned Well: Global Memories of Environmental Injustice*, Lanham, MD: Lexington Books.

Hurstville Local Studies Collection, Hurstville City Library, files relating to Aborigines, Salt Pan Creek and Parklands.

Illert, C. (2003) 'Early Ancestors of Illawarra's Wadi-Wadi People', self-published report, East Corrimal.

James, Ellen (*née* Williams) and Shayne Williams (2005) Interview by Heather Goodall on audiocassette, October 2005.

Kass, T. (2005) *Western Sydney Thematic History*, State Heritage Register Project, NSW Heritage Office, www.heritage.nsw.gov.au/docs-History-WesternSydney.pdf.

Lawrence, J. (1997) *A Pictorial History of The Sutherland Shire*, Sydney: Kingsclear Books.

Maddison, B. (2008) 'Comparing Colonial Commons: Australia, India, Africa', paper presented at the Ocean of Stories Conference, University of Western Australia, Perth, February.

Maynard, J. (2005) '"Light in the Darkness": Elizabeth McKenzie Hatton', in A. Cole, V. Haskins and F. Paisley (eds) *Uncommon Ground: White Women in Aboriginal History*, Canberra: Aboriginal Studies Press.

Molloy, A. (2003) *A History of Padstow*, Australian Media, Padstow.

—— (2004) *Padstow a Brief History in Photos*, Australian Media, Padstow.

Mullins, P. (1995) 'Progress Associations and Urban Development: The Gold Coast, 1945–79', *Urban Policy and Research* 13(2).

NSW Parliamentary Papers of the Legislative Council: Minutes of Evidence before the Select Committee on the Aborigines, 1845: 943–7.

Nugent, M. (2005) *Botany Bay: Where Histories Meet*, Sydney: Allen & Unwin.

Organ, M. (n.d.) 'C.W. Peck's *Australian Legends*', University of Wollongong, www.michaelorgan.org.au/peck1.htm.

Peck, C.W. (1925, 1933) *Australian Legends: Aboriginal Folk-Lore*, Sydney: Stafford and Company.

Read, P. (1988) *A Hundred Years' War: The Wiradjuri People and the State*, Canberra and Sydney: ANU Press and Pergamon.

Report of Protector of the Aborigines, 31 December 1882.

Rosen, S. (1996) *Bankstown: A Sense of Identity*, Sydney: Hale and Iremonger.

Rowley, C.D. (1971) *Outcasts in White Australia*, Canberra: ANU Press.

Schama, S. (1996) *Landscape and Memory*, London: Fontana Press.

Singleman, L. (2002) *Secrets of Sandy Point: A History of Sandy Point*, Sydney: Sandy Point Progress Association.

The Propeller (Hurstville)

The St George Call

The St George and Sutherland Shire Leader

Willey, K. (1979) *When the Sky Fell Down*, Sydney and London: Collins.

Index